What the critics said:

'caustic, obstreperous and insightful – three rare commodities in Australian TV.'

Jon Casimir, *Sydney Morning Herald*

'Current affairs like you've never seen it before. A heartthrob host with a Heston-esque toupée, a vamp reporter who thinks the code of ethics is "Never wear Chanel couture on a grief story" and a producer whose middle name is "ratings, ratings, ratings".'

Michael Idato, *Daily Telegraph Mirror*

'Frontline is, potentially, one of the freshest and best local comedy series we've ever done.'

Robert Fidgeon, *Herald-Sun*

'a bristling satire of the shonky professionalism and dubious ethics of TV current affairs . . . '

Tom Gilling, *The Bulletin*

'a portrait of current affairs telly that should be closely studied by every student of the media.'

Phillip Adams, *Weekend Australian*

'The extraordinary quality of Frontline is that it is more accurate than most documentaries. You keep saying to yourself "yes, that's how it really is out there in the real world".'

Dennis Pryor, *The Age*

'sophisticated, intelligent, modern, with wonderful performances and wonderful writing.'

Charles H. Joffe

FR🔍NT LINE

The story behind
the story . . .
behind the stories

VIKING

Viking
Penguin Books Australia Ltd
487 Maroondah Highway, PO Box 257
Ringwood, Victoria 3134, Australia
Penguin Books Ltd
Harmondsworth, Middlesex, England
Penguin Putnam Inc.
375 Hudson Street, New York, New York 10014, USA
Penguin Books Canada Limited
10 Alcorn Avenue, Toronto, Ontario, Canada M4V 3B2
Penguin Books (N.Z.) Ltd
Cnr Rosedale and Airborne Roads, Albany, Auckland, New Zealand
Penguin Books (South Africa) (Pty) Ltd
5 Watkins Street, Denver Ext 4, 2094, South Africa
Penguin Books India (P) Ltd
11, Community Centre, Panchsheel Park, New Delhi 110 017, India

First published by Penguin Books Australia Ltd 1995

10 9 8 7 6

Cover photographs by Greg Noakes
Cover and text designed by Noel Pennington, design BITE

Printed by Australian Print Group, Maryborough, Victoria

National Library of Australia
Cataloguing-in-Publication data:

Frontline : the story behind the story ... behind the stories.

ISBN 0 670 86768 3.

1. Frontline (Television program : Australian
Broadcasting Corporation). 2. Australian wit and
humor. 3. Television comedies – Australia.

791.4572F

www.penguin.com.au

Contents

In memory of our dear friend
Bruno Lawrence
1941–1995

Preface

It was in the summer of 1993, having completed two successful seasons of 'The Late Show', that we began looking around for a new television project. Around this time we happened to see a '60 Minutes' special posing the question: 'Has the media gone too far?' Australian presenter Jana Wendt hosted an audience-based discussion on the issue with various journalists, executive producers and television presenters pontificating about the social worth of their profession.

This charade of self-criticism continued merrily along until one man, a widower who had lost his wife in a shark attack, stood up and asked 'Why?' Why were he and his family subjected to the horror of current affairs journalism – the relentless prying, the insensitive questioning, the unfettered and voyeuristic invasion of his very private grief?

Well, a lot of journos looked concerned and muttered a few platitudes about 'the public's right to know' and 'freedom of the press'. But no-one there that night answered his simple question. So we thought we'd have a go.

As we began researching current affairs television in this country, we uncovered more and more of these excesses. Gross invasion of privacy, cheque-book journalism, belligerent interviewers, dubious editing tricks – all this was inspired and justified by the relentless pursuit of ratings. Whenever we thought our ideas for Frontline plots might be a little far-fetched, we would meet someone in the industry who convinced us we had not, in fact, gone far enough.

Since Frontline first aired in 1994, to far wider acclaim than any of us could have imagined, current affairs television in Australia has not really changed that much. Executive producers may now cover their tracks a little more effectively, but the same abuses persist. Hidden cameras are still considered legitimate tools, criminals are still offered financial inducements to speak on camera, and programs still cloak their deeds in the veil of 'public interest'.

Which is why Frontline remains so relevant today.

Santo Cilauro, Tom Gleisner, Jane Kennedy and Rob Sitch

Acknowledgements

ACER Computer Pty Ltd

Armadale Apartments

Brashs

City Ford

Ericsson Australia

Geoff Riddell Australia

Iloura

Kingsgrove Apartments

NEC Home Electronics

Sheraton Towers Southgate Melbourne

Sportscraft Sportsgirl Group

Sussan Corporation

The Facility

THANKS TO

Polly Watkins, Deb Choate and Charlie Usher from our office

Lawrie Zion

Julie Gibbs and Katie Purvis from Penguin

Our sensational cast who kindly gave permission to use photos of them

Lydia Livingstone

Australian Broadcasting Corporation

FRONTLINE
Frontispiece

Between 1982 and 1984 I tutored Australian politics at Monash University, and one of my professional challenges was to explain how the media go about determining what will be the political and social issues of the day. Although aided by some very thoughtful and well written texts on the issue, I never had a teaching tool as loaded with insights and explanatory powers as Frontline. Should I ever abandon my own dalliance with the media and return to the front of the classroom,

Rob and Santo at work on Frontline scripts

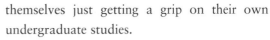
Cast and crew on the Frontline office set

I'd begin any course that dealt with these matters by switching on a Frontline video, and telling the assembled students to watch the screen in front of them. So much for sending everyone off to the library. What a pity that back in those days the Frontline team were

themselves just getting a grip on their own undergraduate studies.

Within weeks of the screening of its first episode on the ABC in May 1994, Frontline had emerged as much more than another hot show. So often was the 'groundbreaking television' accolade deployed to describe it that it quickly became almost a cliché. But 'ground-breaking' is also a strangely inadequate word when it comes to explaining the impact of a series that was written, directed and filmed by a group of people who have worked together since meeting at university more than ten years before.

The Genesis of Frontline

It was during rehearsals for the 1983 Melbourne University Law Revue that Tom Gleisner, Rob Sitch and Santo Cilauro first found themselves collaborating together. The show that resulted was three hours long and had a cast of over twenty, as well as the dubious title of *Legal AIDS: No-one is Immune*. But it also had more than its share of great sketches, and as law revues go, was a conspicuous hit, playing to full houses.

At this stage writing and performing were strictly extracurricular activities for Rob, who was studying medicine, and Tom and Santo, both law students, although Santo was treading the boards in several other student theatre productions. It wasn't until the end of that year that comedy became a potentially more serious interruption to the pursuits of the degree factory. For in response to the popularity of the Law Revue, plans were underway to organise a similar show called *Let's Talk Backwards* that would tour nationally during 1984. To be part of it meant deferring your course. Rob Sitch and Santo Cilauro were amongst the six who signed on.

Everyone enjoys a playback on Santo's camera

With its trade-mark killer sketch which sent up the shaky puppetry of 'The Thunderbirds', the tour was a triumph, and in Melbourne it moved beyond the university venues and ran for an extended season at the Last Laugh theatre restaurant, where the cast were able to develop their comic skills in front of a much broader and often considerably more inebriated audience. Among those watching them there were ABC talent scouts who, sensing potential in what they saw, eventually signed up the

group for a television series which went to air in 1986. It was called 'The D-Generation'.

With a cast that came from other university revues (including Michael Veitch and Magda Szubanski as well as Tom Gleisner, chiefly working as a writer), 'The D-Generation' was presented and marketed as a group of wacky undergraduates majoring in sketch comedy. While mostly true in a literal sense, the implication that this was a crowd of amusing degenerates who would never complete their studies turned out to be way off beam. For almost from the outset, the three D-Generation members who would eventually be involved in the creation of Frontline all showed considerable self-discipline in managing to juggle their studies with increasing work commitments. And they all graduated.

In the years that followed, the D-Generation continued with television projects with both the ABC and the Seven network, while also becoming a major force on EON FM (now Melbourne's Triple M), where they regularly led the ratings with their breakfast show. Reading the news at that time was Jane Kennedy, her task occasionally sabotaged by attempts from the D-Generation to make her laugh. Eventually she decided to quit newsreading and joined the on-air team.

Their next television project was 'The Late Show' in 1992, and also in the group by then were Tony Martin, Mick Molloy and Jason Stephens. With its live Saturday night timeslot, 'The Late Show' was looser and more relaxed in style than their previous sketch comedy programs, and quickly established a cult following for its occasional appearances by Santo Cilauro's octogenarian grandfather, as

Santo and Michael Hirsh at a publishing meeting

streamlined the increasingly complex requirements of organising their professional lives, but as is typical for a group which eschews traditional roles for its core members, his work has evolved in a number of directions which make any conventional description of it somewhat inadequate. Suffice to say, he is now a full partner in their activities, who also happens to be occasionally referred to as their 'Manager' or 'Executive Producer'.

From the outset, Frontline was a bold departure in style and form for what had by now become widely acknowledged as the

well as regular segments like 'Graham and the Colonel' and 'Shitscared'.

'Shitscared' was also one of the first sketches that was filmed and produced by the cast, establishing a precedent which would carry over into Frontline. Santo recalls: 'We just realised that it's a lot easier when you film the stuff yourself, reducing the distance between the inception of the idea and the execution of it.' The first 'Shitscared' episode was shot in the Channel Nine car park using Hi-8 footage and a home video camera that was to be used as a prize for Graham Kennedy's 'Funniest Home Videos' show.

By now many of the team's activities were being managed by Michael Hirsh, who had first met them when he produced a video clip for their satire on jock radio, 'Five in a Row'. Hirsh

most respected and consistent comedy team in Australia. For one thing, they were now creating full half-hour episodes rather than sketches. More significantly still, they had chosen a strategic target – tabloid current affairs television – and built up an armoury of devices with which to take aim, not all of which contained jokes.

Indeed, humour and topical gags did not top the list of priorities when it came to shaping Frontline. Of more immediate concern was the perceived need to dramatise the ways current affairs TV programs are assembled. Frontline was conceived after '60 Minutes' aired a program in late 1993 which posed the question: 'Has the Media Gone Too Far?'

At this time 'The Late Show' was finishing a two-year run, and it was agreed that there would not be a third series. Rob, Jane, Tom and Santo found themselves brainstorming ideas for a new project, as Rob Sitch explains: 'The fact that we were not going to do another "Late Show" came as a shock at the time. We were all tired, but the realisation that we were definite-

Rob Sitch

ly not doing another one came very late and suddenly – in some senses Frontline came out of a real urgency to come up with something. It's probably the fastest we've moved on anything.

'We were sitting one day thinking about other possibilities, and were talking about an old idea we had for a show which originally we were going to pilot at Channel Nine, and none of us were too keen on it, when Santo came up with the idea that comedy about current affairs is boring, but the actual "behind the scenes" has the interest value.'

Once they had worked out the concept of the show they approached the ABC. According to Jane Kennedy, they pitched their idea 'as a satire, a behind-the-scenes look at current affairs. This was after two years of us doing a show with boys running around in underpants, and me doing my best Dannii Minogue impersonation. We also had to tell them that only half the group would be doing it, with only two of us performing major roles in the show, and with Santo as the cameraman. But we were actually really confident about the idea.'

There was also no doubt that the ABC was the only network that could broadcast Frontline.

Jane Kennedy

'Because Frontline was to be about the kinds of current affairs programs you see on commercial networks, we could only do justice to what we wanted to do if we were with the ABC.' Bob Donoghue was the ABC's Network Programmer at the time and thought that Frontline was 'the best idea I'd ever heard for a program, coming from the best group of people I've ever worked with. I don't think there was a moment's hesitation about doing it.'

Debra Choate (Series Two Producer)

The decision to do a show like Frontline may have appeared to be an abrupt change of direction. But it was also in other respects a logical progression from the interests and enthusiasms of a group which had been astute observers of the current affairs treadmill for a decade. In fact they often relied on its output for their own sketch material, both on radio and television. As Jane puts it: 'It wasn't like we started off doing any specific research – I mean we're media junkies anyway.' Jane had also worked as a reporter on a program called 'Body and Soul' where she had been 'taught by the best of them' to 'walk and talk', and do 'noddies', both of which are staged devices used to make the interviewer seem authoritative and in control. Both are hallmarks of her character Brooke's breezy self-confident style.

So once Frontline had been given the go-ahead, the most urgent tasks were to hone in on the specific themes for each Frontline episode, which would be played out by the chronically insecure Mike Moore, and the Frontline staff, headed, of course, by the person who really runs the show, the Executive Producer.

To ensure that Frontline episodes had the requisite degree of dramatic integrity, a great deal of restraint was exercised when it came to scripting jokes. Tom explains that the technique

Tom Gleisner

adopted was to keep the early drafts joke-free, only adding some in at the final stages once everyone was happy with the overall dramatic structure of the script.

This created a deliberate blur between the traditional domains of drama and sitcom, and was heightened by the casting of the series. Suddenly the 'Late Show' members were working alongside so-called 'real actors'. And this wasn't sketch comedy.

Yet to say that they were now in dramatic rather than comedic roles is an oversimplification. Santo Cilauro's appearance as the dull and quietly spoken weatherman, Geoff Salter, was amusing not only because the character was Anglo-Saxon, but also because beneath the mild-mannered deadpan veneer he and Rob

Annie Maver (1st Assistant Director)

Sitch's Mike Moore had effectively repositioned their more garrulous double act, Graham and the Colonel. In both cases the duo make a sport of agreeing with each other's platitudes, although in Frontline, Geoff Salter is far more deferential to Mike Moore, to the point where he is still agreeing with Mike even when it's clear he hasn't got a clue what Mike is talking about. Still this hardly matters to Mike, who only requires Geoff to be a vehicle through whom he can air his considerable aspirations and anxieties.

The casting of other Frontline roles had more explicitly dramatic requirements. The late Bruno Lawrence, by far the best known actor conscripted to the cast, was picked out by Santo for the role of Brian Thompson because of his exceptional abilities as a character actor in films like *The Quiet Earth* and *Utu*. Following Bruno's death in June 1995 a new Executive Producer role was created, and it was filled by Kevin J. Wilson, who had auditioned for the Brian Thompson role the previous year. Most of the other actors were selected by more conventional casting arrangements, after the writing team had established clear guidelines about the requirements for the roles.

The Making of the Series

While Frontline is preoccupied with showing the roles and functions of different individuals within the office of a typical current affairs pro-

Maria McCarthy and Susannah Mott discuss casting

gram, the collaborative process that delivered the show to the screen is itself worth investigating. Although the working unit which began as the D-Generation has taken on different forms in its various projects, it has also maintained an intriguing continuum, due largely to the endeavours of its current core members Rob, Santo, Jane and Tom. In interviews that seek to unravel their group dynamic, they have often stated that they are 'a bunch of friends who

Carrie Kennedy and Ben Morieson (Art Directors) in the Frontline office

simply enjoy working together'. They each have their individual skills, and have developed their abilities within the framework of a collective enterprise. And they have sought to maximise their creative control over as broad a spectrum of their activities as possible.

As a result, most of Frontline has been made independently of any network involvement. Apart from shooting a few specific scenes at the television studios, the ABC's role in producing the program has amounted to little more than flicking on the tape of the show. Most of the real action has been done on the main set inside the rather austere office complex that the Frontline team occupies in an industrial section of South Melbourne. The two-storey block has

the actual sets for the show upstairs, with writing and production offices below. Santo points out that this set-up was favoured because 'we were always looking for a place which would double up as a production office. This ended up being the cheapest and the most practical.'

To the casual observer the two levels often appear to be interchangeable. You wander into what feels like an office, before you realise you're actually on the Frontline set, which is precisely the intention, according to Rob: 'We didn't want to use a studio – there is something about when you film in a studio that it ends up looking like a studio, unless you've got twenty hours a day to fix up lighting set-ups.'

Emma McLean (Series One Producer)

Santo, with his behind-the-lens experience in 'Shitscared' as well as countless Italian weddings and baptisms, became chief cameraman. When it came to deciding how Frontline would look, he points out that they went for a grainy documentary feel which would complement the acting and writing. To achieve this they used a Hi-8 video camera, and then put the footage through the kine process, which takes away the original clean video image and gives it a grainier, filmic quality.

The four creators of Frontline are all involved with writing each of the episodes,

Lawrie Zion (right) and Jane's dog, Jessie (front), sit in on a script meeting

although individual members might take on responsibility for early drafts of a particular script. At a reading for the 'Workin' Class Man' episode, Tom goes through a freshly completed draft, which he's been writing with input from Santo and Jane. After the read-through, there's a range of suggestions from the other three about what areas to develop further. In this case, the focus is on scenes which show how Mike Moore handles being placed in the situation where he's been encouraged to seem more like the common man, so as to attract more working-class viewers to the program. As they dissect the possibilities of plot and script they operate with the focus and purpose of a team of

nuance surgeons. Although dressed in jeans and casual sweaters, they are, in other respects, the white-coat brigade of comedy: they know their patient, and they also know what needs to be done.

This extends, of course, beyond writing and acting to directing and filming. Once a series is being shot, Tom tends to specialise in looking after the writing tasks, while Rob, Jane and Santo all direct the episodes as well as perform, with Santo taking on the additional role of chief cameraman. So while trying to change the approaches of current affairs shows, the makers of Frontline have also been able to change ideas about how television itself can be created. As Phillip Adams pointed out in the *Australian* of 14–15 May 1994: 'What makes the production even more remarkable than its cheek . . . is that the D-Gen is producing the series itself . . . In short, the idiots have taken over the asylum and are setting a precedent for a future approach to low-cost production. Seriously, folks, the D-Gen's approach shows that any group of competent writers or performers could get into the production business simply by buying a bit of Super-8 gear and coming up with a good idea.'

Another fan of the show, Harry M. Miller, points to the strength of the team that creates Frontline: 'I genuinely think it's one of the freshest cutting-edge groups around, and it's the fact that it is clearly a collective endeavour that makes it so exciting.'

While it's a system that creates a lot more work for the quartet who make the show, it has also become a natural way of doing things, just as it is normal for many rock groups to write, perform and engineer their own music. As Tom confesses: 'We enjoy having control of the pro-

Jane, Tom and Santo in their role as directors

duction process – we've been labelled control freaks by various people, and we're happy to wear that banner.'

Rob goes further in explaining the need for this approach: 'There's no equivalent to comedy in television artistic endeavour because comedians genuinely do understand what makes comedy tick better than anyone else. Drama can be run at a number of levels, but generally comedy can't. So it's logical to have the people that are creating the comedy having the rights over its production, because there are so many ways of stuffing it up. In the past, those in charge of the comedy shows have been more responsible for the errors than the com-

edians. So I think it's a mathematical piece of logic to have us governing it.'

Actors who join the cast for guest appearances are often struck by what – in television terms – is a countercultural experience. Andrew Clarke (best known for his role in 'The Man from Snowy River') played the fill-in Executive Producer 'Ed' in the episode 'One Big Family'. He later described the show as 'slick, pulsing, stimulating, erotic, abstract, obtuse, innovative and refreshingly unique. Every actor should endeavour to have Frontline as part of their résumé. It's the first thing any self-respecting producer, director or casting agent will look for.'

Polly Watkins (Publicity)

Reaction to Frontline

Few programs on Australian television have had the kind of impact that Frontline sustained during the winter of 1994. It began with a bang

– the first episode featuring Mike Moore's interview with the embattled Federal Opposition Leader, Dr John Hewson. For Hewson it was one of his more confident appearances during his last months as leader of the Liberal Party – first he ad-libs to Mike Moore about the sweaty effect of the lights on his made-up face. And then he turns the tables on Mike Moore's questions about his poor showing at the polls by pointing out that at least he's doing better there than Moore is with his own ratings. A flustered Mike Moore desperately – and unsuccessfully – tries to regain control of the situation.

The (real) media quickly seized upon this 'virtual' interview. The Hewson appearance dominated the next morning's radio chat shows, especially on ABC metropolitan stations like 3LO and 2BL. Even *New Idea*, not known for its slavish attention to either federal politics or even ABC television programs, ran a feature headed 'The Fall Guy' where it cooed that John Hewson had turned the tables on at least one interviewer. Hewson had needed little persuasion to go on the show, even though at the time

he agreed to appear, Frontline had yet to make its mark, and was still very much an unknown quantity.

Hewson says he 'thoroughly enjoyed' his appearance, not least because 'it was the only time in my life where I got even with the media. I thought the concept of the show was terrific. A lot of those current affairs shows have become gods unto themselves and don't like to be laughed at, even though they spend most of their lives capitalising on other people's problems. I think Frontline served a definite purpose in showing up that soft underbelly.'

Senator Cheryl Kernot, who made a guest appearance in 'We Ain't Got Dames', said she was 'really chuffed' to go on the show, although

Senator Cheryl Kernot on the set with Rob

she felt she was taking a risk 'because I didn't know how my segment fitted into the entire episode'. In retrospect, however, it was 'one of the most hilarious things that ever happened to me – keeping a straight face for one take was all I could manage, but as it

Steven Clode (Make-up) adjusts Rob's wig in the make-up room

turned out I was much funnier than I thought I was going to be.'

She also echoes Hewson's views when it comes to assessing Frontline's contribution to showing how the media works. 'I think it's

done an immense public service for people by decoding how things happen in the media, because when you get so much of your information from it, I think you tend to accord it a status that assumes ethics like honesty, whereas in fact it's just as subjective and personal as anything else – only ten times more powerful.'

For other public figures seeking a bit of high-profile maintenance, Frontline had, after just one episode, become *the* show to be part of. In 'The Desert Angel', Harry M. Miller became Frontline's off-camera opponent in a bidding war for an interview with a beautiful aid worker who had gone missing in the Sudanese desert. In the same episode Brian Thompson tells Mike Moore that

one of the signs that you've arrived in this game is when 'a comedy show does a parody of you'. The wisdom of this insight was certainly not lost on Miller, who responded to the show with a fax.

Within the teams that assembled the shows that Frontline was satirising, there was also some acknowledgement of the old adage that imitation is the best form of flattery. As

John Westacott, Executive Producer of '60 Minutes' chortled in a memo to Brooke Vandenberg, 'Tell bloody Brian to stop stealing my lines. Our Tuesday morning news conferences are starting to sound like last night's Frontline.'

Handwritten fax:

61 6 2773315
JUN 21 '94 10:59AM SENATOR C KERNOT 06 2773315   P.1/1

PARLIAMENT OF AUSTRALIA · THE SENATE

SENATOR CHERYL KERNOT   145 Melbourne Street
Leader of the Australian Democrats   South Brisbane 4101
Australian Democrat Senator for Queensland   Ph (07) 844 8155
Treasury, Aboriginal Affairs, Women, Small Business   Fax (07) 844 3671

                                                        Parliament House
                                                        Canberra ACT 2600
                                                        Ph (06) 277 3745
                                                        Fax (06) 277 3315

To all at Frontline

You had us all rolling on the floor last night [& we weren't watching State of Origin.]

You constructed the context brilliantly. Thank you for inviting me; it was a great thrill.

Love the Bulletin article & adore the flowers.

All the best

Cheryl Kernot.

Typed fax:

HARRY M. MILLER & CO MANAGEMENT

19th May, 1994.

174 CATHEDRAL STREET WOOLLOOMOOLOO NSW 2011 TEL (02) 357 3077
P.O. BOX 313 KINGS CROSS NSW 2011 AUSTRALIA FAX (02) 356 2880

Mr. Michael Hirsh
Executive Producer
Frontline
ABC Television
Melbourne

Dear Michael Hirsh,

It has come to my notice that your production unit included me personally and my company's activities in the most outrageous and scandalous manner last Monday night.

The number of gratuitous mentions were extremely high and having subsequently viewed the tape, one is drawn to two inevitable conclusions.

Firstly, whether it was intended satire or not, the ABC is absolutely in breach of its advertising code and tax payers should not be burdened with what was in fact a blatant (and free) continuous mention of a commercial enterprise.

Secondly, one would have thought the production team would have had sufficient artistic integrity (assuming their dedication to this illegal advertising) to have ensured that certainly, our company's office phone number and probably our fax number, were supered on the screen to co-incide with each mention of my name.

We are distressed and disappointed.

On a more serious note, I thought the episode was really clever, funny and I can't remember having so many people from all walks of life (including a cockney carpenter who is doing some odd repairs at my home) comment to me about the show. You are all to be congratulated.

It is fantastic satire with the terrifying edge of realism hovering above at all times. May your ratings soar to the sky!

Regards,

HARRY M. MILLER

P.S.   You may also mention to the News Chief of Frontline that we in fact have a new story coming up, which we would offer exclusively to Frontline for a figure which would be equivalent to no more than 11 of the Prime Minister's antique clocks.

In this sense Frontline functions in a similar way to Dame Edna Everage's television chat shows, where celebrities are happy to be sent up because they know it's a joke and they want to be part of it. And like Dame Edna, both Mike

60 minutes

3rd June, 1994

Brooke Vandenberg
Frontline
ABC-TV
221 Pacific Highway
GORE HILL   NSW   2065

PERSONAL

Dear Brooke,

Deliver the James Packer profile and you really can blow that fly trap of a programme. By the way, tell bloody Brian to stop stealing my lines. Our Tuesday morning news conferences are starting to sound like last night's Frontline.

Fond regards,

JOHN WESTACOTT
EXECUTIVE PRODUCER

Nine Network Australia Limited
A.C.N. 009 071 167

and Brooke have been able to 'cross to the other side' to the point where they are, in fact, accepted as real people, appearing on magazine covers alongside other current affairs celebrities, and having their private passions chronicled in the *Good Weekend*. It's a transition made possible by their adherence to the credo that the image is the substance.

Not everyone wants to go along with this, however, especially those who see themselves as prime targets of Frontline's encroachment. The Executive Producer of 'A Current Affair', Neil Mooney, was one of the most publicly hostile insiders who took on what he saw as the

Frontline agenda. And Ray Martin's response to the show was a suggestion that it might add a laugh track so that the audience would know when it was being funny. 'Like all current affairs programs, it can only get better', he quipped (*Sun-Herald*, 15 May 1994, p. 140), while the Executive Producer of 'Real Life', Gerald Stone, told the *Age* (*Green Guide*, 7 May 1994): 'I don't cringe at all when I see it. To me it's got as much relevance to "A Current Affair" or "Real Life" as "Fawlty Towers" has to the hotel business.' He left 'Real Life' in August 1994.

Some of this defensiveness came from what the Frontline creators see as a misreading of their intentions. As Santo suggests: 'People maybe thought that the show was an exposé, but it actually wasn't. It really was an observa-

Santo Cilauro

tion. People within the industry thought it was an exposé because it was so accurate.'

Rob adds: 'I think that in some ways that's why a few of the executive producers of current affairs shows reacted with a great sense of indignation. But in actual fact, it wasn't necessarily an attack. To say that it was an attack from our point of view was not right – we were really representing what does go on. And therefore it's trying to sneak out from under the weight of the truth, in a way, to say "Oh, you're trying to attack us." No we're not, we've observed it and we're representing it in a dramatic satirical style, but I think you've got to come to terms with that as the truth, not our opinion.'

One way of looking at this approach is as a kind of televisual literacy drive. So while by the end of 1994 the familiar forms of current affairs shows remained largely un-altered, audiences were becoming wiser to the more obvious tricks like noddies and walkies, as well as the more general processes that determine the composition of such programs.

Still, there was also the odd television reviewer who failed to be impressed by Frontline's arrival. The *Age*'s Ross Warneke said that the show didn't have enough topical humour, and suggested that it 'must be more immediate' as well as more 'zany' like 'Drop the Dead Donkey'.

As the first series unfolded, however, it became clear that the tactic of developing themes and characters rather than simply working over the week's events was paying off. And there was also the occasional bonus when Frontline found itself dovetailing into the

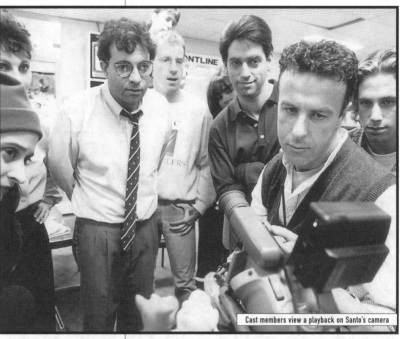

Cast members view a playback on Santo's camera

events of the day. This was not intentional, however, as Jane explains: 'They were complete coincidences. I think they were as a result of us trying to think like a current affairs production team of ideas and what you can do, and coincidentally "Real Life" ran a story on hidden cameras at casinos the night we did an episode on hidden cameras.'

Santo expands further on how this coincidence was misinterpreted: 'There aren't actually all that many current affairs topics floating around, and that week they happened to coincide. And it's part of this runaway train thing, where people go: "Oh, they're amazing – not only have they nailed issues and the way things work, but now they've nailed the actual story – they know when they're going to air." '

There was also some confusion about the origins of the characters who appeared in Frontline. For while Mike, Brooke and Brian began to loom more and more as real people through their appearances in the press and the electronic media, a number of people began speculating about the possibility that Frontline characters were being based on them, although this was never the case, according to Jane: 'We really didn't base anybody on anybody. It was a combination of all the stereotypes of journalists, production workers, publicists.'

Their denials did not quell all the irresistible comparisons. Tom adds that: 'Even minor characters like Santo's Geoff Salter had weathermen taking Santo aside and saying "It's me, isn't it."' And one of the main alleged

Kitty Stuckey (Wardrobe) dresses Santo as Geoff the weatherman

offenders in the 'Hey, that's me you're impersonating' category was the publicist, Jan. 'She's actually not a particularly nice woman but a lot of publicists took pride in thinking it was them and having a bit of a chuckle,' says Jane.

After the first few episodes had gone to air, critical reaction to the program was so positive and widespread that the intensity of the buzz even began to bother the team putting the show together. Tom admits to such anxieties, for instance, when he states that while the response was fantastic, 'I think just towards the

end we started to get a little sensitive that it was starting to go overboard because we feared an inevitable backlash.'

But as well as praising the show, media analysts also started taking a closer look at the style of television that Frontline was satirising. Typical of these 'life imitating art' thought pieces that began to appear in newspapers was Les Carlyon's critique of current affairs, 'Hardly Any Real Life' (*Age*, 20 May 1994, p. 15), where he observed that 'A segment from Sixty Minutes seems straight from Frontline, the splendid ABC spoof on current affairs . . . Promos trumpet the journalistic skills of Ray Martin and Stan Grant. Martin specialises in the smile and Grant in the look. In fairness no-one can do the look as well as Stan, except Mike Moore.'

But what effects did Frontline have on current affairs television itself? By the end of its first series, some commentators were seriously analysing this very question. The demise of the Seven Network's 'Real Life' along with its presenter, Stan Grant, was widely linked to the erosion of its credibility by Frontline's sustained assault of satirical observation of the processes that shape the format and delivery of infotainment shows. On 2 August 1994 the *Age* ran a full-page feature written by Wendy Tuohy called 'When Artifice Imitates Real Life', which began with the question: 'Is Mike Moore Murdering Stan Grant?' Also sprawled across the page was a graph charting the fortunes of the two programs, with the provocative heading: 'How Frontline is Killing "Real Life" in the Ratings'.

Yet in the same article Tom Gleisner also insisted that presenters like Stan Grant were not the real targets of Frontline, which was aiming more for the 'manipulative men' who 'make the

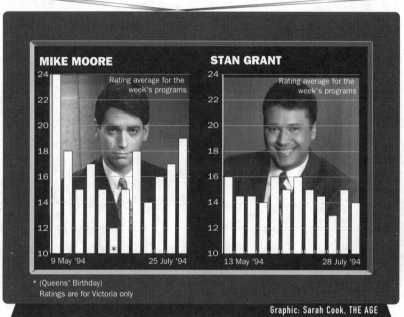

* (Queens' Birthday)
Ratings are for Victoria only

Graphic: Sarah Cook, THE AGE

decisions and wield the power' on current affairs shows. 'There's been a slightly disappointing thing happening in the last couple of weeks – a lot of people have been saying to us, "Obviously Mike is Stan Grant". This is a grave disappointment, because we never meant it to be a straight parody of "Real Life". It's meant to be an amalgam, which also has elements of "A Current Affair" and Ray, and of "Hinch", and even "The 7:30 Report".'

Understandably some of those who make current affairs television are reluctant to specu-

late about the impact of Frontline on the programs for which they are responsible. John Westacott, who is Executive Producer of '60 Minutes', describes the program as 'sobering' and says it worked for him as 'good satire' but claims he is 'too close to judge' whether its influence will extend further: 'I don't think it does us any harm to have such a cynical view of us portrayed, but I think we're too thick-skinned to change our hoary ways at this stage in life.'

Frontline might line up its targets, but there is nothing hateful in the execution of their satire. Harry M. Miller describes the show as 'compulsive viewing' and adds that 'even though their comedy is biting, it is never vicious or malicious.' Bob Donoghue goes further still, claiming that Frontline is the 'best show ever seen on Australian television – I'm its biggest fan, I'm afraid. Its impact went way beyond what most people realised. It has changed current affairs for the better in the way that they're now accountable to the public. Everyone in commercial TV will hotly deny it, but I believe it has happened. The public who chose to watch Frontline cannot be duped any more.'

Frontline's success hasn't been confined to Australia. It has also been shown in New Zealand, and in April 1995 the first series was sold to an American cable network, Comedy Central, which has also introduced that country's audiences to 'Absolutely Fabulous'. The network became aware of the show through Charles Joffe, best known for producing

with wonderful performances and wonderful writing.'

It's a remarkable response for a show which, with its local reference points and behind-the-scenes setting, was at one stage con-

The cast and crew from Series One celebrate with a drink

Woody Allen films, as well as managing the early careers of comedians like David Letterman and Billy Crystal.

Charles Joffe explained to me how he became aware of Frontline. 'There's an American journalist named Sue Karlin who was vacationing in Australia and turned on her television set and saw the show. And she just got all excited about it – and she called the people at the show, and asked Michael Hirsh if he could talk to me about it, and I might be able to do something about it. Well, they sent me copies of six shows and I absolutely fell in love with it. It was sophisticated, intelligent, modern,

sidered by some critics to be even too 'in' for Australian audiences. And it affirms what many of us have long suspected: that the team that brought us Frontline has emerged, in less than ten years, as one of the most innovative and accomplished creative teams that we have ever seen.

Lawrie Zion
July 1995

A note on
the scripts

The scripts that follow are from both the 1994 and 1995 series of Frontline. To me, one of their most striking features is their naturalistic style, and I was surprised that so many of what seemed like ad-libs on the screen turned out to have been calculated pieces of oral sculpture. There are occasional exceptions to this, chiefly with the larger-than-life utterings of Mike and Geoff, and the occasionally over-the-top outpourings from network publicist Jan.

Something to look out for. It appears that the Frontline team are among a select group who use a scripting device whereby some lines or phrases are printed in brackets, which for fairly obvious reasons is called 'bracketing'. But what is it? According to Tom Gleisner, the idea is to impart something between a stage direction and dialogue to the performer. So when Brian talks about possible interview talent with Emma in the 'Desert Angel' episode, the script reads:

BRIAN *(tosses his magazine down)* We're barking up the wrong tree, Em. (Let's go over the facts as we know them.) It's a profile series. We're trying to sell Brooke as the reporter who talks to the big names. It's a flirt piece.

While the italicised line is obviously a stage direction, the other bracketed line is intended to be implied or understood from Brian's actions, rather than spoken. The purpose of this approach is to create a more naturalistic feel to the dialogue, reducing unnecessary words or phrases, with the proviso that the bracketed phrase should be retained if the overall meaning of the passage is in danger of becoming unclear.

You will also find some great scenes that for reasons of length either weren't filmed or were deleted on the cutting room floor.

Lawrie Zion

Character Profiles

Mike Moore:

HOST OF FRONTLINE

Mike's not that far off having the label 'survivor' applied to him. He's been behind the Frontline desk now for quite a few years; in the early days of 'Real Life' he contemplated sitting *on* the Frontline desk, but is now glad he stuck to the chair. With the wisdom born of spending five nights a week watching major world events roll through an autocue, Mike likes to think of himself as a veteran of the industry. Concerned, warm, approachable, hard-hitting, poignant – he can provide a look to match any one of those adjectives. But he's still a dreamer. With all his success and (undercover) car-parking facilities, Mike's arranged to have tapes of his hard-hitting interviews (including the controversial Kamahl walk-out) shipped to producers in the States. Unfortunately, his Executive Producer has arranged for the tapes to be bulk-erased before they leave the country.

Brian Thompson:

EXECUTIVE PRODUCER (SERIES ONE)

Brian Thompson is one of Australia's most experienced news and current affairs producers. Responsible for setting up a new program on an opposition network, Brian is often referred to as a guru. He is somewhat disparaging about the star system, but abides by it to make the show work. He is well paid, respected and treats people fairly, while retaining a healthy cynicism towards the television industry. Brian realises ratings count for everything . . . and he's not the kind of guy to lose sleep over a few suspect stories if it means cracking a thirty.

Sam Murphy:

EXECUTIVE PRODUCER (SERIES TWO)

Following a network shake-up (Series Two, Episode One), former EP Brian Thompson was sacked and replaced by Sam Murphy. Unfortunately the network bosses' attempt at 'making a fresh start' was thwarted when the person they hired turned out to be every bit as conniving as his predecessor. Like Brian, Sam Murphy is cunning, manipulative, cynical and single-mindedly obsessed with ratings. If anything, he's overqualified for the job of Frontline EP. His middle names would be 'journalistic ethics' – but he doesn't have any.

Brooke Vandenberg:

REPORTER

Extremely ambitious, Brooke Vandenberg has had limited journalistic experience (she had a grade C cadetship from the now defunct 3XY radio station in Melbourne), but she looks good on television and can 'ape' that classic interviewer style so well that everyone is fooled into believing she's 'got it'. Brooke is thirty years old, and realises she has limited on-camera life . . . which is why she has her sights set on becoming a reporter for the American '60 Minutes' program as soon as possible (she can't understand why Jana got the gig). She has a very healthy social life, particularly with high-profile, powerful men, and is enjoying her own rising profile through the publicity machine of the network.

Martin di Stasio:

REPORTER

Martin is a hardened journalist who's been in the game since he was a seventeen-year-old cadet. He's done everything from police rounds to a stint in South-East Asia. Not afraid to kick in a door to get a good story, 'Marty' has a lot of respect for the old guard of television journalists in this country: Willesee, Negus, Munro . . . anyone who's done it 'tough'. He used to have it for Ray Martin till he sold out and went to do 'Midday'. He'll never be a 'star' and knows it, but won't shy away from throwing in the odd cutaway of himself in a story.

Emma Ward:

PRODUCER/RESEARCHER

Emma is one of the league of women who work behind the scenes in television, generally for little kudos. She is efficient, intelligent, diplomatic – she gets the job done, particularly under pressure (which is most of the time). She thinks most of the on-air reporters are idiots, but she'd never let on – she's too professional for that. Emma is totally disillusioned by the process by which some women reporters are chosen – basically for looks. She believes she could do the job better than anyone.

Jan Whelan:

NETWORK HEAD OF PUBLICITY

A smart career woman who started in the business as a secretary, Jan has the 'magic touch' when it comes to publicity. She runs a well-oiled machine, and simply adores her network stars. Jan is one of the few women who holds an executive position in television and has no qualms about exercising that power. She is one of the founding members of 'The Coven'.

Geoffrey Salter:

WEATHERMAN

Geoff was born and bred in Mount Gambier. After graduating in Earth Sciences at Flinders University, he immediately took up a job as researcher at the South Australian Bureau of Meteorology. His rise to fame was meteoric – or as Geoff always says, 'meteorological'. Within two years he was the bureau's Environmental Affairs spokesperson and appeared in several nature documentaries. Geoff was snapped up by SES Channel Eight, where he presented the weekend weather for three years before coming to the 'big smoke', where he now enjoys the status of Chief State Forecaster. On air, his affable style and irrepressible sense of humour have earned him a legion of fans – there is even a 'Geoff Salter Appreciation Society' at one particular TAFE college! Geoff drives a Mazda 121 (although on smog alert days he cycles to work), has an Irish setter called 'Bobo', and is quite an accomplished magician.

OTHER CHARACTERS

Stuart O'Hallaran ('Stu') CAMERAMAN

Kate Preston RESEARCHER

Domenica Baroni PRODUCTION SECRETARY

Shelley Cohen EXECUTIVE ASSISTANT

Jason Cotter ('Jase') SOUND

Hugh Tabbagh EDITOR

Elliot Rhodes FRIDAY NIGHT FUNNYMAN

Ian Farmer STATION GENERAL MANAGER

Bob Caville NETWORK GENERAL MANAGER

Khor CLEANER

Colin Konica PHOTOCOPY REPAIRMAN

TEN SCRIPTS
from the First Series

The Soufflé Rises

Day ❶

SCENE 1

MIKE IS ON AIR AT 3AW WITH NEIL MITCHELL.

MIKE I simply feel, Neil, and I'm sure the listeners would agree, that there's a fine line between an interview and an interrogation. (I mean) what's the point in abusing one's guests?

NEIL You prefer being 'Mr Nice Guy'?

MIKE I don't think I'm perceived that way, Neil.

NEIL *(going to calls)* What do you think, Sandra?

SANDRA *(voice only)* About Mike Moore? He's very nice. I saw that Richard Carleton interview you were talking about on '60 Minutes'; it was a disgrace.

NEIL How did it compare to the one Mike Moore did with the Prime Minister last week?

SANDRA I didn't see it.

NEIL Do you watch Frontline?

SANDRA No, but I think he's very nice.

NEIL What about you, Leonie?

LEONIE *(educated voice)* I didn't see it either, Neil. But I think Mike's a very good host. Very fair.

MIKE Thanks, Leonie. I try to present a balanced viewpoint in all matters. But if there's some head-kicking to be done, I won't back away from it.

NEIL *(taking another call)* Toula?

TOULA *(voice only)* Mike, you very nice man. Very kind to people on your show.

NEIL Well, there you have it. Mike Moore – the nice guy of current affairs.

SCENE 2

THE PRODUCTION OFFICE

Marty, Stu and Jase are having lunch around the table area.

MARTY Three weeks later this same chick goes back to the doctor. He looks at the lump on her face and cuts it open. And you know what comes out?

STU Baby spiders.

MARTY You heard this story before?

STU Yeah.

MARTY What about you, Jase? *(Jase nods)* It's bloody true. My sister knows the girl who was nurse at . . .

Mike arrives and speaks to Domenica.

DOMENICA Afternoon Mike!

MIKE Domenica. How are you today?

DOMENICA Fine.

MIKE You, er, hear me on AW?

DOMENICA *(holding up radio)* Never miss it, Mike.

MIKE How do you think I came across?

DOMENICA Nice.

MIKE I didn't sound a bit . . . lightweight?

DOMENICA No! You handled it really well. That's why people like you; you're nice. My mum likes you.

MIKE I didn't know your mother watched.

DOMENICA She doesn't. But from what I tell her, she thinks you're really nice.

SCENE 3

BRIAN'S OFFICE

BRIAN *(on the phone)* Six o'clock. So it's confirmed? Great . . . OK, bye. *(to Emma)* The Hewson interview is confirmed – let everyone know.

SCENE 4

MIKE'S OFFICE

Mike is at his desk, playing with a Gameboy. There is a knock at the door. He pulls a newspaper over the Gameboy.

MIKE Come!

Shelley opens the door.

SHELLEY *TV Week*'s here, Mike.

MIKE Oh, I'm pretty busy. Chuck it over there; I may get a chance to look at it later.

The sound of the Gameboy can be heard faintly.

SHELLEY *(puzzled)* Can you hear something?

Shelley places the TV Week on Mike's desk and leaves. As soon as the door is shut he dives for it. He flicks through to find article entitled 'Mike's Moore Likeable'.

Everyone in the office looks up as they hear Mike scream 'Jesus!' after reading the article.

SCENE 5

GEOFF'S OFFICE

Mike is reading from the TV Week article.

MIKE ' . . . in the hard-hitting world of current affairs, Mike prefers the gentle touch'. They obviously didn't see my run-in with Jackie McDonald.

GEOFF Mate, you nailed her.

MIKE *(continues reading)* 'While Ray Martin and Alan Jones ask the tough questions, Mike takes a softer line . . . ' This is crap!

GEOFF Mate, you ask the tough questions. Remember the time you asked Imran Khan about his new lover?

MIKE Yeah. That was off-air.

GEOFF But it took guts. He's a big man.

MIKE You know who I'm interviewing tonight? John Hewson.

GEOFF Wow! He's tough.

MIKE *(waving TV Week)* I think people are about to see a new side to Mike Moore.

SCENE 6

THE FRONTLINE STUDIO, A FEW MINUTES BEFORE GOING TO AIR

We see Mike and Kate speaking with Dr Hewson and several minders. Mike breaks away from the group and heads over to Brian and Emma who are on the floor going through details on a clipboard.

MIKE Brian!

BRIAN What's up?

MIKE He just said he doesn't want questions about the leadership!

BRIAN So?

MIKE He said we agreed this afternoon not to ask anything about the leadership.

BRIAN Yeah.

MIKE We've got questions, on the autocue.

BRIAN Yeah.

MIKE We'll have to skip them.

BRIAN Mike, these fellas always tell you what you can't ask 'em. Just say 'yes' and ask them anyway.

MIKE So we're going back on our word?

BRIAN Yeah. We're not televising a policy speech – it's an interview. Mike, you're worried about appearing lightweight.

MIKE I am not! Who told . . . ?

BRIAN Domenica. Here's your chance to kick some political head.

MIKE What if he won't come on the show again?

BRIAN Mike . . . when these guys need us . . .

MIKE He might ban us.

EMMA *(checking watch)* Thirty seconds to air.

BRIAN He's an easy target, Mike. Best way for a current affairs host to get credibility is to line up an easy target and nail him. Then you can afford to suck up to Keating. Go get him, tiger.

Brian and Emma head for the control room. Mike and Dr Hewson take their places behind the desk as the floor manager counts down from ten. During these last few seconds Mike and Hewson speak.

HEWSON Still get a little nervous, even after all these years.

MIKE *(light-hearted)* Relax, I'll go easy on you.

FLOOR MANAGER Five, four, three, two . . . *(signals 'one')*

MIKE Good evening, I'm Mike Moore. Welcome to Frontline.

The opening titles run.

MIKE Tonight on the show, the health debate. We're joined live by Liberal Party leader Dr John Hewson. Dr Hewson, thanks for your time.

Widen to reveal Hewson seated with Mike.

HEWSON You're welcome.

MIKE Now, you're about to unveil some major new policy statements in the areas of health and unemployment.

HEWSON Yes, we're very excited by some of the plans . . .

MIKE But before we get to that, let's talk about the leadership issue.

HEWSON *(surprised)* What about it?

MIKE *(producing paper)* Well, according to this opinion poll, your popularity rating is just 32 per cent. Do you really have the support to stay on as leader of the Liberal Party? Surely Bronwyn Bishop's got a stronger claim . . .

We cut to Brian and Emma watching in the control room.

BRIAN Go Mike!

We cut back to John Hewson.

HEWSON Well, perhaps I can ask you a similar question?

MIKE *(thrown)* Sorry?

HEWSON *(producing paper)* What about your ratings? Last I heard less than 18 per cent of people were watching the show. Maybe you should step aside, Mike? I hear Brooke Vandenberg's got a lot of support.

Mike is completely stunned.

Cut to control room. Brian and Emma look on in shock.

BRIAN Oh Christ!

Cut back to Mike.

MIKE *(struggling)* Let's get back to the issues, Dr Hewson. Your new health policy . . .

Cut to control room.

BRIAN Someone call an ambulance.

Day ❷

SCENE 7

THE CAR PARK

Mike arrives in the car park. There are construction workers digging up his car space with a jackhammer. We see him register anger.

SCENE 8

THE PRODUCTION OFFICE

Emma has an open newspaper and is arguing with Kate about a potential story.

KATE *(disagreeing strongly with Emma)* Hang on, a story about an eight-year-old kid who plays the piano? I could play the piano when I was eight!

EMMA Yeah, that was 'Chopsticks'. He plays Chopin.

MARTY *(facetiously)* Chopin wrote 'Chopsticks', didn't he?

Brian looks over Emma's shoulder at paper.

BRIAN How old's this kid?

EMMA Eight. Just been admitted to Melbourne University as its youngest ever part-time student.

MARTY *(aside)* That's in the non-Asian category.

BRIAN All right! Ring the mum and check that no other show is doing it.

EMMA Do we send Brooke?

BRIAN Nah, she frightens kids. Send Marty. Yeah, Marty. *(amused)*

Brian beckons Brooke into his office. Mike arrives with a box under one arm.

DOMENICA Morning Mike.

MIKE Domenica.

DOMENICA Been shopping?

MIKE *(pretending it's nothing)* Oh, just something for the office. It's a cappuccino machine.

DOMENICA I love coffee!

MIKE Gee, tough interview last night.

DOMENICA I thought you were really good. That was mean of him to ask about the ratings. It was an ambush.

MIKE I think I gave as good as I got.

DOMENICA *(pause)* Yeah (sort of) . . .

Mike spots Brian in his office and heads towards him.

MIKE *(interrupting Brian and Brooke's conversation)* Brian, I think we should draft a letter to Dr Hewson's office, tell him he's banned from the show.

BRIAN Wasn't he going to ban us?

MIKE Whatever. He's not coming on the show again.

BRIAN Fine, Mike. *(to Brooke)* You know anyone who's got those silicon breast implants? You know, the ones that leak?

BROOKE Can I count immediate family members?

MIKE Brian, another thing. They've dug up my car space again.

BRIAN *(trying to get rid of him)* Use mine. I'll take yours for the next few days.

MIKE (But) it's all rubble and mud.

BRIAN I've got the four-wheel drive. Why don't you go start that letter?

Mike realises he won't get any more sympathy from Brian, so heads for his office.

MIKE *(as a parting shot)* He's banned.

BRIAN *(muttering, to Brooke)* I hate it when he gets in early.

BROOKE You wanna do a story on breast implants?

BRIAN It's just an idea. If we could interview some of those women who are about to sue, show some breasts and all, no scars, get some models in, show a little . . .

EMMA Gratuitous nudity.

BRIAN Emma, that thought is not worthy of you.

Kate hangs up the phone and calls to Brian.

KATE Our eight-year-old is a goer. I spoke to the mum.

BRIAN She want money?

KATE No.

BRIAN Smart kid. Dumb parents.

Brian is cut off by what sounds like a jet engine taking off in Mike's office, followed by screams of pain. Mike bursts from the door wringing his hands in pain.

MIKE Does anyone know how to set up a cappuccino machine?

SCENE 9

A SUBURBAN LOUNGE ROOM

Stu and Jase record Marty as he interviews an eight-year-old boy and his mother.

MARTY What do your friends think about your piano playing? *(the kid doesn't answer)* Are you looking forward to going to university? *(the kid doesn't answer)* I believe your favourite composer is Chopin.

KID I wanna go to the toilet.

Cut to Marty's look of frustration.

MARTY *(under his breath)* Head first?

SCENE 10

GEOFF'S OFFICE

Mike is showing Geoff his new cappuccino machine.

MIKE I think Domenica said the coffee goes in here and it heats up here. With the steam.

SCENE 11

THE SAME SUBURBAN LOUNGE ROOM

The child is now seated at a piano. The mother sits next to the child trying to coax him into playing.

MUM Come on, we did it this morning. You remember . . .

She plays a bit of Chopin. The kid is uncooperative.

MARTY Don't worry. It's a three-hour tape.

SCENE 12

GEOFF'S OFFICE

GEOFF It's fantastic. *(sipping from mug)* So this brown stuff is chocolate?

MIKE I may have scalded the milk. Just scrape that off. *(changing topic)* You see me with Hewson last night?

GEOFF Tough interview, mate.

MIKE I thought I gave as good as I got.

GEOFF *(pause)* Yeah.

MIKE It was Brian's fault! He made me go into all that leadership stuff.

GEOFF Mate, if the boys upstairs would just leave us on-camera people to do our jobs. One minute they want interstate weather before the forecast, then synoptic charts . . .

MIKE It's crazy. They don't have a feel for it. *(they both sip coffee in silence for a second)* If only I could speak my mind. Then I wouldn't have to be Mr Nice Guy. If I could speak my mind . . .

GEOFF Like Neil Mitchell.

MIKE Or John Laws. I'd love to give my opinion on some of the issues we address.

GEOFF Why don't you?

MIKE (How do you mean?)

GEOFF Do an editorial. Show 'em you've got a mind of your own.

MIKE Brian would kill me.

GEOFF Mike! It's your show. Just do it. You feel strongly about an issue? Make a comment about it.

MIKE All right. I will. *(pause)* What's an issue I feel strongly about?

SCENE 13

THE PRODUCTION OFFICE

Domenica, Kate, Emma and Shelley are chatting.

DOMENICA And then the doctor cut her face open and you know what came out?

GIRLS What?

DOMENICA Baby mice.

The girls are suitably nauseated.

GIRLS You're kidding. Yuk! That's not true.

DOMENICA It is! Marty's sister knows the nurse who . . .

They are interrupted by Brian, who comes out of his office.

BRIAN Any word from Marty?

EMMA He rang half an hour ago. Said they're still taping.

DOMENICA She's still got the mice. It was either mice or a possum . . .

SCENE 14

A SUBURBAN DRIVEWAY

Marty, Stu and Jase have just got into their car.

MARTY Well, that was an afternoon well spent with Young Einstein.

Stu turns key in ignition. The car fails to start.

MARTY Bloody fantastic!

They all get out and go around to open the car's bonnet. They stare for a second at the engine.

STU Do you know anything about cars?

MARTY Nuh.

STU Jase?

Jase shakes his head.

MARTY Shit.

STU I know it shouldn't be smoking.

A child's voice is heard.

KID I think it's your alternator.

The three boys look down to see our child prodigy.

SCENE 15

MIKE AT THE FRONTLINE DESK

We hear Marty presenting a story on Greek-Macedonian hostility. Mike is having his make-up checked. Over his shoulder we see an autocue reading 'That report from Martin di Stasio. After the break, we pucker up for more on the art of kissing. (Smile, shuffle papers.)'

MARTY *(voice only)* . . . continues to simmer. With both sides blaming each other, the hostility shows little sign of easing.

We cut to the control room where Brian and Emma watch.

MIKE *(through monitor)* Mmm, that report from Martin di Stasio.

FLOOR MANAGER *(mimes)* To the break in five.

MIKE And it's certainly a complex issue, though if you ask me . . .

As Mike continues, we cut to Brian and Emma registering shock.

BRIAN No we didn't.

Mike continues his editorial.

EMMA It's the final scene of *Tootsie*.

BRIAN I'm gonna kill him.

Cut back to Mike.

MIKE . . . the Greek people of Australia have only themselves to blame. Their stubborn refusal to recognise Macedonia's right to its own flag and symbols is short-sighted, if not immoral. It ignores centuries of autonomy in the former Yugoslav Republic of Macedonia, and blame for the recent spate of violent attacks must rest fairly with our Greek community. Still, Macedonia survived 800 years of the Ottoman Empire; a few months of Greek protest will do little. *(changing his serious tone to a light-hearted one)* After the break – we pucker up for more on the art of kissing.

SCENE 16

BRIAN'S OFFICE, AFTER THE SHOW

Mike is being bawled out by his boss.

BRIAN What the fuck were you doing?

MIKE I think it's an important issue, Brian.

BRIAN You're not paid to think, Mike. You're paid to sit there and read what we tell you to read. That little political announcement of yours put us forty seconds over time. You know how much forty seconds is worth on this network? A hell of a lot more than your bullshit opinions.

MIKE I happen to feel very strongly about the Macedonian cause.

BRIAN And so do the Greeks. Those wogs are crazy; they burn down houses.

MIKE Well I'm sorry Brian, but I stand by my comments.

BRIAN Switchboard's already received death threats.

MIKE *(shocked)* What? Against who?

BRIAN You.

MIKE Me? *(confused)* I just thought . . .

BRIAN I don't think there was much thought.

MIKE I just didn't want to be seen as a lightweight.

BRIAN Would you forget this 'lightweight' bullshit? Everyone in current affairs television is a lightweight. Ray Martin, Stan Grant, that red-haired mate of yours on the ABC, with the pen. None of these people have real balls; it's just image.

MIKE Jana Wendt has balls.

BRIAN Ah. You don't reckon that 'perfumed steamroller' crap didn't come straight out of Channel Nine publicity? I heard Jana wanted to stop it, but she was too weak. Current affairs hosts do not give their own opinions.

MIKE Jana does.

BRIAN What is this 'Jana' bullshit? Mike, Jana Wendt has never expressed a personal opinion in her life. She interviews someone from the Greek community about racial violence. She'd never go 'I think you're a bunch of psychos'. She'd say 'It's been alleged you're a bunch of psychos'. 'Prime Minister, people say your business dealings are dubious'. 'Michael Jackson, some are suggesting you sleep with eight-year-old boys'. 'People are starting to ask questions'. 'People think you're a prick'. What people? No people! That's the trick, the beautiful trick. You can say anything as long as it's not you saying it. The only TV commentator arrogant enough to say what he personally thought was Derryn Hinch – and look where he is now. Flogging denture cream on the 'Midday' show. *(softening)* Mike, don't fall for this lightweight crap. You're a good host, you've got cred as a journo. OK?

MIKE Sure. *(pause)* Is 'Midday' a good job?

Day ❸

SCENE 17

BRIAN'S OFFICE

Brian and Emma are running through details of tonight's show.

EMMA . . . she actually went to the Magistrate's Court and got an order giving her custody of the dogs.

BRIAN *(a little bored)* And then hubby runs off with them.

EMMA That's about it.

BRIAN Can we stage a showdown?

EMMA We can try.

BRIAN All right, give it to Marty. And . . .

Brian cuts himself off as he notices a promo for 'A Current Affair'. He turns up the volume with his remote.

VOICE-OVER *(fading up)* . . . just how safe is your airconditioner? Plus, we meet one of Australia's last living legends.

The vision for this promo consists of shots of various rooftop airconditioners, followed by footage of Maurie Fields. Telemation throughout reads '6.30 tonight'.

VOICE-OVER That's 'A Current Affair', 6.30 tonight on Channel Nine.

Brian turns the volume down.

BRIAN Since when is Maurie Fields a living legend? Lucky to qualify on either count.

EMMA *(continuing with list)* We've got a possible studio interview at two. Woman who claims she was sacked for being diabetic.

Brian is distracted.

EMMA *(testing him)* At two o'clock the woman is prepared to come on topless. *(still no reaction)* Brian?

BRIAN Can we find a living legend by tonight?

EMMA Brian! *(referring to TV promo)* We can't afford to let them set the agenda.

BRIAN But we can't ignore them either. Geez, they shit me. They put Ray Martin and a celebrity together; it always rates. I don't know why, maybe opposites attract.

EMMA What do you suggest?

BRIAN Get me a living legend for tonight. All I'm asking for is some old showbiz bastard who doesn't mind spending the afternoon perving at Brooke – and there's our story. Get Kate to help. I want . . .

As Emma leaves the office she mimes Brian's next words to herself.

BRIAN . . . a promo by four o'clock.

SCENE 18

THE PRODUCTION OFFICE

Mike arrives. He notices a policeman in the office speaking to Shelley.

DOMENICA Hi Mike.

MIKE *(indicating cop)* What's . . . (a policeman doing here?)

DOMENICA *(quite excited)* We've been receiving bomb threats.

MIKE When? Who?

DOMENICA (I've got a log.) *(checking clipboard)* Started last night, 6.48. 'Mike Moore will die'. 'Macedonia guilty of genocide'. 'Frontline host is dead'. Aren't people rude? Ooh, nasty. 'Slav-Macedonian conspiracy clear'.

Stu leans across.

STU 'Bring back Star Trek'.

DOMENICA That's not really there, Mike.

MIKE Where's Brian?

DOMENICA In his office.

Mike heads towards Brian's office. Marty stops him en route.

MARTY Morning Derryn.

MIKE Look, Marty . . .

MARTY Hey, very brave move. I mean, a lot of people would back away from making themselves a target, but mate, you've got balls. Actually, that's the bit they cut off first.

We follow Mike across to Brian's office. Brian is meeting with Emma and Kate.

MIKE *(interrupting)* Brian, is everything all right? There's a cop . . .

BRIAN I told you. There are some issues you don't buy into.

MIKE Have you seen the log? They wanna kill me.

BRIAN So do I. Jan's organised for you to do an interview with some local wog paper; that should smooth things over a bit.

MIKE Great. Any word on my car space?

BRIAN They're still digging it up. I don't mind using it for the rest of the week.

KATE *(looking through magazines)* Frank Thring?

BRIAN Too . . . Thringy.

KATE Noel Ferrier?

Brian gives the thumbs down.

EMMA Well, we've ruled out the entire 'Blankety Blanks' panel.

MIKE Maybe we should look at increased security?

BRIAN *(has an idea, to Emma)* Not quite. Funny bloke . . . glasses, cigar, pommy accent.

MIKE Ugly Dave Gray.

EMMA Oh you're not . . . (serious)!

BRIAN It's twenty to eleven. We don't have much choice. *(reaching for phone)* See if you can find his agent. I'll get onto archives to . . .

There is a loud bang. Mike gets a shock. Marty steps into shot with a burst balloon.

MARTY Sorry mate, the pin slipped.

SCENE 19

MIKE'S OFFICE

Mike is being interviewed by two Greek journalists. One asks the questions and then translates Mike's answers to her (presumably monolingual) colleague.

MIKE Well, I know a bit about Greece. I mean, I once spent two weeks on the island of Corfu. Absolutely beautiful.

GREEK #1 But you have never formally studied the history of Greece?

MIKE Well, how accurate were those epic theatres? *(Mike's joke is met with silence)* Not formally, no. At school we studied the Pantheon. No, what's it called? Partheon. I mean, I'm obviously a bit scratchy now. Pythagoras, we did one of his plays.

Greek #1 translates this answer to her colleague, who writes it down. The translation takes a little longer than Mike's answer would seem to have warranted.

GREEK #1 Are you aware there is a world of difference between the cultures of Greece and those of the northern Slavic Macedonians?

MIKE Who makes the dips? *(more silence)* Seriously, of course, I think there's two sides to every issue.

Greek #1 translates for her colleague. Greek #2 responds in Greek. Aggressively.

MIKE *(over the top of Greek #2's reply)* I mean, obviously it's a complex issue. I feel very strongly about that. What exactly are you writing . . . ?

SCENE 20

BRIAN'S OFFICE

Brian and Jan are meeting.

JAN *(agitated)* I've had every editor of every daily in the country on the phone! We are going to have to soften this, show that Mike is not anti-Greek.

BRIAN What do you suggest?

JAN He has to be seen with Greek people, shaking hands. I've lined up a photo opportunity this Saturday at a soccer match with Con the Fruiterer.

BRIAN He's not Greek.

JAN Isn't he?

BRIAN It's Mark Mitchell.

JAN Oh really? Now I get the joke. Tell me, does he have any Greek friends? George Donikian?

Brian shakes his head, 'no'.

JAN George Kapinaris?

Brian shakes his head, 'no'.

JAN George anyone? We'll find someone. Oh, SBS phoned; they want to interview him on 'Face the Press'.

BRIAN Mmm, an interview. It means he has to open his mouth.

JAN *(seeing his point)* You're right. But we should get some value out of this. What about a promo? 'Mike Moore – the man who speaks his mind'?

BRIAN Yeah. Provided he doesn't speak.

SCENE 21

A SUBURBAN HOUSE

Brooke is interviewing Ugly Dave Gray at a table. In the background are awards and other showbiz paraphernalia.

UGLY So this bloke comes back in and says: 'If that's his missus, I'd hate to see their dog.'

Brooke laughs without a lot of conviction.

BROOKE What are your earliest memories of TV?

UGLY Telling my mother-in-law to get out of the way. She had an enormous arse, we couldn't see the screen . . .

BROOKE *(laughing)* But seriously . . .

UGLY I used to say, 'Here's something you've never seen before. Your feet.' And could that woman eat.

She was on a seafood diet. She'd see food and want to eat it. I remember one time . . . Have you got enough? I'll give you a few more. My mother-in-law . . .

We cut as Ugly goes on. It is quite clear Brooke would rather be somewhere else.

SCENE 22

THE EDIT SUITE

Brian, Kate and Hugh are viewing archival footage of Ugly Dave Gray. It is accompanied by a voice-over.

VOICE-OVER Tonight on Frontline, we meet one of this country's last living legends.

Hugh stops the tape.

BRIAN Actually, can you make that black and white? *(Hugh adjusts monitor to black and white)* Great. It makes him look like more of a legend.

SCENE 23

UGLY DAVE'S HOUSE (OUTDOORS, BY THE POOL)

Brooke walks into shot and talks.

BROOKE For almost fifty years now he's been a shining light of the Australian entertainment industry. The wise-crackin', cigar-smokin' funnyman we know simply as 'Ugly Dave'. But is there a sad face behind the happy clown?

Brooke's final position brings her next to Ugly, who is seated. He reaches out and gives her bum a slap.

UGLY Speaking of behinds . . .

BROOKE Dave!

Ugly gets up to chase her.

UGLY Come on darlin'. Make this sad face happy . . . *(wheezes)*

Brooke restrains herself. Stu speaks from behind the camera.

STU Are you all right, Dave?

Ugly sits.

UGLY Just the old ticker.

BROOKE Maybe you should cut down on the smoking.

UGLY I have. I've taken up drinking.

SCENE 24

MIKE'S OFFICE

Mike is reading TV Week *when his phone rings. He hits the speaker-phone button and speaks.*

MIKE Hello.

Nothing is said.

MIKE Hello?

VOICE You will die.

MIKE Who is this?

VOICE You will die.

Mike rushes over to his office door and opens it. Marty is over by the photocopier. He looks at Mike innocently. Mike returns to his phone. We see Marty pull a mobile phone out of his pocket and speak into it.

MARTY Horrible death . . . painful . . .

SCENE 25

BROOKE ON A MOBILE PHONE OUTSIDE UGLY DAVE'S HOUSE

BROOKE Emma, it's Brooke. Well, we've finished shooting. Small problem. Can you change the voice-over from 'Tonight we meet a showbiz legend' to 'Tonight we remember a showbiz legend'?

We widen out to reveal Ugly Dave Gray on a stretcher being loaded into an ambulance by two paramedics. There is a sheet over his face.

SCENE 26

THE CONTROL ROOM

Brian and Emma watch the last few seconds of the show. Elliot Rhodes is performing at the Yamaha keyboard.

ELLIOT Malcolm Turnbull
He's sure got pull
He'll change our flag
Call the Queen a bag
And give old England the flick
So we become an Aussie re-pub-lic.

Cut back to Mike.

MIKE *(laughing)* Ha, ha. Elliot Rhodes taking another light-hearted look at the week that was. That's all for Frontline this week; join us Monday when we pay special tribute to another funny man they called 'Ugly'.

Cut to a preview of Brooke's interview with Ugly.

BROOKE What are your earliest memories of TV?

UGLY Telling my mother-in-law to get out of the way.

As Ugly continues (voice only), we cut back to Mike.

FLOOR MANAGER In five. Stand by to laugh.

UGLY *(voice only)* She had an enormous arse. We couldn't see the screen.

MIKE *(laughing)* Until then, have a great weekend.

Closing music. In the control room, Emma takes a phone call.

BRIAN Well, it's been a beautiful week. John Hewson's creamed us, Mike's incited a wave of racial violence and Brooke's killed a living legend. I might go home and get drunk.

EMMA Brian. It's the gatehouse. Someone jumped the fence and tried vandalising Mike's car.

BRIAN Well, it's not all bad news.

EMMA Um, only Mike's car wasn't parked in his spot. Yours was.

Brian slumps.

Episode 2

The Desert Angel

Day 1

SCENE 1

THE PRODUCTION OFFICE

Marty is pointing a remote control at the main office monitor and is spooling through a tape. The crowd has obviously got a bit restless while they are waiting for Marty to find the right bit.

MARTY Hang on, hang on, it's just after this bit. Here it is, here it is.

Cut to program on TV monitor. We see a crappy version of the Frontline graphics, then an actor dressed as Mike Moore sitting behind a mock-up of the Frontline desk.

MIKE MOORE CHARACTER Hello and welcome to Front-Up.

Pull back to reveal the Frontline staff standing around the monitor laughing.

MIKE MOORE CHARACTER Later we speak to a chiropractor and ask the question: can he get my neck to straighten up? But first, my caring expression, because this story involves somebody old, or sick, or possibly both . . .

DOMENICA Quick, Mike's coming.

They turn off the VCR and scramble back to their seats. Mike walks in. There are general greetings. He fiddles with the mail in his pigeonhole.

MARTY Did you watch 'The Comedy Bunch' last night?

MIKE *(feigning unconcern)* No, was it any good?

MARTY Yeah, yeah . . . They did a very funny piece on Frontline.

MIKE Oh really? I must try and get a tape . . .

Mike heads straight into Brian's office.

MIKE *(agitated)* Did you see 'The Comedy Bunch' last night?

BRIAN Yeah.

Mike turns and shuts the blinds.

MIKE What did you think?

BRIAN Pretty funny.

MIKE Really?

BRIAN *(slightly dismissive)* A bit undergraduate . . .

MIKE Were they having a go at me?

BRIAN (Well) sort of.

MIKE I don't always have my head at . . .

BRIAN (Don't worry about it) Mike, all it says to me is your profile's lifting.

MIKE But if I'm not going to be taken seriously . . .

BRIAN Mate, you should be celebrating.

MIKE But if I'm not able . . .

BRIAN Sit down, Mike. (Look) there are two signs that you've arrived in this game: a comedy show does a parody of you, or Channel Nine tries to poach you.

Emma knocks and comes into the office holding a fax and a videotape.

EMMA Remember the Desert Angel?

Brian and Mike don't really react. They've spent the last two weeks doing stories on the Desert Angel and are a bit bored with the story.

EMMA The young aid worker who went missing in the Sudanese desert five weeks ago, and who we pronounced dead . . . *(thinks)* oh, just last week.

Brian and Mike haven't moved.

EMMA She's been found alive.

BRIAN No shit!

EMMA Half dead, but she's going to make it.

BRIAN *(grabbing the fax)* That cannot be true.

EMMA *(telling him what's in the fax)* A Sudanese army helicopter picked her up five hours ago.

MIKE But we held a memorial service for her. I did the eulogy.

BRIAN *(still reading)* Holy cow.

MIKE *(somewhat in his own world)* You know what this means . . . The Comedy Bunch are going to have a field day.

BRIAN Play the tape, Em. *(reading under his breath)* Five weeks. What a kid.

Emma puts the tape in the VCR. The tape opens with Mike on the set of Frontline.

MIKE Today, sadly, it became official. Authorities have given up hope of finding Australian aid worker Jessica Steckle, the 'Desert Angel', alive. Frontline put together this tribute . . .

Opens on a photo of Jessica, and follows with other photos and a bit of home video footage.

MARTY *(voice only)* Jessica Steckle was the carefree kid everyone loved. Straight A student, sports champion, captain of her school. Jessica wanted to study medicine.

Sad, classical guitar music ('Cavatina' from the movie The Deer Hunter) starts over a collage of shots.

EMMA Was she a straight A student?

BRIAN Nah, we fudged it.

EMMA How was she going to do medicine?

BRIAN We didn't say she was going to do it; we said she wanted to do it.

MARTY *(voice only)* But she gave it all up to be an aid worker in the Sudan. The carefree kid became the caring kid. Three weeks ago this modern-day Florence Nightingale failed to return from a mercy mission. Today authorities officially gave up their search for the girl known as the 'Desert Angel'. During a memorial service held at St Paul's Cathedral, Frontline's Mike Moore read the eulogy.

MIKE *(on screen)* I never met Jessica, but I feel I know her.

Cut to Mike looking through his fingers at the screen.

MIKE *(on screen)* For us, it ceased being a story and became a crusade. But today, the heat and the sand – things that mean leisure and relaxation in our country – meant death in Sudan. Those sands were like sands of an hourglass and so too were the final days of her life. She spent forty days in the desert . . .

Mike grabs the remote control and fast-forwards the tape.

MIKE I'm gonna look like a fool.

BRIAN Forget it, Mike. She gave us our best figures of the year.

EMMA *(with an excellent memory for detail)* Peaked twenty-six Melbourne, twenty-fives Sydney, Adelaide . . .

BRIAN Thanks, Em. OK, she's alive. It's an inconvenience. *(to Mike)* But let's forget about having egg on our face. In fact . . .

We see Brian staring at the angelic face of the Desert Angel on the monitor.

BRIAN I'm glad she's alive. This is going to be huge. If this girl gave us twenty-sixes when she was dead, what's she gonna do for us now?

Brian looks around the room while it all sinks in. Emma has innocently taken the remote out of Mike's hand as though she is actually moved by what's on the tape.

EMMA Just one more bit.

She hits the button and the last ten seconds of the show play.

MIKE *(on screen)* That's all from us tonight. Goodnight. *(looking solemnly heavenward)* Goodnight.

Brian can't help but sneak a private half-smile.

BRIAN Get onto her Mum. *(Emma is already leaving)* Make sure it's exclusive. *(he reiterates, shouting)* Em, exclusive!

Mike leaves and walks back through the office. Domenica shouts to him.

DOMENICA Mike, there's a John Smith on the phone.

MIKE What does he want?

DOMENICA I dunno, but it sounds important.

MIKE I'll take it in there.

Mike walks into his office and hits the speaker-phone.

NEIL It's Neil Byrne here from Channel Nine, Mike. Sorry about the John Smith bullshit . . . couldn't exactly give my real name.

MIKE What can I do for you, Neil?

NEIL Are you alone?

MIKE Uh-huh.

NEIL Mate, a few of the big boys here have been talking a lot about Mike Moore lately, and er . . . We were wondering whether we could have lunch and a bit of a yak.

MIKE Neil, I'm actually tied to Frontline.

NEIL I know that, mate. It's just a yak. Strictly confidential, 100 per cent private. You have my word on it.

MIKE Neil, I . . .

NEIL Mate, it's just a yak.

MIKE When?

NEIL Twelve-thirty at Tre Scalini.

MIKE Shouldn't we meet in private?

NEIL A table up the back. There's no drama.

SCENE 2
BRIAN'S OFFICE

Emma walks into the office.

BRIAN Did you speak to her mum?

EMMA Yeah *(pause)* and so did Harry M. Miller.

BRIAN *(looking up)* No!

EMMA We're going to have to bid for it.

BRIAN We organised the fucking memorial service.

EMMA So we could film it.

BRIAN She doesn't know that.

EMMA But Harry M. does.

Brian leans back in his chair.

BRIAN He'll bust our balls.

EMMA She's gonna be huge.

BRIAN 'Cause we made her huge. Now Channel Nine'll come along after we've done all the hard work. Sure, they can pay a lot of money. They've got about ten different shows they can put her on. How else can we use her? What, are we going to have her spinning the wheel for Captain Hairpiece?

EMMA But if she's good talent, we could stretch it over a week.

BRIAN If she's good talent we can stretch her over a month, but if she's a sullen bitch we'll do our dough.

EMMA Everyone I've spoken to says she's fantastic.

BRIAN Jesus, this is going to cost us . . . *(he pauses for a second, thinking)* Is she definitely going to live?

SCENE 3
GEOFF'S OFFICE

Mike is in with Geoff talking about his day.

MIKE The waiter says, 'Mr Moore' . . . knew my name . . . 'Come this way.' Takes me over to the very front table and there's the big three sitting there.

GEOFF You deserve this, Mike.

MIKE Anyway, we eat . . .

GEOFF What'd you have?

MIKE Umm . . .

GEOFF Tell me later.

MIKE They say, 'We've got someone we'd like you to meet.' There's a limo takes us to the Hyatt, we walk into the penthouse suite. A big bloke gets up from the sofa – Kerry Packer – walks up to me and says, 'So you're the bastard who's been causing us trouble.'

GEOFF Wow.

MIKE Said he's watched every show for the last four weeks . . .

GEOFF And this is still Packer?

MIKE Yeah. Reckons there's only two true stars on Australian television – Ray Martin and me. Said they want me at the network, they had a new show in mind, they'd pay a sign-on fee, a development deal . . .

GEOFF A development deal! You can get your docos up.

MIKE Exactly.

GEOFF I'd love those smart arses at the Comedy Bunch to hear this. Undergraduate smart arses . . . Thank God I'm a regional celebrity. They can't touch me.

MIKE Mate, you can't tell anybody. They really don't want this to get out.

GEOFF Of course they don't.

MIKE Top secret as far they're concerned.

Geoff nods meaningfully.

SCENE 4

BRIAN'S OFFICE

Brian, Emma and Kate are going through women's magazines searching for stories.

BRIAN What kind of name is Dimitriades anyway?

EMMA *(Actually)* he'd be a good story.

BRIAN What does he do?

KATE He's in that 90210 rip-off.

BRIAN *(He)* looks a bit young. Gary Sweet.

EMMA Overexposed.

BRIAN Alex Papps.

EMMA *(dismissively)* 'Where are they now?'

KATE Michael Crawford.

EMMA *(into her magazine)* If he can be surgically removed from Ray Martin.

BRIAN *(tosses his magazine down)* We're barking up the wrong tree, Em. (Let's go over the facts as we know them.) It's a profile series. We're trying to sell Brooke as the reporter who talks to the big names. It's a flirt piece.

EMMA Sorry?

BRIAN It's a flirt piece.

KATE You know, like Tracey Curro on '60 Minutes'.

BRIAN *(Exactly.)* She's cute and blonde and if she plays it right they'll flirt with her, (and) there's your promo, and you run it all week. Doesn't matter if the story's crap. Everyone'll tune in to see Bono hit on Tracey Curro.

KATE Jana Wendt and Dustin Hoffman.

BRIAN Most famous flirt piece ever . . . *(changing back to the matter at hand)* Big names, that's the key. (What have been) the big interviews this year? *(clicks his fingers repeatedly)* (Come on, think.)

KATE Greg Norman on 'Real Life'.

BRIAN Yep, big interview . . . and a flirt piece.

EMMA Shane Warne on '60 Minutes'.

BRIAN Another flirt piece.

KATE *(facetiously)* Carl Lewis on Alan Jones.

BRIAN *(practically)* That interview saved Alan Jones's arse . . . We're onto something. Think sport.

EMMA Andrew Ettingshausen.

BRIAN Yeah, but rugby . . . not big in Melbourne.

EMMA Who cares?

BRIAN That's the attitude that got 'A Current Affair' into trouble.

KATE He's national.

BRIAN No, his penis is national . . . *(thinks briefly)* Actually, go international.

KATE Jeff Harding?

BRIAN *(impatiently)* Boxing – no appeal to women.

EMMA Wimbledon's coming up.

BRIAN *(That's)* good, good, very good.

KATE Don't we have the world doubles champions or something?

BRIAN *(slightly pained)* Doubles?

KATE The Woodies, they're the world . . .

BRIAN Nooo.

KATE Wally Masur.

Brian shakes his head like he's bitten into a lemon. Emma starts laughing to herself. They stop and notice her.

EMMA I know. Pat Cash.

Brian and Kate immediately break into broad sneaky smiles.

EMMA You said you wanted a flirt piece.

KATE There's no way . . .

BRIAN Would he do it?

EMMA If he knew it was with Brooke.

KATE What if it's just a rumour?

EMMA It's not.

KATE I'm sorry?

EMMA (I know) it's not.

BRIAN All jokes aside, if we could get him (it'd be huge). Make the call, and speak to him, not his dad.

EMMA *(halfway out the door)* So Brooke Vandenberg is actually going to interview Pat Cash!

Kate shakes her head in juicy disbelief. Mike pokes his head in the door, as if to say 'Did you want to see me?' Brian waves him in.

BRIAN People are going to watch that for sure.

MIKE *(oblivious to the innuendo)* Absolutely. He's such a great tennis player.

Brian and Kate look at Mike to check that he's joking.

MIKE Well, he is.

He's not joking. He genuinely doesn't get it. They continue their business.

KATE I'll come back later, Brian. *(she leaves)*

MIKE You wanted to see me (right?)

Brian nods him to a seat. Mike takes a seat as Brian fiddles with a bit of paperwork on his desk.

BRIAN How did the meeting with Channel Nine go?

MIKE (What . . . how did . . . ?)

BRIAN You did have a meeting?

MIKE Neil Byrne rang, said he just wanted to have a private chat.

BRIAN A private chat? The front table at Tre Scalini? That's not private, it's a press release.

MIKE Did Geoff speak to you?

BRIAN Geoff! Mike, I've already had three different phone calls, and one of them came during your entree. Jesus, the front table. The last person to fall for that trick was . . . you when we got you from the ABC.

MIKE Is that how you . . . ?

BRIAN They set you up.

MIKE No, this was different.

BRIAN (Uh-huh . . .) What did Packer have to say?

Mike is stunned. There was no way Brian could have known he met with Packer. Brian's gaze hasn't flinched.

BRIAN Yeah, really different. (Well, come on) what did Packer have to say? No, no, no, let me guess. 'There's only two stars on Australian television, Jana Wendt and Mike Moore.'

Mike gives a sheepish 'not quite' look.

BRIAN 'Ray Martin and Mike Moore.'

Mike gives a tiny acknowledgement that that is correct.

BRIAN Then he would have stood up and looked out the window. *(he gets up and walks to the window)* 'We've got a lot of plans at Nine . . . ' Then he would have turned around . . . *(he turns around and points at Mike)* 'and we want you to be a part of it.' (Don't you realise?) Frontline is hurting 'A Current Affair' so they poach the host.

Emma appears, but stops at the door.

BRIAN (It's all right.)

EMMA *(surprised)* We just heard on the radio you're going to '60 Minutes'.

Mike has a look of disbelief at the way his secret meeting at Tre Scalini has snowballed into a major story.

BRIAN *(explaining)* Nine would've rung 'em.

MIKE Have I made a tactical error?

BRIAN *(to Emma)* What have you got?

EMMA Pat Cash said yes.

BRIAN *(with relief)* Great . . . and the ex-con?

EMMA Mr Miller said fifty thousand.

BRIAN *(whistle)* Fifty?

EMMA Not negotiable. Nine definitely want it.

Brian leans back and takes in the ramifications of that amount.

BRIAN I'll have to get approval.

MIKE Sorry. We're not going to pay for the story.

BRIAN Don't have a choice. Your mate Kerry wants it as well. *(in a pointed manner at Mike)* Seems like he thinks he can buy anything.

SCENE 5

THE CAR PARK

Stu and Marty are unpacking the unit van after getting back from a story. The cellular phone goes. Stu picks it up.

MARTY *(continuing the conversation already in progress)* They overvalue all the prizes, so when they say 'This holiday valued at thirteen thousand dollars', it's actually worth about seven or eight.

STU Yeah . . . we're actually in the car park. Uh-huh . . . You're kidding . . . you're kidding! Emma! OK. *(hangs up)*

MARTY Story?

STU Guess who Brooke's doing a profile on tomorrow? *(pausing for effect)* Pat Cash.

MARTY *(shaking his head)* You're kidding.

STU That's what I said.

MARTY You're kidding.

STU That's what I said.

MARTY You are kidding.

STU I said that too.

MARTY Does she know?

STU *(looking off to the side)* She's about to find out. *(shouts)* Brooke!

MARTY I don't think I can stay for this.

Brooke arrives.

STU *(to Brooke)* We've got another profile tomorrow morning. We're going to leave here about ten.

BROOKE *(nastily)* So you're the producer now.

STU *(quickly)* It just came through on . . .

BROOKE Who is it?

STU Er . . . Pat Cash.

BROOKE *(the slightest of pauses)* Fine. I'll just get the background. See you at ten.

She walks away. They watch her without changing their gaze.

MARTY She's cool.

STU She is cool.

MARTY She's cool.

STU Very cool.

MARTY She represents a definite drop in temperature.

SCENE 6

GENERAL MANAGER'S OFFICE

Ian Farmer, the station General Manager, is in his office when the secretary's voice comes over the speaker-phone.

KELLY Mr Farmer, Don Willesee to see you.

FARMER *(desperately)* No, Kelly, I'm not in.

Brian walks in the door smiling and Farmer realises he's been got again.

FARMER I don't know how you keep thinking them up. *(moving around his desk to the armchairs)* Thought you were never going to top Grant Dodwell.

They both sit down.

FARMER (Now) I had a think about this Desert Angel and basically we're prepared to pay a lot. *(he picks up a photo of the Desert Angel)* You're close and you're getting closer. I know for a fact they're worried.

BRIAN It'll get out we paid.

FARMER *(shrugs)* We'll leak a false figure.

BRIAN I also wanted to talk to you about Mike.

FARMER The Nine offer? *(he explains his knowledge)* A journo just rang.

BRIAN What d'ya reckon?

FARMER They're spoiling.

BRIAN (Are) they serious?

FARMER Probably.

BRIAN How do we handle it?

FARMER Same way they do. Bullshit a bit. The real trick is to offer a few trinkets, make him feel like he's earmarked to be the network star.

BRIAN *(puzzled)* As in . . . ?

FARMER *(reaching into his coat pocket as he speaks)* I've had to do this so often I actually wrote them down one day. You can offer him weekend news, 'Earthwatch', the lotto draw – actually I keep that list for weathermen. Here we go. Hosting tribute nights, royal command performances . . . *(scratches that one out)* I've got to update this.

BRIAN What about 'Carols by Candlelight'?

FARMER Try prying that away from Mr Waxy Fingers. (Here's one) a guest spot on 'Getaway' . . . er, 'Holiday'. What's our one?

BRIAN 'Vacation'.

FARMER I thought we axed that.

BRIAN No, that was the lifestyles show.

FARMER Oh God, that was awful. *(thinks)* Why don't you just say the network has a lot of things in mind, we see his role expanding . . . What's his soft spot?

TOGETHER Documentaries.

FARMER (Need I ask.) I must add that to the list. What in particular?

BRIAN Asia, sailing . . . Could we get him to do a doco on . . . ?

FARMER Brian, there's no part of the Australian coastline that's yet to be documented by this country's news presenters.

BRIAN *(he shares a small laugh)* Could he host 'This World'?

FARMER Just promised it to Mr Game Show.

BRIAN What about something on Asia?

FARMER What's this Asian thing?

BRIAN He just spent three weeks in Vietnam. Thinks he's done the grand expedition.

FARMER My fifteen-year-old daughter's been to Vietnam!

BRIAN (I know but what can you do?)

FARMER *(thinking)* Tell him we're very keen to have a six-part series on 'Emerging Asia', 'Our Neighbours of the North'. Talk about a development deal.

BRIAN What timeslot?

FARMER Timeslot? (Are you crazy?) We're not going to screen it!

SCENE 7
THE EDIT SUITE

Stu is labelling tapes while Marty waits for them.

MARTY Did you mark my close-ups?

STU I stopped after the first fifty.

MARTY *(protesting)* Hey, it's the way it's done.

STU Oh, I'm not suggesting there's an ego component.

Mike walks in.

MIKE Did you hear Brooke's doing Pat Cash?

STU Actually I think she's already done him.

They all laugh, but Mike is less convincing.

MIKE She hasn't interviewed him before.

MARTY (Well) it won't be so much an interview, more a reunion.

They all laugh again.

STU Actually, will it be a closed set?

They laugh again, Mike joining in uproariously after a few seconds.

MIKE Set, tennis set. Very funny.

Mike moves off, none the wiser. Completely bewildered, Marty and Stu watch him go.

SCENE 8
BRIAN'S OFFICE

Brian is on the phone.

BRIAN It's too much. I'm not paying that kind of money.

Mike appears at the door. Brian waves him in.

BRIAN I want an answer by this afternoon. *(he hangs up)* Yeah?

MIKE Look, I'm sorry I didn't tell you about the meeting.

BRIAN That's OK, Mike. I know how they work. They talk big about projects: *(listing)* development deals, packages – and nothing ever comes of it. They warehouse you, mate.

MIKE Sure.

BRIAN You've got a big future here, Mike. The network has a lot of things in mind. They see your role expanding. They've earmarked you to be the next network star.

MIKE Really? (Actually) I heard the host job for 'This World' is coming up.

BRIAN Mate, that's a job for a game-show host.

MIKE I just thought . . .

BRIAN Mate, if you want it, I'll ring 'em now *(picks up the phone)* They asked me if you'd like to do it.

He punches the numbers with purpose.

MIKE Well no, hang on, hang on. If you don't (think it's a good idea) . . .

BRIAN *(confiding)* They're actually after a six-part series on Asia.

MIKE That's right up my alley!

BRIAN That's what I said.

MIKE And?

BRIAN And if they ever find out about that Packer meeting they'll freak.

MIKE Forget it. It never happened as far as I'm concerned.

BRIAN They'll find out you met with someone.

MIKE Brian, I don't want to go to Nine!

BRIAN You've made the right move.

MIKE I'd never get my Asian documentaries up there.

BRIAN That's the difference between us and them, Mike. We're serious.

Mike gets up to leave. Brian is about to get back to what he was doing, but Mike turns around.

MIKE (Actually) one more thing. Is there something going on with Brooke at the moment?

Brian gives him a look as if to think 'Is he joking? Surely he knows.' He doesn't.

BRIAN Mike, shut the door.

SCENE 9
GEOFF'S OFFICE

Mike enters Geoff's office in a hurry.

MIKE Geoff, you're not going to believe this, but guess which television star had a fling with Pat Cash a few years back?

GEOFF Brooke Vandenberg.

MIKE *(deflated)* How'd you know that?

GEOFF Everyone knew that. I just always thought that it's common knowledge.

MIKE What do you mean everyone knew that?

SCENE 10
BRIAN'S OFFICE

Jan is sitting at the desk with pen and paper.

JAN I'm so glad, Brian. Publicity's been in an absolute spin, and Mike's such a sweetie. I love him.

BRIAN He's confirmed his commitment to the network. In addition he'll be working on . . . *(he searches for the right words)* special projects.

JAN Documentaries?

BRIAN Yeah, but don't say that.

JAN No, darling, I know . . . Now, we need a quote from Mike.

BRIAN *(with no sense of deception)* OK, let's think one up . . . 'I'm looking forward to a long and fruitful relationship with the network . . .'

JAN 'Exciting new developments . . .'

BRIAN 'Exciting new developments . . .'

JAN And I can add those: prime-time specials, on assignments, guest spot on 'Holiday', 'Getaway' . . . What's our one? I always forget.

DOMENICA *(voice only, on speaker-phone)* Line one, Jan.

Jan picks up the phone, knowing full well who it will be.

JAN Mandy darling, all wrong, sweetheart. He's definitely staying here. *(pause)* They're silly old pricks, that's what they . . . In fact I was just speaking to Mike this second. He said *(obviously reading)* I'm looking forward to a long and fruitful relationship, with my role expanding . . . *(pause)* Well, he always gets formal when he's excited . . . He's very excited about his guest spot on 'Holiday' and . . . well, you know the one I mean.

Day ❷

SCENE 11

THE PRODUCTION OFFICE

There is a production meeting. A few of the staff are gathered around the fax machine, waiting.

MARTY I don't know. It's a lot of money.

STU She's good.

MARTY Fantastic. But I'm just saying you can turn anyone into good media fodder . . . Look at yourself. You play indoor cricket.

STU Yeah?

MARTY Well, if you went missing in the desert tomorrow you'd be *(pompously)* 'an aspiring sports star cut off on the verge of national selection'. *(everyone laughs)* Ever bought something at an op shop?

STU Yeah?

MARTY 'Community-minded, a humanitarian who gave of himself' . . . Your old man's got superannuation?

Stu nods. Brooke is reading the paper while eating.

BROOKE *(without looking up)* 'Heir to a fortune.'

STU Brian can have my story for fifty grand.

MARTY Only one problem. You're as ugly as sin.

The others laugh. Jase, who has said nothing but listened to everything, giggles.

MARTY Isn't that right, Jase? *(Jase nods)* And that's one thing you can't fudge, although we did manage to do it once. We had one girl who died, had it all but ugly as a cow, so we cut a photo of a model out of *Cleo* and said that was her. Two days before someone picked it up.

Everyone reacts.

STU Who's Brian talking to?

EMMA He's on the phone. *(the fax paper starts to feed)* I think it's Harry M. Miller.

MARTY You know what the 'M' stands for?

He leans across to Stu and whispers the answer in his ear. Stu laughs.

MARTY It's true. Isn't it, Jase?

Jase nods. They crane their heads upside down to see the ratings figures.

EMMA Frontline nineteen, twenty; 'A Current Affair' twenty-two, twenty-two . . .

MARTY *(whistles)* Bloody close. They'll be shit-scared.

EMMA 'Real Life' fifteens . . .

MARTY *(grabs the sheet from Emma)* Gee, that 'Bob Morrison Show' is proving me wrong.

Brian speaks from the doorway.

BRIAN We lost her. *(there is audible disappointment)* 'A Current Affair'.

EMMA How much?

BRIAN Seventy-five grand.

MARTY *(he whistles)* We're going to get crunched.

There is a general rabble of disappointment and suggestions.

MARTY They'll clean up. We're done.

BRIAN *(quietening them down)* Just because we haven't got the rights from Harry M. Miller to interview her doesn't mean we can't do a story on her.

MARTY We're going to spoil?

BRIAN (You) bet your arse we are. OK people, (listen up) we need a story on the Desert Angel tonight, an angle if you will.

BROOKE *(musing)* Maybe the Angel has a darker side.

BRIAN Does she have a darker side?

EMMA *(reading efficiently)* Aid worker, school captain, considered becoming a nun . . .

STU We know she's got a boring side.

MARTY Nothing about table-top dancing?

STU Do you recognise her?

BRIAN *(Brian shoots them a glare)* Come on, we're on to something.

MARTY You know, when you think about it, five weeks in forty-degree heat, with no supplies, sounds a bit suss to me.

BRIAN Sounds real suss . . . So we do a James Scott on her.

EMMA (protesting) We can't have a go at her.

BRIAN Don't need to. Get someone else to do that.

MARTY Grab an expert. Ask him a few pertinent if somewhat ambiguous questions.

EMMA I don't believe I'm hearing this.

MARTY What church was she with?

EMMA Latter-day Saints.

MARTY (hamming it up slightly) Very kooky.

EMMA We were gonna canonise her twenty minutes ago.

BRIAN (in mock shock) That was before I found out about all that shonky stuff.

MARTY Now we're finding out about the real Desert Angel.

BRIAN Cut a promo.

EMMA (protesting) We haven't done the story.

BRIAN When's that stopped us? 'Tonight on Frontline . . .'

MARTY 'Growing doubts . . .'

BRIAN 'Growing doubts over the Aussie aid worker', some actuality and then . . . (thinks)

BROOKE 'Desert Angel or Desert Devil.'

BRIAN Bang. That's my girl.

Mike walks into the meeting carrying a car magazine.

BRIAN Desert Angel out.

MIKE How?

BRIAN I'm not paying for stories. I told 'em to shove their cheque-book journalism up their arse. (he leaves)

Mike gives Brian a proud look and then speaks to Marty.

MIKE I've got a lot of respect for him.

SCENE 12

THE CAR PARK

Marty and Stu are loading up and chatting. Jase doesn't say anything but nods assertively. Brooke walks over to the car and gets in. Marty drops his voice.

MARTY She still hasn't flinched.

STU I reckon, just quietly, she's happy the story's got out.

Marty looks doubtful.

STU (Look at it this way.) These days chicks haven't made it in TV until there's a rumour about them and some rock star or (in this case) sports star.

MARTY (Eh?)

STU They know they're only glorified mouthpieces.

MARTY Hang on, mate.

STU Not you, you're different. But people like her, any profile's good profile, so a rumour like this, it's an investment in the future. Her and Pat Cash, I reckon she wanted it to get out.

MARTY (on the back foot a little, but then decisive) Nuh.

Stu looks at Marty as if to say, 'Maybe it's true'.

SCENE 13

THE EDIT SUITE

Brian and Emma enter.

BRIAN (to Hugh) Give us a look.

EMMA Here's the bit we want to use.

The footage plays. A man in a white coat behind a desk is asked a question from behind the camera.

MARTY *(voice only)* Can a human being survive thirty days in the desert?

DOCTOR No way, impossible. However in Jessica's case it's a bit different, because we know she had some water, she's extremely fit, young, knew the basics of survival.

BRIAN Forget all that water, fit stuff. Take it back.

Hugh takes it back.

MARTY *(voice only)* Can a human being survive thirty days in the desert?

DOCTOR No way, impossible.

BRIAN That's the bit to use. *(turning to Emma)* I want you to get it on quick and run the crap out of it. OK, let's have a look from the top.

VOICE-OVER Tonight on Frontline, doubts arise over the Aussie aid worker.

MARTY *(voice only)* Can a human being survive thirty days in the desert?

DOCTOR No way, impossible.

VOICE-OVER 'Desert Angel or Desert Devil?', tonight on Frontline.

BRIAN Great.

SHELLEY Brian, urgent phone call from Harry M. Miller.

Brian looks around to Emma and then to Hugh.

BRIAN Just hang on.

SCENE 14

MIKE IS ON AIR AT 3AW WITH NEIL MITCHELL.

NEIL Anyway, let's look at tonight's show. You won't be talking to the Desert Angel? Big story.

MIKE No, we're quite firm about this now. We won't pay people for stories.

NEIL You paid the topless hairdresser.

MIKE Yeah, but . . . That was for the haircut.

NEIL *(polite but still obviously circumspect)* All right, that's Frontline tonight with Mike Moore, and just before we go, what are these rumours about you going to Nine?

MIKE Oh, just that, Neil, rumours. No, I'm very happy where I am.

NEIL *(OK,)* back after the break.

They both remove their headphones. Mike, oblivious of the fact that he sounded less than convincing, immediately starts up a bit of friendly private banter.

MIKE Speaking of rumours, guess which television reporter had a dalliance with a certain Pat Cash a few years ago?

NEIL *(flatly, as if to say 'Why are you asking me something everyone knows?')* Brooke Vandenberg.

MIKE How did you know that?

NEIL I thought everyone knew that.

SCENE 15

A GARDEN

Brooke is interviewing Pat Cash. They are both seated on director's chairs.

BROOKE And finally, how do feel about being Pat Cash, the sex symbol, again?

PAT *(laughing)* I think I'm only a sex symbol to the elderly.

BROOKE Pat Cash, thanks for your time.

STU That's great. (While you're there) can we get your cutaways?

They film while Brooke apes her previous reactions: flirting, the pen to the mouth, concern, doubt, etc.

STU Great. Thanks, everyone.

Brooke gets up. There is suppressed giggling and muttering among the crew. As Stu walks away, Pat sidles up to Brooke.

PAT *(half-whispering)* Is there something going on with the crew?

BROOKE There's a rumour that you and I slept together.

PAT *(shocked)* But this is the first time we've met! *(Brooke shrugs)* Who would have started that rumour?

BROOKE I did.

SCENE 16

THE PRODUCTION OFFICE

Mike arrives back in the office.

DOMENICA You sounded great, Mike.

MIKE Thank you.

DOMENICA Really strong.

MIKE I made a stipulation when I came from the ABC that I wouldn't be involved in anything that challenged my journalistic integrity. But Brian is the real hero.

Brian and Emma rush into the office.

BRIAN Quick, Mike. We've got the Desert Angel!

MIKE For free?

BRIAN For what we offered last. Nine pulled out.

MIKE *(aghast)* You paid?

BRIAN Yes.

MIKE (But) I've just been saying we wouldn't indulge in cheque-book journalism.

BRIAN Well you're going to look stupid then, aren't you?

MIKE I can't go on now and . . .

EMMA It's fine, Mike. We'll work something out.

MIKE What do you mean?

EMMA *(thinking fast)* We won't pay her. We'll put it in a trust, for when she grows up. That's not paying her – she can't take it out until she's twenty-one.

MIKE She's twenty now.

BRIAN Lucky girl.

MIKE Brian . . .

BRIAN Mike, we'll sort something out. It's going to be a live cross from the airport.

As they walk out of the office, they hear a promo.

VOICE-OVER Tonight on 'A Current Affair' doubts arise over the so-called 'Desert Angel'. Could she really have survived that long? 'Florence Nightingale or Fraud?', tonight on 'A Current Affair'.

BRIAN Bastards.

SCENE 17

THE FRONTLINE STUDIO

Cut straight to Mike behind the desk.

MIKE Hello, and welcome to this very special edition of Frontline. In a few moments we're going to cross live to speak with someone who's captured the hearts of Australia, someone who became known as the 'Desert Angel'. In an incredible story of survival against the odds, the young and beautiful aid worker Jessica Steckle, who went missing for five weeks in the searing Sahara desert, turned up alive just yesterday. This miracle maiden with the model looks chose to talk to Frontline exclusively, and she joins me now live via satellite from Perth.

Cut to Emma and Brian in the control room.

BRIAN This could crack it for us. We can run stories on this kid for a month and nobody's gonna get tired of her.

EMMA I can't believe 'A Current Affair' just pulled out like that.

BRIAN They're feeling the pressure. They're starting to make mistakes.

Cut back to Mike.

MIKE Good evening, Jessica.

JESSICA G-g-g-good ev-v-v-ening M-m-m-mike.

Mike looks stunned.

Cut back to control room. Brian and Emma look stunned.

Episode 4
She's Got the Look

Day ❶

SCENE I

BRIAN'S OFFICE

Music: 'She's Got the Look' by Roxette. We see sexy shots of female athlete Nikki Burke: in the gym, sweat strategically dripping down her boobs; running shots; sitting on a bench drinking Lucozade – this could be a commercial.

BROOKE *(voice only)* Nikki Burke. She's only nineteen, with a sexy smile and supermodel looks to match. She could easily be at home on the catwalks of Paris. But rather than 'walking', she's in the running as one of our main hopes at the 1996 Olympics.

NIKKI *(voice only)* Yeah, the training's hard. But I guess I want to do this not just for me, but for Australia as well.

Widen to reveal Brian and Marty watching Nikki on video.

MARTY She is (definitely) good-looking.

BRIAN Her voice is a bit Jo Bailey. Mind you, we can fix that . . .

MARTY What did this rate?

BRIAN *(calling out)* Em, the Olympic athlete piece. What did it rate?

EMMA *(without checking notes)* Twenty-two Sydney, twenty-one Melbourne, Brisbane twenty-four, Perth . . .

BRIAN *(cutting her off)* Thanks. *(to Marty)* She's a spunk, all right. She's on her way in here now.

Brian spools back through tape and lets it run again.

MARTY She's definitely good talent.

Mike enters, interrupting as usual. He carries an invitation.

MIKE Brian, 'Sale of the Century' are having a celebrity super-challenge . . .

BRIAN It's not for you, Mike.

MIKE Really?

BRIAN You've got too much cred, mate.

MIKE Yeah.

Brian is concentrating once more on the video of Nikki. Mike's attention is also drawn to the screen.

MIKE Nikki? Are we doing another story?

BRIAN We're thinking about an on-air role.

MIKE As a reporter? On Frontline? But . . . we can't just pull someone off the street and turn them into a journalist. It's taken me fifteen years to become what I am.

BRIAN *(with a warning look at Marty to keep quiet)* Mike, I know what you're saying, and I think you've got a point . . . but I happen to think that the girl's got it. I know how to spot talent.

He walks over to the VCR and presses 'Pause' on a stunning close-up of Nikki. Marty is standing in front of a blown-up photo of Mike.

MARTY *(adopting the same pose as Mike's photo)* Obviously you've made the odd mistake.

BRIAN The fact that she happens to be, er . . . good-looking is an added bonus.

MIKE She's an athlete. She's got no journalistic experience.

BRIAN Mate, no-one's saying it's gonna be easy, but she's about to enrol in the best school of journalism in this country. She'll be learning from pros like you.

MIKE *(pondering this)* Yeah . . . But look, I just want to flag my reservations right from the outset about this whole idea of hiring good-looking girls instead of serious journalists. I hate this whole bimbo trend.

During this speech Emma enters and places a piece of paper on Brian's desk. As she is leaving she speaks.

EMMA Well said, Mike.

MIKE We didn't hire Emma for her looks.

MARTY Not so well said, Mike.

Emma exits.

MIKE Well, you know what I mean.

SCENE 2

THE PRODUCTION OFFICE

EMMA No-one likes Billy. How can you like him?

KATE I like Michael.

EMMA But he's such a bastard.

DOMENICA My cousin's just come back from America and she told me what happens at Billy and Alison's wedding.

KATE AND EMMA No! Don't tell us!

KATE Does she die?

Nikki enters. Emma notices and signals Domenica.

DOMENICA Sorry, can I help you?

Nikki is wearing skimpy running shorts and a midriff top which shows an obscenely taut and tanned stomach. Her hair is gorgeous. Out of nowhere, Mike appears.

NIKKI I've got an appointment with Brian Thompson.

DOMENICA Sure.

MIKE You must be Nikki Burke.

NIKKI Yeah. And you are . . . ?

MIKE Mike Moore.

Mike coolly shakes her hand.

NIKKI Hi! Sorry, I'm a bit sweaty. Brian called and told me to get here like, now, and I'd just come home from a run.

MIKE Yeah, I'm a bit of a runner myself . . . I often jog to work. *(the other girls exchange smiles)* How many k's did you do today?

NIKKI Um, fifteen or twenty.

Mike whistles. The girls in the office are suitably unimpressed.

BRIAN Nik! Come on in.

NIKKI Bye!

Mike stares at her in a sleazy way.

MIKE *(to Emma)* Before you say a word, I'm totally with you on this one.

EMMA What do you mean?

MIKE I mean, the girl's had no experience.

EMMA *(slightly panicked)* She's not becoming a reporter?

Mike gives a dorky shrug and exits.

EMMA *(almost to herself)* Unbelievable.

SCENE 3

GEOFF'S OFFICE

MIKE So did the news director actually tell you you had to do this?

GEOFF No, he just said maybe I should update my look a bit.

Geoff tries on spectacle frames.

MIKE Just tell him 'no'. Your old frames suit you.

GEOFF Nuh, I'm trying not to rock the boat. My urban wildlife documentary is looking promising. Farmer's got a 6.30 Sunday timeslot free.

MIKE Really? Great . . . 'cause I saw that Tina Dalton thing on 'Deadly Australians'. How easy is that!

GEOFF Been done.

MIKE People wanna know what's in their backyards.

GEOFF Yeah, so I'm not gonna make waves.

MIKE It'll be good. Speaking of looking good . . . seems the Frontline team will be expanding. Brian's pretty keen to hire this athlete. She's a bit of a spunk.

GEOFF Yeah?

MIKE I've flagged my reservations. She's got no journalistic experience, but Brian thinks she's got 'it' . . .

SCENE 4

BRIAN'S OFFICE

JAN I don't see why you're so against this. The

General Manager wants him to do it, the network's very keen . . .

BRIAN I don't want him on.

JAN But 'Celebrity Sale of the Century' is a publicity bonanza. It's cross-network promotion.

BRIAN I'm trying to run a current affairs show here and I don't want the people out there finding out Mike's not the intelligent, knowledgeable host we sell him as.

JAN Brian, it's not 'Mastermind', it's 'Sale of the Century'.

BRIAN Hey, have a chat to him some time. Ask him to name some capital cities.

SCENE 5

THE PRODUCTION OFFICE

A production meeting is in progress.

BRIAN You've got the rundown, Em?

EMMA Still putting together tonight.

Mike arrives.

MIKE Is there a meeting?

BRIAN *(under his breath)* Shit. *(to Mike)* Mike, we were just starting. Grab a seat. All right.

MIKE *(going into his office)* Just hang on a second.

Brian goes to continue but is interrupted again, this time by Mike wheeling a very squeaky ergonomic chair out from his office. No-one says a thing.

BRIAN Who've we got for the celebrity profile series?

EMMA It's looking a bit thin at the moment, but I . . .

BROOKE *(cutting Emma off)* I've got James Packer – 3.30 today.

MARTY You're kidding.

BROOKE No, I am not.

MARTY You kept that one under your hat.

MIKE *(amid squirms and hidden giggles from the rest of the staff)* That's amazing! How did you get him to agree . . . ? Well done, Brooke. Congratulations.

THE REST OF THE STAFF *(mock congratulations)* Yeah, well done.

BRIAN Well, that takes care of our profile series. Now we need . . . Is anyone sitting on a good sports story? Something uplifting . . .

MIKE *(having just been told the James Packer story by Marty)* You're kidding!

BRIAN Guys, bit of focus. Marty, have you finished that shonky lawyer story yet?

MARTY Still going.

BRIAN What?

MARTY It's almost there. He won't talk.

BRIAN *(cutting him off)* Don't waste any more time on this arsehole. Do a foot-in-the-door.

KATE But if he's refusing to talk?

BRIAN If he's refusing to talk then get footage of him refusing. Don't phone. Rock up, stick the camera in his face, hope for a bit of push-and-shove and BANG!

KATE Bang what? You still haven't got an interview.

MARTY Don't need an interview.

BRIAN Don't want an interview. Bastard may sound reasonable. A refusal makes him look guilty.

EMMA We reverse the presumption of innocence.

BRIAN Exactly.

EMMA That was a criticism.

BRIAN OK, that's solved. Now, I want a sports story. It's for the new girl we're trying out. You might have seen her around . . . *(he pretends to search for her name)*

MIKE *(immediately)* Nikki Burke.

BRIAN She's an athlete. What's a story that would suit her?

EMMA Something without many verbs?

MARTY Nah, we keep them for Mike.

BRIAN I was thinking something about sport.

KATE What about something on handicapped sportspeople?

BRIAN Yeah, good 'n uplifting.

KATE There's the wheelchair tennis . . .

BRIAN No wheelchairs.

KATE What about the blind pentathlete?

Brian shakes his head. Cut to Emma looking unimpressed.

KATE What about that deaf marathon swimmer?

BRIAN Yeah, he's good. Actually that'd be a chance to get Nikki in some togs . . .

Everyone starts to pack up and leave. Emma hangs back and approaches Brian, who is heading for his office.

EMMA So am I to understand that you have employed Nikki?

BRIAN I'm thinking about it.

EMMA I didn't realise there was a vacancy in the on-camera reporting department.

BRIAN *(distracted)* There wasn't. I made one.

Emma nods and goes to leave, then thinks better of it.

EMMA What would you say if I told you I wanted an on-air position?

BRIAN *(looking up)* Em.

EMMA *(angrily)* Why? Why couldn't I be a reporter?

BRIAN Whooaaah!

EMMA I'm good . . . You say I'm good.

BRIAN As a producer, Emma. You're the best.

EMMA Yeah, but I . . .

BRIAN Emma. You understand how it all works.

EMMA I thought I did, but how do you explain how a girl with no experience is suddenly on camera?

BRIAN She's a high-profile, intelligent . . .

EMMA Don't patronise me . . . *(not letting Brian get a word in)* I'm not blind. Yes, she's very attractive, but if I got a bit of make-up, a suit . . . I write all that shit. I'm more a journalist than she is. I'm more a journalist than Brooke, or Marty . . . and they all get paid five times my salary and I'm stuck here. I write their questions. I do the research. I set it all up and what do I get? Nothing. And when I want an opportunity – nothing. It's treated as a joke. 'Em become a reporter? You've gotta be kidding . . . ' *(she has worked herself up)*

BRIAN Are you finished?

EMMA I think so.

Emma goes to leave. As she goes out of the office Mike enters.

BRIAN Brian, I've been thinking about this 'Sale of the Century' thing, and I reckon I should do it.

BRIAN Mate, I'll come clean with you. I want you to do it. It's network politics. The boys upstairs . . . The trouble is, it's on another station.

MIKE *(he can't believe it)* Oh, it's so short-sighted! These cowboys spend their year off at TV conferences in . . . what's the capital of Belgium?

BRIAN Brussels.

MIKE Brussels. They've got no idea.

BRIAN Mike, sit down. Mate, network politics – had 'em up to here. You know what I keep in my top drawer? *(pulls out envelope)* My resignation. And one day when they push me too far, I'm gonna walk in and just slap it down on their desk, 'cause I've had a gutful.

MIKE *(panicked)* Hey, mate, not over 'Sale of the Century'. Put it away. Let's not let them win. Stuff 'em. I'm not going on.

SCENE 6

THE LADIES' BATHROOM

Emma is standing in front of the mirror. Her face is red and swollen from tears. Brooke walks in, looking immaculate. She smiles fleetingly and heads for a cubicle.

EMMA Am I attractive?

There is a pause, then the flush of the toilet. Brooke emerges.

BROOKE What an odd question.

EMMA Well, am I?

BROOKE Yes.

EMMA Do you think I'd be a good television reporter?

BROOKE *(now understanding where she's coming from)* Yeah, but you're a great producer.

EMMA Doesn't it piss you off that a girl whose only experience on television is a Lucozade commercial gets to all of sudden become a journalist on a current affairs show?

BROOKE Yeah, it does. But it's not going to change the way things are. She looks good on camera. If you've got the looks, you get the gig.

EMMA Marty's no oil painting.

BROOKE Neither is Laurie Oakes or Jim Waley. They're blokes, Emma. It's completely different for women in television – looks are everything. Unfortunately I've only got about ten years left before I'm considered over the hill. And as for Jana – tick, tick, tick. Stick to producing, Emma. You'll be around a lot longer than I will.

She exits with a cool smile. Emma continues to stare at herself in the mirror. She blows her nose with toilet paper.

SCENE 7

A SUBURBAN STREET, OUTSIDE A HOUSE

Marty is in a car with Stu and Jase. They're eating McDonald's. They look like cops on a stake-out.

MARTY Come on. We'll knock this over in ten.

STU Hang on, I haven't had my apple pie.

MARTY You must be the only person in Australia who gets sucked into buying an apple pie.

STU I like 'em. Well I do.

MARTY OK, all we need here is a bit of hustle and bustle, and him refusing to talk to us. Then we can piss off. Understand?

STU Yep.

MARTY Jase? *(Jase nods)* Let's go. Start rolling the camera now.

They leave the car. Stu is shooting. Marty gives a quick nod to Stu and knocks on the door of the house. We see through Stu's viewfinder what we will eventually see at home on TV.

BOWMAN *(heard through door)* Yes?

MARTY Mr Bowman? My name is Martin di Stasio from Frontline. *(aggressively)* I was wondering if I could speak to you about the $250,000 that's gone missing from your clients' trust funds.

Pause. Marty smiles at Stu as if to say 'Beauty, just what we're after.' Then the door opens.

BOWMAN All right. Come in.

Marty is stunned. This was not supposed to happen.

SCENE 8

THE PRODUCTION OFFICE

Mike is quietly relating a story to Domenica, Shelley and Kate.

MIKE . . . so I'm in Brian's office, and you'll never guess what he pulled out of his top drawer.

SHELLEY AND KATE His resignation.

Mike is a little deflated that everyone seems to know his story. Emma and Nikki walk past. Emma is showing Nikki around the office.

EMMA Magazines . . . newspapers . . . mainly research stuff . . . *(sarcastically)* You probably don't need to worry about that. Tea, coffee, biscuits . . . Oh, you probably don't eat biscuits.

NIKKI No, I don't.

MIKE *(coming back from the bathroom)* Hello there! Guided tour going well? Welcome to the trenches . . .

EMMA We've just finished. Excuse me.

MIKE This is probably a bit of a change of environment from the Institute of Sport.

NIKKI I guess so . . .

MIKE You must have got sick of eating all that Kellogg's Sustain . . . *(he laughs weakly)*

Nikki laughs politely. There is a pause.

MIKE Actually I would have loved to have gone there. No such thing around in my day. I wasn't a bad fencer at uni . . .

NIKKI Oh really?

MIKE Mmm . . . Also played a bit of tennis. *(he mimes tennis shot)* Do you play?

NIKKI Not really. Well, I can play a bit, I guess.

MIKE We should have a game.

NIKKI *(reluctantly)* Yeah . . . OK.

MIKE Well, I better get back to work . . .

He mimes tennis shot again.

SCENE 9

BOWMAN'S HOUSE

BOWMAN Well, come in.

Marty gestures for Stu to move the camera around a bit as if there's a slight struggle.

MARTY I think we've got all we need.

BOWMAN You haven't asked me any questions.

MARTY Mr Bowman, please. I think we can discuss this calmly, Mr Bowman . . .

Marty and crew are now moving towards their car. Bowman is chasing them.

MARTY *(pretending to be scared)* Christ! Quick, get in the car.

SCENE 10

IN THE CREW'S CAR

STU But he said he'd speak to us . . .

MARTY Stu, we came here with him refusing to speak to us. Christ! He practically invited us in for a beer . . .

STU So? Why didn't we go in?

MARTY He was about to talk! Brian'd kill us. Turn that up, will ya? I love this song.

SCENE 11

THE PRODUCTION OFFICE

EMMA *(handing Nikki a tape)* Take this to the edit suite. Hugh will give you a hand.

NIKKI I'm sorry, I've forgotten where the edit suite is.

Mike bursts in from his office.

MIKE I'm on my way there now. I'll show her.

EMMA *(to the other girls)* Radar ears.

SCENE 12

THE EDIT SUITE

Marty and Hugh are viewing footage. Mike and Nikki walk in.

MIKE Here's the engine room of the show. I spend a lot of time down . . . Hugh, I thought we agreed this was a designated non-smoking area.

HUGH I thought we agreed you'd never come in here.

MIKE *(laughs)* He's a character. This is Nikki Burke. Nikki, this is Hugh, our editor. You know Marty.

HUGH G'day.

There is a pause.

MIKE Well, these boys look a little busy. Why don't we go get a coffee?

NIKKI Sure.

Mike and Nikki leave. Marty and Hugh get on with their work. They are viewing footage of Bowman answering the door.

MARTY It's useless. I was gonna say *(reading)* 'no sign of the money and no sign of an explanation from Mr Bowman'. And the bastard says 'Come on in'. We'll have to dick it.

HUGH Maybe not. What if we reverse the footage? *(Marty looks puzzled)* Read the line again.

As Marty re-reads 'no sign . . . ', Hugh reverses the footage to make it look as if Bowman is in fact shutting the door on Marty.

MARTY You're a genius.

SCENE 13

BRIAN'S OFFICE

Brian and Jan are in a publicity meeting. They are staring at a colour shot of Nikki.

JAN I think in Nikki's case – being so attractive – we'll really need to push the credibility angle.

BRIAN Hey, she's a high-profile sports star. This isn't Rachel Friend from 'Neighbours' suddenly popping up on 'A Current Affair'.

JAN We can pop some glasses on her.

BRIAN Nah, nah . . . We gotta get a good look at her.

JAN What are her academic qualifications?

BRIAN *(flipping through cv)* She left school at

fifteen. *(protesting)* She's been training every day of her life.

JAN Never mind. Any journalistic experience?

BRIAN She once wrote for her school newspaper.

JAN Mmm, I've worked with less.

BRIAN She's travelled a bit. Commonwealth Games in Edinburgh, Auckland . . .

JAN *(writing)* Already travelled the world's hot spots. Now, does she have a boyfriend?

BRIAN Yeah, but don't mention it. I want every bloke in Australia to think he's in with a chance.

JAN Of course.

BRIAN The fact is, the moment she appears on air we're going to cop the bimbo angle.

JAN Yes.

BRIAN *(he remembers something and starts laughing)* Remember when you were at Nine and you said Ian McFadyen was the ideal host for 'Cluedo' because he once studied criminology?

JAN *(roaring with laughter)* Yes, that was a masterstroke.

BRIAN Well, let's do the same. Let's enrol her in a uni. Then we can say she's studying for a degree.

JAN I think high school might be a prerequisite for university, Brian.

BRIAN What about Open Learning?

JAN *(laughing)* Oh, Brian!

SCENE 14

THE FRONTLINE STUDIO

End of story going to air. Footage of crying, disgruntled client.

CLIENT We lost the lot . . . $250,000. He said he's put it in a trust fund . . . and it's just disappeared.

Cut to Marty approaching Bowman's house. Voice-over continues over image.

MARTY *(voice only)* . . . no signs of the money and no signs of an explanation from Mr Bowman.

MARTY *(on screen)* Mr Bowman, why won't you speak to us about the thousands of dollars that have gone missing from your clients' trust accounts?

There is an obvious edit, followed by reverse footage of door shutting.

MARTY *(voice only)* It appears Mr Bowman wants to shut the door on the whole case.

Cut to Mike.

MIKE Mmm, Martin di Stasio there, with a pretty shady character. Coming up after the break, Brooke Vandenberg goes head to head with James Packer.

Day ❷

SCENE 15

THE PRODUCTION OFFICE

Domenica walks through the office with a huge bunch of classy flowers. She puts them on Brooke's desk. Brooke does not look up. She is reading a newspaper. Domenica waits a bit to see if Brooke will read the card, then walks off.

KATE *(curiously)* How'd the Packer interview go?

BROOKE Fine.

EMMA He looks pretty up himself to me.

BROOKE Actually, he's a very easygoing, funny guy.

KATE *(almost under her breath)* And thoughtful . . . *(she indicates the flowers)*

BROOKE *(still not looking up)* These aren't from James.

EMMA But you haven't even looked at the card.

Brooke holds out her wrist to display a chunky gold bracelet, probably worth a few grand.

BROOKE This is.

Mike staggers up to reception. He is in running gear, sweating, and panting heavily.

DOMENICA Mike!

MIKE *(barely able to speak)* Morn . . . Dom . . .

DOMENICA You didn't run to work?

Mike nods 'yes' and staggers into his office. Brian enters the production office just in time to see Mike go into his office.

BRIAN *(holding an* Australian *newspaper)* Well, there's bugger-all in here.

EMMA What about the relief effort in Rwanda?

BRIAN Boring.

KATE I've found something. *(she holds up a copy of* Australasian Post, *a bit embarrassed)* It's not exactly highbrow.

BRIAN Keep talking.

KATE *(reading)* 'Aussie Farmer's Work of Fart. It may be a case of beauty being in the nose of the beholder, but for Horsham farmer Allan Hogg, it's time to kick up a stink. His statues, or stat-poos, are . . .'

BRIAN Can we get to the point?

KATE Farmer makes animal sculptures out of shit. Sheep out of sheep shit, cows out of cow . . . You think it's worth sending someone down there?

BRIAN We don't have much else for the rest of the week. Make sure the guy's there first. And that no-one else has got him.

Kate picks up the phone to start organising the story.

BRIAN *(to Emma)* We send Marty?

EMMA He's pretty flat out. *(mischievous pause)* Brooke's free.

Brooke puts her head up in disgusted horror.

BRIAN *(to Kate)* Lock him in. Make sure nobody else is doing it. It's just the sort of bullshit story 'A Current Affair' would do.

Kate flips through the telephone directory. Brooke takes Brian aside.

BROOKE Brian, I think I've moved on a bit from there. I've just done James Packer and now I'm doing wacky, zany stories?

BRIAN Come on, Brooke.

BROOKE Shit.

SCENE 16

A GOLF COURSE

FARMER First it was 'Good Blokes and Superstars', then 'Top Sorts and Sheilas'. Now they've decided they don't even need Ray Martin. They've got Mike Munro trotting out some old '60 Minutes' interviews.

BRIAN You want us to give it a go?

FARMER These clip shows are so cheap. Saw that interview with Packer last night. Brooke would have a few big names on the shelf.

BRIAN Sure.

FARMER See what you can put together. Maybe a 6.30 Sunday night. Oh, and do it soon. *(Brian looks puzzled)* Geoff Salter's heard there's a gap; wants me to play his urban wildlife documentary. I need an excuse.

BRIAN Geoff . . . ?

FARMER Our weatherman.

BRIAN Oh, Mike's mate. I'll see what I can do.

FARMER How's our new girl going?

BRIAN Nikki? Potential's there. Her looks are dynamite.

FARMER She got legs?

BRIAN Up to her neck. She's gonna be huge.

FARMER Expensive?

BRIAN *(demeaningly)* Her coach manages her.

FARMER All right, stitch her up before someone else gets to her.

BRIAN Three-year deal?

FARMER Yep.

SCENE 17

THE PRODUCTION OFFICE

Emma has several large cue cards and is about to leave the office. Mike stops her. He is wearing brand-new tennis gear.

MIKE Em . . .

EMMA Hey, nice outfit.

MIKE Just my old tennis gear. You seen Nikki?

EMMA Gee, you've changed your tune. What about 'I'm with you on this one, Em. She's got no credibility.' Thanks, Mike.

MIKE Emma. Can I have a word with you (in private)?

They go into the kitchen.

MIKE Em, I've flagged my reservations about Nikki's appointment from the very start. I know she has no qualifications to do this job. I know she was hired for her looks . . .

EMMA It's just pathetic, this obsession with looks. You name me one woman on Australian TV who's not good-looking.

MIKE Well . . . there's that matron from 'A Country Practice'.

EMMA Mike! The way I see it, you get any good-looking girl who's got a bit of confidence and can string a few words together and you could put her on '60 Minutes'.

MIKE *(laughing)* Oh Emma, you're so wrong.

EMMA Mike, it's true. And who do they get to write all their questions and do all the research? People like me.

MIKE Are you telling me every presenter on Australian television is an empty-headed bimbo?

EMMA No, I'm just saying . . .

MIKE It's a bit far-fetched, Em. Do you think I was hired just because I look good?

There is an awkward pause.

MIKE Now we both know Nikki is here for her good looks. And as much as it's against my journalistic integrity, I think we have to accept that.

EMMA *(seeing through him)* It's so obvious you're keen on her.

MIKE *(laughing)* Oh Emma, Emma, Emma. All I'm doing is attempting to make Nikki feel welcome in this office – which is more than I can say for you girls. She plays tennis . . .

He turns to leave.

EMMA Mike. Your tag's showing.

SCENE 18

A COUNTRY PUB

Brooke, Stu and Jase enter. There is only one drinker and the barman in the bar.

BROOKE Hello?

BARMAN G'day.

BROOKE *(pulling out* Australasian Post*)* We're looking for this man – Allan Hogg.

The barman and lone drinker exchange smiles.

BARMAN Oh, the sculptor guy. Not here. Shot through last week.

BROOKE He's not in town? But my producer rang . . .

BARMAN Sorry, love.

BROOKE Great. *(to Stu)* Incompetent little bitch.

STU Well, I guess we head back . . .

BROOKE *(meanly, to Stu)* Excuse me. We've driven three hours. We're not going back without a story. *(smiling, to barman)* I guess you'd get a lot of characters round these parts.

BARMAN Oh yeah . . .

BROOKE *(shaking hands all round)* I'm Brooke Vandenberg from Frontline, the television show.

BARMAN Yeah, sometimes we get you on Southern Cross.

BROOKE We'd love to do a story on anyone round here who's a little bit . . . you know . . . unusual. Bit of a character.

DRINKER There's Cliff. He's a character.

BROOKE Great. What does Cliff do?

DRINKER He's a plumber. Real character.

SCENE 19

THE CAR PARK

Through viewfinder we see Nikki standing in network car park. We hear Brian directing her.

BRIAN OK. Now walk toward camera, not too fast, and start talking.

NIKKI What, at the same time?

Cut to shot of Emma rolling her eyes, holding cue cards above her head.

NIKKI *(woodenly)* And despite his disability, it was at this time Neil decided to take the pledge and prove he could face the challenge that lay ahead.

BRIAN Great. Now use your hands to emphasise 'this time' and 'take the plunge'. You actually said 'pledge' . . .

NIKKI And *despite* his disability, it was at *this time* Neil decided to *take the plunge* and prove he could face the challenge that lay ahead.

She walks far too close to the camera.

BRIAN That was great. It'd be terrific if you could stop walking on 'face the challenge that lay ahead'.

Nikki looks completely flustered, as does Brian.

SCENE 20

OUTSIDE PUB

Brooke watches in disbelief as Stu and Jase record a piss-weak yokel attempting to crack a stockwhip.

YOKEL I'll get it in a tick.

STU *(to Brooke)* This is shithouse.

BROOKE Stu, we were going to interview a man who makes sculptures out of animal droppings. I don't think our standards are that high.

YOKEL It's the humidity.

SCENE 21

THE CAR PARK

BRIAN So we'll just use this as a marker, so you know when to stop. All the pros do it. And in your own time . . .

NIKKI So despite his disability, it was at this time Neil decided to take the plunge and face the challe . . .

She trips over marker. At the same time, in the background, we see Mike on his racing bike in full racing gear. He rides past, waving.

MIKE Looking good!

SCENE 22

OUTSIDE A FARMHOUSE

Brooke watches, arms folded, as Stu and Jase record another yokel just winding up his bird-whistling act.

YOKEL #2 And finally, this is the Major Mitchell cockatoo. *(he screeches like a cocky)* How was that?

BROOKE Fantastic. Thank you very much.

The bird-whistler departs as Brooke and Stu confer.

BROOKE Did you get that?

STU Nuh.

BROOKE Good. Well, it's been a productive afternoon. Let's just recap. The whip-cracker – spellbinding. The bush balladeer – could've listened to him for hours. Oh, not forgetting the incredibly talented woman who plays the recorder with her nose. I'll get a Walkley award for this.

STU Don't forget the bloke who reckons 'Blue Heelers' was based on him.

BROOKE Brian's gonna explode.

STU It's not our fault the shit-sculptor shot through. At least no-one else is gonna get him.

Brooke lifts her head at the noise of a tooting Channel Nine unit van driving past with a large statue of a kangaroo made out of kangaroo droppings on the roof-rack. The Channel Nine crew call out affectionate greetings to the Frontline crew.

SCENE 23

THE PRODUCTION OFFICE

Brooke arrives back from her story, looking hot and tired.

EMMA How was the country, Brooke? Phew!

The staff ham it up as if Brooke has brought a shocking smell with her. The camera follows Brooke to the bathroom. Nikki is already in there. She has been crying. Embarrassed she's been sprung crying, Nikki tries to laugh it off.

NIKKI Phew. I'm finding this really hard. I don't know how you do it.

BROOKE *(maniacally washing her hands)* You just do it.

NIKKI I'm so stressed.

BROOKE Why do you want to be a reporter?

NIKKI *(pause)* I don't know. Brian wants me to sign this three-year contract.

BROOKE Three years? How many years have you been training?

NIKKI Since I was about nine.

BROOKE You wouldn't have had much time to train lately.

NIKKI Well, my coach is a bit pissed off.

BROOKE Sorry. I just find it all a bit confusing. 'Cause you know there are much easier ways for you to make it big. You know what I'd do if I were you? *(Nikki shrugs)* Stick with your training. Go to Atlanta. An Olympic athlete with your looks? You'll be a national celebrity. Everyone will be knocking on your door. You'll have a Rexona commercial before you get off the plane.

NIKKI I guess so.

BROOKE *(conspiratorially)* I'm not planning to be around here much longer myself. Got a call from John Westacott.

NIKKI Really? Who's he?

BROOKE Executive Producer of '60 Minutes'. Apparently they're wanting to expand their on-air line-up. I don't want to be stuck here doing poo stories for the next five years. '60 Minutes' means travel, you get your own producer, they write all your questions, great interviews . . . That's where I could really make my mark. Just like you can if you stick with sport.

Brooke goes to leave.

NIKKI Thanks, Brooke.

SCENE 24

GEOFF'S OFFICE

GEOFF Had a meeting with Farmer about the urban wildlife doco. Can't be done.

MIKE What?

GEOFF Apparently your EP wants a clip show of Brooke's interviews in the timeslot. Farmer's ropeable.

MIKE Oh.

GEOFF Farmer doesn't want to know it, but Brian's threatened to resign.

MIKE I can believe it. He's had network politics up to here. Oh well, I got Brooke back for you this afternoon. When she came in from the story we all went 'Phew!'

Geoff laughs obviously.

MIKE You know the story she's been doing?

GEOFF No.

SCENE 25

THE PRODUCTION OFFICE

Emma, Kate, Marty and others are working. Brian can be seen in his office on the phone. Brooke enters and goes to speak with Emma.

BROOKE *(conspiratorially)* I don't think our little blonde athlete friend will be bothering us any more.

EMMA What . . . ?

BROOKE Had a quick chat earlier. I think I convinced her she was eminently more suited to running around a track than current affairs television.

EMMA Brian will freak.

BROOKE He just wanted someone round to soothe his midlife crisis. He'll get over it.

EMMA Were you feeling threatened by her?

BROOKE Oh Emma, please. She may have a cute arse but you do need slightly more than that to make it as a journo. She might pick up a job on 'Man O Man', but . . .

BRIAN *(slamming down the phone)* Shit!

Everyone looks towards Brian. He emerges from his office.

BRIAN *(to Emma)* What did you say to Nikki?

EMMA *(surprised)* What do you mean?

BRIAN Come on, Em.

EMMA *(defensive)* I hardly spoke to the girl.

BRIAN Well, someone did. She's just called to say she doesn't want to do the show. Some crap about the Olympics.

Brian returns to his office.

BROOKE *(to Emma)* Mission accomplished.

SCENE 26

THE FRONTLINE STUDIO

Elliot Rhodes is just winding up his usual song.

ELLIOT Oh dear, who will become our chief?
Hewson, Bronnie or Peter Reith?
The Liberals will find they get no relief
Till Johnny decides who's the boss.

MIKE Ha ha ha. Our Friday night funnyman Elliot Rhodes there, with 'The Leadership Limbo'. We're

back next week. Don't forget this Sunday, Brooke Vandenberg presents 'Men of Substance'.

We roll a few seconds of Brooke interviewing Gary Sweet. Cut back to Mike.

MIKE Looks good. Have a great weekend.

SCENE 27

THE PRODUCTION OFFICE

The staff are having a drink.

SHELLEY I thought it was funny.

MARTY 'The Leadership Limbo'? Come on . . .

KATE He's all right.

BRIAN And he's cheap. If we . . .

Brian's attention is diverted by a '60 Minutes' promo on the office monitor.

BRIAN Turn that up, Domenica.

VOICE-OVER . . . talks exclusively to Richard Carleton. And this week '60 Minutes' introduces its newest recruit – specialist sports reporter, Olympic athlete Nikki Burke.

Cut to shot of Nikki doing an almost perfect walk to camera using hands, with an obviously disabled athlete in shot.

Cut to various reactions from staff. Brian is pissed off, Emma is smug and Brooke is in complete shock.

EMMA *(whispering to Brooke)* Mission accomplished.

Episode 5
The Siege

Day ❶

SCENE 1

BRIAN'S CAR

Interior shot of Brian driving a four-wheel drive. The radio is reporting news of a siege. Brian is on the speaker-phone.

RADIO Three or possibly four children are being held hostage. At this stage it appears he has a sawn-off shotgun, and neighbours say that there's plenty of ammunition in the farmhouse. Police say the gunman, Gavin John Forbes, and his estranged wife, Vanessa, are involved in a custody battle . . .

The radio report continues under Brian and Emma's conversation.

BRIAN Em, you got the radio on?

EMMA *(voice only)* The siege? I'm already in the office.

BRIAN Unbelievable, isn't it? We gotta move fast on this one. Wake Marty and Brooke up.

EMMA You want Marty in the chopper?

BRIAN Yep, someone in the air, someone on the ground . . . and get some background on this gunman.

EMMA I think I've teed up his mum. We'll send Brooke out.

BRIAN Great.

EMMA *(pause)* What about Mike?

BRIAN All right, you better get him in.

SCENE 2

THE PRODUCTION OFFICE

Brian walks briskly through the office. There is a flurry of activity – phones, faxes – everyone's working on the siege.

EMMA Can't get hold of Mike.

BRIAN *(writing on whiteboard)* Keep trying. Production meeting now, guys. Come on, I wanna try and get the whole half-hour out of this. Shelley, how'd you go with that map? Keep the radio on. OK. What do we have?

KATE We've got onto the bloke's mother. Brooke's on the way.

BRIAN You got a crew?

KATE Freelance.

BRIAN What about Marty?

SCENE 3

AN AIRPORT, AT THE NETWORK'S PRIVATE HELICOPTER PAD

Marty, Jase and Stu are loading camera gear into a helicopter.

MARTY Mate, these things are safe.

STU I hate things with one engine. What if it conks out?

MARTY It won't.

PHIL *(shaking hands)* Marty; fellas.

MARTY Phil's a pro. Last job was flying Christie Brinkley to the snowfields.

By this time they are climbing aboard with the pilot, Phil.

MARTY Smooth ride ahead?

Phil winks.

MARTY *(to Stu)* What did I tell you?

Phil turns round from the cockpit with a bottle of Wild Turkey.

PHIL You guys wanna drink?

SCENE 4

THE PRODUCTION OFFICE

SHELLEY Brian, Caroline's on the phone.

BRIAN Tell her to leave a message. *(to Kate)* Just in case this thing falls over, we need some stand-by filler . . . an expert on psychos and stuff.

KATE Who?

BRIAN Jesus, Kate, ring the university.

SHELLEY Brian . . . *(reading note)* Your son will be here at lunchtime.

BRIAN Oh shit! School holidays. (Of all the days . . .) *(to Shelley)* Ring her back. Tell her we've got a crisis and . . . *(he runs out of steam realising this won't work)* Forget it. *(to Emma)* Where the hell is Mike?

EMMA I'm trying to get through to him. *(pissed off)* This answering machine . . .

MIKE *(voice only; a pathetic Joh Bjelke-Petersen impersonation)* You, you, you, you know who this is. It's Sir Joh, and young Mike can't come to the phone, so leave a message or I'll, or you'll . . . Yes, Flo will bake you some pumpkin scones . . . *(beep)*

EMMA I think it's supposed to be Sir Joh.

BRIAN *(to machine)* If you're not here in half an hour I'm gonna shove those pumpkin scones up your arse.

SCENE 5

IN THE COUNTRY, AT THE SIEGE SITE

Actual footage shows a large media contingent and police presence. Marty stands in front of Stu's camera, ready to present a report.

MARTY Just pathetic. A five-kilometre exclusion zone. Who do the cops think they are?

STU They just don't want anyone getting shot.

MARTY Can hardly see the bloody farmhouse. Mind you, look who's grabbed the prime position.

We look where Marty indicates. Actual footage of Mike Munro doing a report to camera.

STU You wanna do an intro?

MARTY Why not?

STU You right, Jase?

SCENE 6

THE FRONT DOOR OF A SUBURBAN HOUSE

BROOKE *(ringing doorbell)* What did you guys do last?

CAMERAMAN Been on sport for the last month . . .

BROOKE Just be ready and start rolling as soon as we sit down.

The door is opened by a middle-aged woman.

BROOKE Mrs Forbes? Brooke Vandenberg, Frontline. I believe the office rang about doing a short interview? *(entering)* I'm so sorry to hear about your son and grandchildren . . .

SCENE 7

THE PRODUCTION OFFICE

KATE Brian, we're still struggling to find a psychologist specialising in siege-related trauma.

BRIAN Well, we need someone.

KATE We've got a psychology, er, student.

Brian walks away.

KATE *(calling)* He's mature-age. He's got a beard.

BRIAN (All right.) Interview him in front of a bookcase.

SCENE 8

A SUBURBAN LOUNGE ROOM

Brooke is brushing her hair in a mirror which is hanging over the fireplace. Mrs Forbes is seated, reading a document.

BROOKE It's a standard procedure, Mrs Forbes. I'll just get you to sign here . . . just an exclusivity clause.

MRS FORBES So I mustn't talk to anyone else?

BROOKE Some shows are very unscrupulous. It's not so much to protect us – it's to protect you.

Mrs Forbes is convinced. She signs the paper. Brooke takes it from her and immediately snaps from 'caring' into 'professional' mode. She nods to crew 'Are you rolling?' The cameraman indicates 'rolling'.

BROOKE *(sensitively)* Mrs Forbes, how would you describe your son?

MOTHER He's not a bad person. He just loves his kids and . . .

BROOKE Take your time, Mrs Forbes.

She's really sobbing now. Brooke is rapt.

BROOKE But he wouldn't want to harm the children in any way.

MOTHER No . . . never . . .

BROOKE Mrs Forbes, what would you like to say to your son Gavin?

She indicates to crew, 'You better be getting this big juicy teary scene.'

MOTHER Gavin . . . Come on love, give yourself up. Let the kiddies go. LET THEM GO . . . *(huge sobs)*

At this moment the sound guy is desperately twiddling knobs and pointing to his headphones. Brooke sees this; she is not impressed. He mimes to her 'no sound'.

BROOKE Just one moment, Mrs Forbes.

She turns to crew and whispers something to them. They whisper something back. She pauses, obviously pissed off, then speaks.

BROOKE Mrs Forbes. Would you have any nine-volt batteries?

SCENE 9

THE EDIT SUITE

Brian and Hugh are viewing a piece Marty has sent back from the siege site.

MARTY *(on screen)* Just a few kilometres through those trees, the gunman is holed up with his three children and a cache of weapons. It's a tense stand-off, with police fearing one wrong move could spark . . .

Brian stops the tape.

BRIAN He's too far away. Might as well be in the studio. I want some chopper shots. I'm gonna call him.

Brian exits to the production office, where Emma meets him, holding a small piece of paper.

EMMA Brian, I've got the number.

BRIAN (What?)

EMMA I've got the number of the farmhouse.

BRIAN Ring it, ring it!

Shelley's voice is heard.

SHELLEY Brian. Someone here to see you.

We reveal that Shelley has entered with Damien.

DAMIEN Dad.

BRIAN G'day, mate.

SCENE 10

THE SIEGE SITE

MARTY When do we get our station parkas?

STU Got mine.

MARTY When?

STU Last week.

MARTY Shit. I always miss out. You get one, Jase? *(Jase nods)* Shit. Why aren't you wearing them?

STU 'Cause they're rank. Green and pink shit all over them. Look like ABC sports.

MARTY *(looking around)* Nine's are good. Navy, simple.

STU Classy. *(his mobile phone rings)* Hello? Sure. *(he passes the phone to Marty)* It's Brian.

MARTY Thommo . . . Yeah, well, the cops have thrown a five-kilometre exclusion zone round the whole place. It's the closest we can get. Yeah, it's still here . . . You serious? All right, we'll give it a go. *(hangs up)*

STU Story?

MARTY Wants us to get closer.

STU But the cops won't . . .

MARTY Wants us to fly over in the chopper.

Stu looks stunned. Jase runs off to be sick.

SCENE 11

THE PRODUCTION OFFICE

Brian enters with Damien.

BRIAN Domenica, have you met my son Damien?

DOMENICA Hi, Damien. How are you?

No response from Damien.

BRIAN Could you maybe get one of those computer-game things happening on . . . *(he indicates one of the office computers)*

DOMENICA Sure. *(to Damien)* Do you like Mortal Combat?

Domenica leads a reluctant Damien over to a computer terminal.

EMMA We found Mike. He was practising for the go-kart celebrity race . . . *(pre-empting Brian)* He's on his way here. *(she's still trying the farmhouse number)* Shit! It's ringing. Hello, this is Emma Ward from Frontline televi . . . Sorry? *(to Brian, in a mimed whisper)* It's him! It's the gunman!

A hush falls over the office, except for Damien's computer game. Emma rips the plug out of the wall.

EMMA Yes. Yes. I understand, Gavin. Would you be prepared to do an interview? *(pause)* No. We'd be happy to put your side of the story to air.

BRIAN Get Mike in the studio now. Oh fuck! Where is he? Find him.

KATE He's five minutes away.

EMMA OK, Gavin. Now I have to change the phone line over. Gavin, will you . . . *(Brian gestures 'No!' Emma brushes him away defiantly)* Gavin, I'll call you straight back on the other line. Now when I say 'Hang up', I want you to hang up . . . Hang up!

She quickly hangs up and picks up the Commander phone line. The staff around the office hold their breath.

EMMA Gavin? Great. OK, we're going to interview you straight away.

SCENE 12

AN AIRBORNE CHOPPER

Stu is filming.

MARTY This is good. We can see the farmhouse.

PHIL We got trouble. Police chopper. Gotta bail. Whisky Mike Tango. Message understood. Delta Bravo. Piper departing east.

MARTY You got enough, Stu?

STU Yeah!

PHIL They're not happy.

MARTY *(smugly)* We got our shots.

SCENE 13

MRS FORBES'S LOUNGE ROOM

The audio problem has been fixed and Brooke is attempting to get the interview with Mrs Forbes happening again.

BROOKE Thanks for the batteries. Now, Mrs Forbes . . . *(caringly)* Just in case that very moving message you gave to Gavin before didn't come out, do you mind if we go again?

MRS FORBES All right.

BROOKE And feel free to be just as open as before. Gavin will know you're very upset. You could really turn things around . . .

MRS FORBES Gavin, if you're listening, I just wanna say . . . Give yourself up. It'll be all right.

Pause.

BROOKE Would you be able to cry again?

SCENE 14

THE PRODUCTION OFFICE

Emma is at her desk, still on the phone.

BRIAN We're gonna go over to the studio. We'll take the line from there. Is he in there yet?

DOMENICA He swears he's on his way.

BRIAN Tell him we'll meet him at the studio.

DOMENICA *(on the phone)* Mike, Brian says that you should meet him at the studio . . . He wants to know if he can stop at McDonald's.

Brian grabs the phone.

BRIAN *(angrily)* Move it.

EMMA *(on the phone to the gunman)* I see. Yes, I can imagine . . . Well, I couldn't imagine, Gavin, but you . . .

She indicates to Damien to turn the sound of the TV down.

EMMA Uh-huh. And where do you originally come from? Oh, that's a pretty spot.

SCENE 15

THE SIEGE SITE

An informal press conference has been called, with a cop addressing a gathering of journalists.

COP We cannot stress the importance of media cooperation enough here. Already negotiations have been jeopardised by one media organisation breaking the air-exclusion zone.

Marty and Stu exchange surreptitious smiles.

COP There are people's lives at risk here. Negotiations with the gunman via the telephone have been halted, as we are now unable to get through to him. It appears he has taken the phone off the hook. I'm afraid that's all I have for you at the moment. Please stand well back – the man is armed.

The press conference breaks up.

MARTY *(to Stu)* Phone's off the hook my arse . . . Hey, Terry! *(catching a journo's attention)* Your mob's got through, haven't they? You bastards.

TERRY It's not us, mate.

Stu answers his mobile phone and leaves shot.

MARTY *(aggressively)* You bastards. It's not right. You're risking people's lives here, mate.

TERRY I'm telling you, it's not us.

MARTY Well who is it?

TERRY I dunno. *(he walks off)*

MARTY They've crossed the line.

STU *(very quietly)* Brian just rang. It's us.

MARTY You beauty.

SCENE 16

THE FRONTLINE STUDIO

Emma is still talking on the phone.

EMMA Just a few minutes now, Gavin, and you'll be talking to Mike Moore. You can tell people your side of the story.

Mike enters, dressed in spanking new Grand Prix racing gear.

MIKE I haven't been to make-up.

Barely does he have these words out than make-up and wardrobe start to transform him for an on-camera appearance.

KATE His name's Gavin. The farmhouse is in Weeaproinah. Four kids, three are his. Custody battle. He's got a sawn-off shotgun . . .

MIKE Wee-a-p . . . p . . .

KATE Wee-a-proi-nah. We've written it out phonetically for you.

MIKE Questions?

Brian enters. Everyone is shouting frantically.

BRIAN Where the hell have you been?

MIKE It was a charity event.

BRIAN Jesus, Mike. Listen to me. Let him do all the talking. Take it easy on him, and don't let him hang up on you. Let's go.

MIKE Hang on. Am I on camera the whole time?

BRIAN We'll cut to a map if we have to, but yes. The camera is on you. It's a pre-record.

Brian leans over and starts to adjust Mike's tie.

BRIAN Makes it look like it's on the run.

Last-minute camera checks. Mike checks himself out in the monitor with the phone receiver in his hand. All is pandemonium.

FLOOR MANAGER Five, four, three . . .

BRIAN Let's go!

DOMENICA They're set. Now.

EMMA *(into phone)* Just passing you through to Mike now.

FLOOR MANAGER . . . two, one . . . and cue Mike.

SCENE 17

THE FRONTLINE STUDIO

Mike is recording the interview.

MIKE *(suddenly calm, after all the shouting)* Well, just a few moments ago I managed to make contact with the gunman himself, Gavin Forbes. Hello, Gavin. It's Mike Moore here from Frontline.

GAVIN *(voice only)* Hello.

MIKE Gavin, why are you holding your children at gunpoint?

GAVIN Listen, mate, I have to let everyone out there know that this is . . . totally unfair. It's . . .

MIKE It's what, Gavin?

GAVIN It's just going to destroy me. They're my kids. I'm trying to make a point here, and . . .

MIKE Gavin, isn't this perhaps taking matters a bit too far?

Cut to Brian in control room.

BRIAN Nice work, Mike.

Cut back to Mike.

GAVIN I want people to understand what I'm going through.

MIKE How are the kids at the moment, Gavin?

GAVIN They're fine.

MIKE So you haven't harmed the kids, Gavin?

GAVIN No.

MIKE Gavin, can I speak to one of the children?

Cut to Brian.

BRIAN Great, Mike. Great stuff.

Cut back to Mike.

GAVIN Yeah, just a minute . . .

KID *(voice only)* Hello?

MIKE Hello. Who's this?

KID Amy.

MIKE Hello, Amy. My name's Mike Moore. Do you know who I am?

KID No.

MIKE Amy, are you afraid?

KID No.

MIKE Have you enjoyed this adventure?

KID Yes.

Cut to Brian.

BRIAN Guns . . . guns.

MIKE Is Daddy pointing the gun at you?

BRIAN Sensational.

KID No.

Cut back to Mike.

MIKE Can you put Daddy back on the line? *(pause)* Gavin, wouldn't it be a good idea to put the gun away, let the kids go, and just talk this through with the police? Gavin?

GAVIN They won't listen.

BRIAN *(voice only)* Wrap it up now . . .

MIKE They will, Gavin . . .

GAVIN *(getting hysterical)* They won't listen! No-one listens!

Mike looks stunned: 'What do I do now?'

Cut to control room. Emma enters.

BRIAN *(to the floor)* OK, that's enough. *(to Emma)* Emma, take the phone. Keep him on the line.

EMMA *(taking the phone)* Gavin, I'm sure everyone in Australia will sympathise with you . . .

BRIAN *(to the floor)* Mike, sensational.

MIKE *(through control-room monitors)* Could we try a take two?

EMMA . . . you must be feeling a bit stressed right now. You don't want to be bothered by anyone at the moment. It's probably a good idea to take the phone off the hook, at least for an hour or so . . . just so you can get your thoughts together. There's no rush.

SCENE 18

THE SIEGE SITE

Marty and Jase are standing around. Stu arrives with takeaway food.

MARTY Egg-and-bacon sandwich?

STU Yep. Got a couple each. Jase?

Jase shakes his head.

MARTY I think Jase left one in the chopper. On the roof, from memory.

Jase smiles weakly.

MARTY Just talking to some blokes from Seven. They've got nothin'. Big fat zero. Moore's done the pre-record with our gunman, mate.

STU Cops are gonna pop when they find out.

MARTY Yeah, probably.

SCENE 19

THE FRONTLINE STUDIO

Mike is at his desk, rehearsing the autocue. His image goes completely out of focus, then back again. We hear Brian's voice.

BRIAN Damien!

We reveal Damien playing with one of the studio cameras. He reluctantly stops.

BRIAN Go and help Nicole with the autocue.

Damien is sent over to the autocue machine. He begins playing with it.

SCENE 20

THE SIEGE SITE

It is now dark. Marty, Stu and Jase are setting up for a live cross.

MARTY How about if I crouch down like this?

STU What for?

MARTY *(as if it's a stupid question)* To make it look like I'm in danger.

STU But the gunman's five kilometres away.

MARTY Shut up. It's dark. Who's gonna know?

STU *(joking)* Sure you don't want a flak jacket?

MARTY Actually, that's a bloody good idea. See if we can borrow one from the cops, will ya?

SCENE 21

THE FRONTLINE STUDIO

Mike is at the desk. We can hear the final part of the interview with the gunman he pre-recorded that day.

FLOOR MANAGER In five, four, three . . .

MIKE That exclusive was recorded just moments ago. Now for the very latest at the siege site, we cross live to our man on the spot, Martin di Stasio.

Live cross to Marty. He is crouching.

MARTY Thanks, Mike. Well, the siege is now into its ninth hour with still no breakthrough. Police have managed to make contact with the gunman and trained negotiators are currently speaking to him.

Cut to Mike in the studio.

MIKE Have any shots been fired?

Cut back to Marty.

MARTY Not at this stage, though police are warning the media out here of the very real dangers. We believe he is heavily armed, and we are just confirming reports that Forbes is a former war veteran.

MIKE So we could have a Rambo situation?

Cut to control room.

BRIAN *(surprised)* Go Mike!

Cut back to Marty.

MARTY That's not out of the question.

MIKE Thanks for that, Martin. Keep safe.

MARTY Sure.

We cut back to the studio.

MIKE Martin di Stasio reporting there live from the line of fire. Coming up after the break, we speak with . . .

There is the faintest of pauses in Mike's delivery. A reverse shot shows his autocue is moving oddly, backwards and forwards. Mike struggles on.

MIKE . . . a psychologist specialising in . . . psychology. That's next on Frontline.

We go to a break. Reveal Damien playing with the autocue machine. He is grabbed from behind by his father.

SCENE 22

THE PRODUCTION OFFICE, AFTER THE SHOW

Emma, Kate, Shelley, Domenica, Brooke, Hugh and possibly even the photocopier man are sharing a drink. Champagne is evident. Brian enters, smiling.

BRIAN Great stuff, everyone. What did 'A Current Affair' do?

BROOKE Some pissy farmhouse shots. Then they dragged out some old David Koresh footage.

BRIAN Piss-weak. 'Real Life'?

BROOKE Some more farmhouse shots. Not much else. *(she shrugs)*

BRIAN Pathetic. '7.30 Report'?

EMMA Should Melbourne have the Grand Prix.

General laughter.

KATE Who wants a beer?

General party atmosphere starts. Enter Mike. Big cheer, clapping. He is chuffed.

BRIAN Good stuff, mate. Talking to the kids – sensational!

MIKE I'm still recovering. It was pretty gruelling.

BRAIN Mate, you entered the big league tonight.

MIKE I hope those kids are OK. Imagine threatening to kill your kid!

BRIAN *(none too subtly looking at Damien, who is playing with a Gameboy)* Yeah.

Mike goes over to Damien.

MIKE Damien. Caught us on a pretty exciting day.

Damien is not so impressed. He continues playing Super Mario.

MIKE *(looking over Damien's shoulder at the game)* What kingdom are you up to? *(no response)* Watch out for the spider things.

BRIAN Hey, they're doing a cross.

One of the girls turns up the TV. We see our network's generic news update opener, and a generic newsreader.

NEWSREADER Good evening. And in this update, it's just been confirmed the gunman at the Weeaproinah siege has given himself up. For the latest we cross to Frontline reporter Martin di Stasio, who has been at the farmhouse since the early hours of this morning. Martin, what's the latest?

Cut to Marty on location. There is a cheer from the staff when Marty appears on screen.

MARTY Brian, about five minutes ago, the gunman, Gavin John Forbes, gave himself up to police. There was no sign of a struggle, and the children are safe and well. Gavin Forbes was immediately taken away from the scene by police and is likely to appear in court tomorrow.

NEWSREADER And the children are safe?

MARTY Physically, yes. Of course, who knows what psychological scars they may bear from this incident?

Cut back to newsreader.

NEWSREADER I guess only time will tell. And there'll be a full report on the aftermath of the siege tomorrow night on Frontline.

Cheer from the office.

BRIAN First plug we've got from the bastards this year.

NEWSREADER Of course, earlier today Frontline host Mike Moore spoke exclusively to the gunman.

Cut to Mike on phone; grab from interview.

MIKE *(watching)* Brian, do I get royalties for my interview being repeated?

Day ❷

SCENE 23

THE PRODUCTION OFFICE

Action starts on fax machine pumping out figures. The staff are gathered around Brian.

BRIAN Melbourne thirty-four, thirty-six . . . Sydney thirty-four, thirty-four . . .

There is general elation.

MARTY The other one?

BRIAN *(reading)* We bloody creamed 'em.

Emma enters with a bottle of Moet and a tradesman carrying a crate.

EMMA Crate of Moet, if you don't mind!

General enthusiasm from staff.

BROOKE *(reading)* . . . The host of the current affairs programme, Mike Moore, is being blamed by police for the hold-up with negotiations, and for putting the lives of the child hostages at risk. Executive producer Brian Thompson denies police dealings were placed in jeopardy, and says that Moore acted in a responsible and calming fashion.

DOMENICA Cool, Mike! Front page news!

BRIAN Where are the Sydney papers? *(he notices Damien hanging around)* Shell, get him some McDonald's, will you?

MIKE *(aside)* Brian, they're really pointing the finger at me. You don't think that I went a bit far with the kids and . . . ?

BRIAN Mate! Look at this! You've bloody made it. We have struck the jackpot.

He holds up the Age with 'Siege ends . . . TV Program Blamed' headline.

SCENE 24

MIKE IS ON AIR AT 3AW WITH NEIL MITCHELL.

MIKE No, Neil. No, I won't deny that it was good television.

NEIL That may be so from a ratings point of view, because you certainly got high figures . . .

MIKE Yes. Thank you.

NEIL . . . but judging from the reaction of callers we've had this morning, what you did was totally irresponsible, endangering the lives of those children.

MIKE Now wait a minute . . .

NEIL You are not a professional negotiator.

MIKE I'm not a professional negotiator, you're right, but no-one came to any harm. In fact I believe I had a calming effect.

NEIL What makes you qualified to negotiate with an obviously unstable and highly emotional person holding four small children at gunpoint?

MIKE (smiling) I understand what you are saying, but look, Neil, I've been in the business for fifteen years. I've interviewed everyone from the Dalai Lama to Sharon Stone . . . I think that helps.

NEIL Well, Mike, there's a lot of people who don't share your confidence, including Commissioner Frank Grey, who we have on the line now. Good morning, Commissioner Grey.

Cut to Mike's shocked reaction.

SCENE 25

BRIAN'S OFFICE

MIKE All I'm saying is, I was put in a very compromising position. He was really having a go at me. Maybe we should reconsider Neil and those spots.

BRIAN Michael, listen to me. Look at the figures. Highest this show's ever had – highest this station's had in years . . .

MIKE What about what the press are . . . ?

BRIAN Wake up, mate. They're pissed off they didn't get the interview themselves.

MIKE But the police . . . That police commissioner was really angry that I spoke to the kids.

BRIAN Those kids didn't even cry. It was a big adventure for them. Mike, the police are embarrassed. We made them look like fools.

Jan enters.

JAN (making a big entrance) Hello Mike, sweetie. You are a star! Are you ready for this? Sydney Morning Herald want an interview . . . Green Guide, Courier-Mail, Herald-Sun . . . Ernie and Denise . . . I'd think about that one. The Bulletin . . . Somehow we're going to have to fit them in today. It's so exciting, isn't it? (hugging him) Inside gossip is that Stan and Ray are livid.

Mike has perked up now.

JAN Now which picture would you like us to use?

She holds up a 'serious' Mike pose, and a smiley 'cowboy boots' Mike.

MIKE Did you hear that, Brian? Stan and Ray are really livid.

SCENE 26

OUTSIDE A COURTHOUSE

Brooke is with Stu and Jase, waiting for our gunman, Gavin, to appear. There are a number of other reporters and crew also. Brooke and Stu stop talking and exchange surreptitious glances when one of the reporters approaches them.

JOURNO Reckon he'll get bail?

BROOKE (guardedly) I imagine so. Kids weren't hurt . . . first offence.

JOURNO Yeah. So you guys all still celebrating?

BROOKE What about?

JOURNO What about? Last night's figures. Good get. Our EP freaked this morning. Ray's chucked a nervy turn. (Brooke shrugs) Just tell me. Did you tell him to keep the phone off the hook after you did the interview? You know we were trying to get through all day as well.

BROOKE Look, I don't know. I'm not the producer.

Someone yells, 'Here they come!' There is a bit of pushing and shoving as reporters try to get a statement from our criminal. Brooke remains quite calm. The criminal and his lawyer make a beeline for Brooke. She ushers Gavin into a waiting car.

BROOKE Thanks, Gavin.

Gavin, Brooke and crew jump in the car. The other journos look on in envy.

SCENE 27

GEOFF'S OFFICE

GEOFF I swear. Everyone's talking about you.

MIKE Really?

GEOFF I was just in the canteen and I was standing behind Helen from sales and she was saying something about 'Well, thanks to Moore, the rate-card's up a thousand bucks a spot.'

MIKE Mate, I've already done six interviews today.

GEOFF You deserve this, Mike.

MIKE I mean, some have been tough, really tough on me. What do you think? I didn't put those kids in danger, did I?

GEOFF No! No!

MIKE Really?

GEOFF Mike, you saved those kids' lives. The police should be thanking you. *(pause)* I reckon you'll be asked to host the Logies next year.

SCENE 28

BRIAN'S OFFICE

Chief Commissioner Grey is talking heatedly with Brian.

GREY I'm warning you. I know you don't give a fuck what I say now – you've got ya ratings, and ya champagne *(holds up bottle of champagne)* 'cause you got away with it.

BRIAN Mate, everyone was safe.

GREY It might not've ended like that. You know and I know that you risked those kids' lives.

BRIAN You're getting a bit dramatic now, aren't you?

GREY *(angrily)* You took a risk. We knew that guy was nuts . . .

BRIAN Mate, nothing happened.

GREY But it could've. You endangered people's lives. And if the broadcasting laws in this country weren't so piss-weak, you'd be taken off air.

BRIAN Message received.

GREY Bullshit. *(leaving)* Fuckin' cowboys.

Grey exits. Through Brian's venetians we see Mike lurking outside the office. He enters.

MIKE Is everything . . . ?

BRIAN Yeah.

MIKE We didn't go too far, did we?

BRIAN I want to show you something.

Brian throws a copy of Time *with Mike on the cover onto the desk. The caption reads 'Has the Media Gone Too Far?'.*

MIKE Wow!

BRIAN Australian *Time*, but still pretty bloody fantastic. Now what did you want to say?

MIKE *(smiling at copy of mag)* Nothing.

SCENE 29

THE PRODUCTION OFFICE

There is a framed, blown-up picture of Mike from the cover of Time *in the office.*

MARTY *(staring at photo)* It's just too tempting, isn't it?

He is holding a whiteboard marker, indicating that he could easily vandalise the photo.

EMMA Marty.

Enter Brooke with crew.

BRIAN How'd ya go?

BROOKE Fine. Should've seen the faces on the other guys.

BRIAN And the interview in the car . . . ?

BROOKE Smooth as.

Brian moves over to Kate. Everyone starts to get on with things.

EMMA *(to Brooke)* What was Gavin like?

BROOKE *(thinks)* Absolute nutcase.

TWO WEEKS LATER

SCENE 30

THE MAKE-UP ROOM

Mike is sitting in a make-up chair. Emma is running through what's in the show.

EMMA . . . So that's a four-minute story. Then straight to 'Are older women sexier?'

BRIAN *(rushing in)* Mate, in the studio now. We've got ourselves another siege, and the guy's asked for you.

Emma is in slight shock.

MIKE Wow!

BRIAN It's a gift, mate. *(sucking up to him)* He's asked for you.

MIKE Righto, who is it? Where is . . . ?

BRIAN Kate's got all that. Mike, we're going to air live with this one . . . straight up. The news is going to throw to us. *(they're all now heading towards the studio)* How's the old ticker, mate?

MIKE Fine. *(he is completely confident)*

BRIAN *(as Kate is passing on info)* You're an old pro at this. The police'll be asking for you now . . . Here we go!

FLOOR MANAGER In five, four, three, two, and . . .

MIKE Welcome to Frontline, and an exclusive tonight. As we still reel from the drama of the Weeaproinah siege two weeks ago, another siege is taking place right now. A 36-year-old Brisbane man has taken four hostages in a city law firm. The man has contacted Frontline, and is on the line, live from the building in William Street. Are you there, Lee?

LEE *(voice only)* Yes I am, Mike.

MIKE Lee, you've specifically asked to speak with me.

LEE Yeah.

MIKE Well, you've got the whole of Australia watching and listening. What do you want?

LEE I want you to hear this.

Three shots ring out. Screams. Then to black.

Episode 6

Playing the Ego Card

Day ❶

SCENE 1

BRIAN'S OFFICE

Brian is waiting on the phone. Mike is pestering him.

MIKE Come on, Brian. It'll be good for the show.

BRIAN *(into the phone)* No, I'll keep holding. *(to Mike)* Why are you so early?

MIKE I had to do an interview (I've been promising for the past few weeks).

BRIAN Schoolkids?

Mike nods meekly. Brian gives him an admonishing 'I've told you about that before' look.

MIKE Brian, I need to cover a big overseas story. I've got to break free from that desk.

BRIAN It's where you belong. You are the host. The focus. You're not the cog in the wheel. You're better than that.

MIKE Yeah, (I know). You've told me that before, but I'm more than just a host. When I was at the ABC . . .

BRIAN *(into the phone)* Yes, hello. Brian Thompson here. Concerning your letter dated the ninth of April – do you have a copy in front of you? Good. Then shove it up your arse. *(he hangs up)*

MIKE That's no way to treat our viewers.

BRIAN It was my wife's lawyer.

MIKE (Really?) Everything OK with you and Pam?

BRIAN Couldn't be better. We've separated. (Forget about that.) Now, what were you on about?

MIKE I want to do an overseas story.

BRIAN Fine, as long as you do it from your desk.

MIKE No, not throw to a story. Actually go somewhere.

BRIAN Go where?

MIKE Bosnia?

BRIAN Past its use-by date, Mike.

MIKE New Caledonia?

BRIAN Sounds like Club Med.

MIKE There's a civil war . . . *(Brian shakes his head)* It's in our region.

BRIAN First smart thing you've said – close to home. Apart from that, it's a dud.

MIKE But you don't even know about it.

BRIAN That's why it's a dud, Mike. Why don't I know about it? 'Cause I haven't seen it on the TV. Why haven't I seen it on the TV? 'Cause there's no vision. Pictures, Mike, pictures.

MIKE Oh, I know pictures are important . . .

BRIAN Important? Listen mate, a pub brawl in Manly is better than a massacre of millions if you've got the pictures. And if you don't have the pictures it sure as hell better have Australians.

MIKE Bougainville!

BRIAN Where?

MIKE Bougainville. The Australian copper mine they're fighting over; it's Australian-owned.

BRIAN Pictures, Mike. You gonna send me vision of a quarry?

MIKE Don't underestimate our viewers, Brian.

BRIAN I've built a career on it, Mike. I think there's someone to see you.

At the door are two public-school boys with a tape recorder. Emma is with them. Mike leaves with the kids.

SCENE 2

FARMER'S OFFICE

Farmer, Jan and Brian are meeting. Brian is reading a document.

FARMER Makes interesting reading.

BRIAN *(dismissively)* They're only focus groups.

FARMER Mmm. Yeah.

BRIAN What are you thinking, Fez?

FARMER Brooke's come out looking pretty good.

JAN Extraordinary.

FARMER The punters love her.

BRIAN So?

FARMER Could she host for a week?

BRIAN (*somewhat interested*) So we can get a look at her? It has crossed my mind.

JAN Oh, wonderful. 'Brooke into the Frontline'.

BRIAN (It's a) good idea. But . . .

FARMER But what?

BRIAN Mike.

FARMER What?

BRIAN His nose would be out of joint.

FARMER Isn't he due for holidays? (*Brian shakes his head, 'no'*) Would he take off for a week?

Brian suddenly has an idea.

BRIAN I've got an idea. Leave it with me.

JAN Do we ease off on Mike's publicity and promotion?

FARMER AND BRIAN No!

FARMER Do the opposite. Mike Moore has this network's 100 per cent support . . . right up to the day we sack him.

SCENE 3

THE PRODUCTION OFFICE

Brian enters. Mike is still in his office with the schoolkids. Mike sees Brian go past his window and immediately tries to wind up his interview with the kids. Brian goes over to Emma and speaks confidentially.

BRIAN Book Mike on a flight to Port Moresby after Friday night's show. Send Stu and Jase this afternoon.

EMMA What?

BRIAN I'll explain later.

Mike is at the door of his office, ushering the kids off.

MIKE Oh, and say hello to Father Stephenson for me.

KIDS He's dead.

MIKE Oh, that's terrible.

Brian is by now in his office. Mike follows him in.

MIKE Brian, I've been thinking about Bougainville.

BRIAN Mike, you are not leaving this place.

MIKE But Brian!

BRIAN No. (*he pretends to reconsider*) OK, talk me into it.

MIKE Brian, it's a civil war. An entire country's economy as well as a billion-dollar Australian mining company's been brought to its knees, all by a small bunch of rebels. It's a revolution on our doorstep.

BRIAN Mmm. You'd be away for a week.

MIKE I could do it in a couple of days.

BRIAN No, no, you'd need a week. All right, we'll book a flight and . . . Hang on, what am I thinking? Have I lost my mind?

MIKE What?

BRIAN Farmer will never allow this. Who am I gonna get to host while you're away?

MIKE Marty?

BRIAN Oh, he's a bit hard-edged.

MIKE Brooke?

BRIAN Come on, Mike . . .

MIKE What? She can do it.

BRIAN She's green. You know how hard it is to host this program, follow someone like you.

MIKE But Brian!

BRIAN (*reaching for phone*) All right, I'll see what they say. Farmer's gonna freak.

Brian dials and waits for an answer. We cut outside where Emma's phone rings. She picks it up.

EMMA Hello.

BRIAN Fez, it's me. Brian.

EMMA (You've dialled the) wrong extension, Thommo. It's me. Em.

BRIAN Not bad, and you?

Emma turns to Brian through window.

BRIAN Thanks, mate. Yeah, show is looking good. He's doing very well. I'll pass that onto him. Now, mate, speaking of Mike, how would it be if we sent him away overseas? (*exuberant reaction from Emma*) Come on, Fez – it'd only be for five days.

(Emma elatedly mouths 'five') Look, calm down. There's no need for that . . . We'll put Brooke in as host. I know she's green. Mate, I appreciate this. I owe you one. Done.

MIKE Great!

BRIAN Hey, let's keep this absolutely hush-hush. Don't want this place going into a tailspin when they realise you won't be in the chair next week.

SCENE 4

THE EDIT SUITE

Brooke is with Hugh looking at footage.

BROOKE That's the cutaway I want to use.

The phone rings. Hugh answers.

HUGH Yeah? *(passing phone to Brooke)* It's Emma.

BROOKE Yes? *(to Hugh)* No, cut there. *(to Emma)* Why? I've already done a promo this week. What's this one for? Right.

Brooke hangs up, thinks, then dials again.

BROOKE Em? Sorry if I sounded a bit short then – I'm a little in shock. I just wanted to say thanks for all the help you've given me.

SCENE 5

MIKE'S OFFICE

Domenica knocks on Mike's door and walks in carrying an army outfit on a coat-hanger.

DOMENICA Hi Mike. Wardrobe sent this down for you.

MIKE Oh, they found one. Great. *(proud but secretive)* You know what it's for?

DOMENICA Your trip to New Guinea?

MIKE Who told you?

DOMENICA Um . . . *(points vaguely at office)*

MIKE It's hush-hush, OK?

Mike spots Stu, who is at Brooke's desk reading her address book. Mike leaves his office and goes across to him.

MIKE Oh, Stu, I need a word. What are you doing?

STU Looking through Brooke's address book. Can you believe this? Greg Norman's home phone number.

MIKE Stu, when Brooke gets in, tell her I need to speak with . . .

STU She's in. Can you believe this? The number's got an asterisk next to it – 'any time'.

MIKE What do you mean she's in? It's just gone ten. Brian doesn't want any of us in before lunch.

STU (shrugging) Anyway, she's in. Saw her in the studio, doing some promo. (still looking at book) Christ, Wayne Gardner.

MIKE I've got to talk to her about something.

STU (absorbed in the book) God, it's true about Paul Mercurio!

MIKE Stu! What if Brooke knew you were looking through her stuff?

STU She'd be rapt. Why do you think she leaves this lying around?

MIKE Don't be silly.

STU Don't be naive. She's a smart woman, Mike. Hear she's hosting while we're in Bougainville.

MIKE Bougainville? But . . . how do you know?

Marty walks in from the kitchen, eating a bowl of cereal.

MARTY I hear you guys are going to New Guinea.

STU (looking at the book again) Bingo! Told you, Marty – Michael Hutchence.

MARTY (to Mike) Got a minute?

Mike follows Marty into the kitchen. Marty shuts the door.

MIKE Marty, we're trying to keep this whole thing a bit hush-hush. Don't want people spinning out about me being away.

MARTY I gotta say, mate, I got a little respect for you.

MIKE Thanks, Marty.

MARTY Putting your dick on the line for a real story.

MIKE Well, it's not . . .

MARTY You don't mind Brooke taking over?

MIKE Well, she's not 'taking over'. She's just filling in for the week. And who told you . . . ?

MARTY Just great, isn't it? I sit here with twenty-one years' experience, playing second fiddle to some show pony who's schmoozed her way into the network's good books.

MIKE Marty, I wanted you to host next week.

MARTY I don't care, mate. I'm like you – not into profile shit. I'm into getting real stories.

MIKE Farmer didn't want Brooke to host.

MARTY Bullshit, Mike. He loves her. They all love her. Ask anyone around the station what they think of her. All the people that count – she's got them wrapped around her finger. She's smart.

MIKE That's what Stu said . . .

MARTY I'm warning you, Mike. When you're away next week working in the jungle, she'll be back here workin' the room.

MIKE How do you mean?

MARTY Here's some friendly advice. Never let anyone fill in for you who might be capable of taking your job. Why do you think everyone gets Peter Luck to do their show for them every summer? No threat to anyone.

MIKE You don't think Brooke . . .

MARTY Who knows? Don't get into that game. You know what really matters, after all the magazine covers and celebrity stuff, what really matters? Open the top drawer of my desk some day.

MIKE The top drawer?

MARTY Just open it. In the meantime, watch your back.

Marty exits.

SCENE 6

THE FRONTLINE STUDIO

Brooke is sitting at the desk, lost in thought. Kate enters.

KATE OK, let's go. You set in there, Em?

We see Emma taking a seat in the control room.

BROOKE What do I say in this promo?

KATE Nothing. There's a voice-over. You just turn to camera.

BROOKE What does the voice-over say?

KATE Hasn't been written yet.

BROOKE Uh-huh. Well, what kind of look?

KATE Brian said give us three. We'll sort it out later. *(checking notes)* All turns to camera. *(calls to camera crew)* Version one – 'Concerned Look'.

Brooke does a concerned look.

KATE Bought. Version two – 'Reassuring Look'.

Brooke does a reassuring look.

KATE Bought. Version three – 'Smart Look'.

BROOKE What's that supposed to be?

KATE I think it's this one. *(does a face)*

BROOKE What? What's that?

Cut to control room.

EMMA Keep recording. Version four – 'Absolute Bitch Look'.

SCENE 7

BRIAN'S OFFICE

Marty walks into Brian's office.

BRIAN What? *(pause)* What? *(pause)* Don't be ridiculous.

MARTY I've been here twenty-one years, Thommo.

BRIAN Yeah, so you should know how things work.

MARTY Twenty-one years, Thommo. She hasn't even been here twenty-one months.

BRIAN She's struck a chord with the viewers.

MARTY Struck a chord with you and everyone else that matters in this station.

BRIAN You're the best reporter in the country.

MARTY So why don't you treat me like one? Where's the respect, Thommo? Where is it?

Outside, we see Mike walk pensively into the production office from the kitchen with coffee. He sees Marty in Brian's office.

MIKE *(to Domenica)* Amazing guy, Marty, isn't he?

DOMENICA Yeah, he's funny.

MIKE Certainly speaks his mind.

Mike goes over to Marty's desk. He slowly opens the top drawer. He pulls out a banana. At first he is confused, then he holds it up in admiration.

Cut back to Brian's office.

BRIAN . . . I don't trust her either, Marty – but we'd be crazy not to give her a go.

MARTY So Mike's about to get the dick?

BRIAN No. He is going to do an overseas story.

MARTY (But) is he coming back to do any?

BRIAN Listen to yourself.

MARTY Listen to *your*self.

BRIAN It's not my job to listen to myself – it's to listen to people above me, and as much as I hate to pull rank, you are not one of them. Understood?

Marty exits. As he goes past Mike's office, Mike gestures to him through the window and with great deliberation places a banana in his top drawer. He gives Marty the thumbs up, to which a confused Marty replies with an uncertain nod.

SCENE 8

BRIAN'S OFFICE

Emma enters with a tape.

EMMA Brooke's promos.

BRIAN Great.

EMMA Thommo, is Mike about to be dumped?

BRIAN Why does everyone think Mike's about to be dumped? Cowboys upstairs just wanna give Brooke a run; see how she handles it.

EMMA And that's why we're sending Mike to the *(referring to promo)* 'Battlefields of Bougainville'?

BRIAN He wanted to go.

EMMA But a week of reports from New Guinea? It's a dud story.

BRIAN Hey, it's a bigger story than you think. Terrorism. Guerrilla warfare. Australian nationals threatened on our very doorstep. A war that cannot be won. Em, it's practically another Vietnam.

EMMA I think you're overstating it.

BRIAN I hope so.

EMMA OK, assuming it is another Vietnam. Why send Mike? We've got a bureau up there. They could send us vision.

BRIAN You know what vision without a reporter is? A documentary.

EMMA A documentary?

BRIAN A reporter has to be in the story – part of it. Why did '60 Minutes' send Richard Carleton to Baghdad?

EMMA They wanted him dead?

BRIAN Closer to the truth than you think. But they also wanted him to be part of the story.

EMMA So they don't really have to be there?

BRIAN 'Course not – it's part of the drama. You tell me. Who was the most prominent figure in the Gulf War?

EMMA Saddam Hussein.

BRIAN Peter Arnett – a news reporter.

EMMA Great. So Mike becomes 'our man in the danger zone – the fearless war correspondent'.

Mike enters without knocking. He holds a piece of paper.

MIKE *(worried)* Brian, I've gotta have injections.

EMMA Your weatherman friend's looking for you.

MIKE *(impatiently, as if she ought to know this)* Geoff – his name's Geoff.

EMMA He's on the roof.

MIKE The roof.

Mike exits.

EMMA Wanna see the promo?

She puts the tape in the VCR and presses 'Play'. We see a promo for the show, with a collage of news pictures.

VOICE-OVER She's the woman with the stories. The names. The courage to tell it like it is. He's the man with experience. Next week on Frontline, while Mike Moore reports exclusively from the battlefields of Bougainville, Brooke Vandenberg will keep you informed with what's happening here at home. Frontline – the winning team.

Brooke turns to camera.

BRIAN Beautiful.

EMMA On air tonight?

BRIAN Nah, tomorrow. Don't want Mike spinning out.

SCENE 9

THE ROOF OF THE TV STATION

Mike is eating a sandwich and Geoff is adjusting the time-lapse camera.

MIKE So that's the time-lapse camera?

GEOFF Uh-huh.

MIKE Guess where I'm off to next week?

GEOFF Bougainville.

MIKE Who told . . . ? How does everyone know things round here?

GEOFF Got some info on the climate if you want.

MIKE Yeah. Yep.

GEOFF *(surveying city skyline)* You tell people it's a smog-alert day, suggest they leave their cars behind. It's as if no-one's listening to you.

MIKE What do you think of Brooke?

GEOFF Brooke? Fabulous lady. Very smart.

MIKE You think she's smart?

GEOFF Oh yeah. Smart enough to understand what I do. Thinks my work is innovative. Not many people pick that up . . .

MIKE She's told you that?

GEOFF Yep. Didn't have to say it, but she did. Went out of her way to compliment me.

MIKE So you two talk a lot?

GEOFF Oh . . . not a lot. Come on, she's a busy woman – she's got no time to sit around and talk with a weatherman.

Mike looks uncomfortable.

MIKE Well, I'd better get a move on . . .

GEOFF Sure, you're leaving tomorrow night.

MIKE How did you know when . . . ? Anyway, keep it quiet. It's hush-hush.

GEOFF Yep. She'll be a great fill-in.

MIKE How did you know she's . . . ?

GEOFF Heard the promo is great.

SCENE 10

BRIAN'S OFFICE

MIKE *(in a bit of a state)* Brian, I thought we agreed to keep this quiet. You've already cut the promo.

BRIAN Hey, we wanted to promote your overseas story.

MIKE But I'm not even in it.

BRIAN Yes, you are.

MIKE But not at the end, when she does the turn and you say 'team' but I'm not even there. I could have sat at the desk and she could have stood behind me, and we could have looked at each other and then turned like this. *(turns to imaginary camera, then lowers voice)* Brian, I don't wanna be out of line here, but I'm worried about Brooke. This whole thing; she's not doing it for the show. She's looking after herself.

BRIAN So? What's wrong with that?

MIKE She wants my job, Brian.

BRIAN Mike, I can assure you the network is 100 per cent committed to you.

MIKE Really?

BRIAN Hey, would we have organised this front cover for you if we weren't?

Shows him cover of TV Week with picture of Mike playing guitar.

MIKE She's smart. (I'm telling you) she wants my job.

BRIAN Sit down, Mike. Listen carefully (because I don't have time to repeat this). Yes, Brooke is smart, bloody smart. Probably smarter than you and me put together. (She's) got a head start – she's a woman. But I'll let you in on a secret. She's too smart to want your job. All she wants to do is look like she could do your job.

MIKE Same difference. In the end, she wants my job.

BRIAN Wrong. In the end, she wants Ray Martin's job.

MIKE (So why are you letting her get away with it?) Tell her you know what she's up to.

BRIAN Mike, this network spends millions each year cockteasing an audience. Now we find someone who has the nous to do it herself – and you want us to put the brakes on her?

Kate knocks and enters.

KATE Mike, you're due at the doctor's in half an hour.

MIKE *(not convinced)* She's very cunning . . .

SCENE 11

DOCTOR'S SURGERY

DOCTOR Brooke? Very warm. I think she comes across as a caring kind of person. Although I've heard some things . . .

MIKE Like what?

DOCTOR Just things. About her and certain male celebrities. Come on, you probably know a lot more than I do.

MIKE There are lots of rumours – like the one about her being a real bitch. *(laughs, hoping the doctor will take the bait)* You would have heard that one.

DOCTOR No. *(he gives Mike an injection)* This one's for typhoid. It might hurt for a couple of days.

MIKE Ow!

DOCTOR Look, I understand if you don't want to – please say no . . . My nurse is a bit of a fan. Would you mind if she got an autograph?

MIKE *(very pleased)* No, bring her in.

DOCTOR *(calls)* Helen.

Helen, the nurse, enters clutching autograph book.

HELEN Hi. Really appreciate you taking the time. My husband and I are big fans.

MIKE Not a problem. *(taking book)* Who to?

HELEN If she could write 'To Vic and Helen from Brooke', that would be great.

Mike does not look chuffed.

SCENE 12

MIKE'S OFFICE

Mike is at his desk as Domenica appears at the door, putting on her coat.

DOMENICA Don't work too late, Mike.

MIKE Oh, still got research to do for this Bougainville assignment. Don't forget . . . hush-hush.

DOMENICA (But) isn't it exciting?

MIKE Oh, bit of a pain in the arse really. Brian insisted I cover this story; couldn't let him down. Domenica, what do you think of Brooke?

DOMENICA I think she's a bit nuts. 'Night, Mike.

MIKE Goodnight, Domenica.

Domenica exits. The cleaner, Khor, appears with his vacuum.

KHOR Working late, Mike?

MIKE Oh, just some research.

KHOR When you leave for New Guinea?

MIKE How did you . . . ?

KHOR Brooke gonna be new boss lady. Very beautiful. Very smart.

Day ❷

SCENE 13

BRIAN'S OFFICE

JAN Yes, Brooke. The promo will be on air today. *New Weekly* are doing a 'My Favourite Fashion Accessory' list. *(Brooke shakes her head)* There's a photo.

BROOKE All right.

JAN *Telegraph Mirror* are running a 'Celebrity Stars and Baths'. Famous people in the bath . . . *(Brooke shakes her head 'no' again)* I tend to agree.

Emma enters with a tape.

EMMA Footage from Bougainville. Just in off the satellite.

BRIAN Shit, when did Stu get there? *(indicating for Emma to play the tape)* Sorry girls, we're gonna have to wind this up.

Brooke and Jan exit. They speak to each other as they leave Brian's office.

BROOKE He's not seriously going to run a week of these reports.

JAN Where is Bougainville, darling?

SCENE 14

MIKE'S OFFICE

Mike is in his office when Brooke passes by. He calls her in.

MIKE Brooke, can I have a word with you?

BROOKE Yes?

Brooke goes into Mike's office. Jan leaves.

BROOKE Mike, even though I'm at the desk, I think it should look like you're still running the show.

MIKE Hey, I'm not precious. I've got no problems with you fronting the show.

BROOKE No, I think for the sake of the show, it should look like the spotlight's still on you.

MIKE Oh, yeah, whatever.

BROOKE It's such a good story you're doing.

MIKE Well, it's what being a journo is all about.

BROOKE Really?

MIKE Yeah, go and take a look in my top drawer some time. That's what really matters.

Brooke looks confused.

SCENE 15

BRIAN'S OFFICE

Mike is impatiently trying to talk to Brian about Brooke. Brian is worriedly looking at the pictures Stu has sent back.

MIKE Is an up-grade likely? I mean it's not for me – it's for the sake of the show.

BRIAN *(into the phone)* Stu, this is crap.

STU *(voice only)* (I) can't help it, Thommo. It's where the army blokes are taking me. But they reckon that road's booby-trapped.

BRIAN Yeah, well, it just looks like a road, Stu. That's boring vision.

MIKE I mean, I mean . . . I don't mind travelling economy. I just think it looks a bit low-rent. It'd reflect badly on the show . . .

BRIAN *(to Stu)* Forget the Australian army, Stu. Go to the rebels – they're mad. They'll show you guns.

Brian hangs up and leans back in his chair, exhausted.

MIKE Don't worry, Brian. I'll be there in twelve hours.

This thought is too much for Brian.

SCENE 16

OUTSIDE TOILETS

Mike bumps into Marty.

MARTY What time's your flight?

MIKE Eight-thirty.

MARTY Lady Macbeth driving you to the airport?

MIKE Hey, Marty. I think you're being a bit harsh on Brooke.

MARTY Oh, she's done a job on you too.

MIKE She said I should still be in the spotlight.

MARTY Ever been rabbit-shooting, Mike?

MIKE But . . .

Mike follows Marty out, but stops short at his door when he realises that Brooke is talking to Shelley in his office.

BROOKE *(to Mike)* You don't mind if I use your office this week, do you?

SCENE 17

THE FRONTLINE STUDIO

Elliot Rhodes is just winding up another musical comedy milestone. Mike and Brooke are at the desk

waiting for him to finish. There is a frosty atmosphere around them. Mike reminds Brooke to smile at the end of the song. Brooke disdainfully indicates she already knows. The floor manager indicates five seconds to go.

ELLIOT . . . her eyes were glintin'
Hillary's hair was tintin'
They all were chasing Clinton
For a White House rendezvous.

MIKE Ha ha. Friday night funnyman Elliot Rhodes there, with the 'White House Rendezvous', winding up another week here on Frontline. Next week I'll be filing a series of reports from the battlefields of Bougainville and, well, I couldn't think of a better person to fill in behind this desk than senior Frontline reporter Brooke Vandenberg.

BROOKE Thanks, Mike. And we look forward to some fascinating reports from our troubled northern neighbour.

MIKE Be sure to join us for that. Until then have a safe weekend. And good luck for next week, Brooke.

Lights dim and final theme music rolls. Brooke and Mike stand and leave without any conversation or even eye contact.

THREE DAYS LATER

SCENE 18

BRIAN'S OFFICE

Mike and Stu are talking from the speaker-phone. On the VCR, Brian is watching a scruffy native New Guinean talk pidgin English.

BRIAN Yes, Monday morning here as well, Mike – we're actually in the same time zone. Look mate, the stuff you beamed down last night was very interesting but it's not right. Didn't Stu take you to meet some rebels?

MIKE *(voice only)* Yeah, yeah, we will. This RAAF big wig organised a meeting with a local chief. I got a spear!

BRIAN Mike, can I talk to Stu?

STU *(voice only)* Plenty greetings, big chiefee-chiefee.

BRIAN What is the story, Stu? I told you to stop talking to the army and meet some rebels.

STU *(quietly)* Thommo, it's a snow job. It's like they don't want us around. That air force bloke's made Mike shit himself about going into the jungle . . .

MIKE I'm not shitting myself, Brian. It's really, really dangerous out there.

BRIAN Guys, maybe the army is playing games with us. I don't care. Just give me vision. Vision. Does big chiefee make himself cleary-cleary? I want to see soldiers with rifles. You know, guns – big sticks that go boom boom.

Brooke enters.

BROOKE Is that Mike?

MIKE Yes.

BRIAN *(calls)* Em, call Canberra. Defence Department. I want to talk to the minister. Something's not right.

BROOKE Mike, can you start all your stories with 'Thanks Brooke'? I've worked out a bit of a throw.

MIKE (I've) already written your throws and faxed them down to Brian . . . *(Brian indicates that he's thrown them in the bin)* After you say, 'Caught in the crossfire, Mike Moore', I'll open with 'Mike Moore, reporting from Bougainville'.

BROOKE That sounds more like a signing off.

MIKE No, I close with 'That's all from Mike Moore, here in Bougainville'.

BROOKE No-one says their name twice during a story. Why don't you get straight into it, after I've thrown with 'In Bougainville, Mike Moore joins us'?

MIKE 'Joins us'? I'm the host. If anything, you're joining me.

BROOKE Mike, for a week I am actually the host.

MIKE *(pause)* Can I talk to Brian?

Brian has his head in his hands. He is sick to death of this dispute.

SCENE 19

THE FRONTLINE STUDIO

Brooke is behind the desk.

BROOKE Welcome to Frontline. I'm Brooke Vandenberg. Tonight, Bougainville: idyllic island or bloody battleground? Kate, you can roll that autocue quicker. I read faster than Mike.

We reveal that Brooke is only rehearsing.

BROOKE They say it's the war that cannot be won and it's right on our doorstep. Emma, I think we should mention Vietnam here. Otherwise it's too boring. *(pause)* Emma, are you listening? *(pause)* Is anyone up there?

KATE Hang on, she's on the phone with Brian.

EMMA *(over PA)* Brian says we're not running anything from Bougainville tonight.

BROOKE Good call.

Brooke exits.

SCENE 20

THE PRODUCTION OFFICE

Emma walks in from the studio.

EMMA *(to Marty)* We're gonna run another of your pieces.

MARTY Bougainville didn't work out? *(shakes head)* Too many show ponies. *(referring to Brian)* His house of cards is about to fall down on him.

EMMA *(going into Brian's office)* Thommo? No good footage from New Guinea?

Brian hits 'Play' on the VCR and shows footage. Mike is crouching in front of two soldiers with automatic machine guns in a jungle trench.

MIKE *(on screen)* Here in the foothills, the National Guard is constantly under attack from the secessionist rebels. *(turns to them)* Excuse me, can you shoot when I talk?

manipulation

The soldiers shake their heads uncooperatively.

BRIAN *(to Emma)* PNG government's gonna bill us for the bullets.

The footage continues with Mike in the same position.

MIKE This is take two . . . Here in the foothills, the PNG National Guard is constantly under attack from the secessionist rebels. *(Mike turns to them)* Why didn't you shoot? When I talk, you shoot . . .

The soldiers start firing wildly. Emma is laughing.

BRIAN I'm glad you find this funny.

The footage continues to run. We see Mike interviewing two poorly dressed rebel soldiers.

MIKE How many hard-core BRA do you think there are up in the hills?

SOLDIER #1 *(pause)* I couldn't tell the number.

MIKE Are they well armed?

SOLDIER #1 Yes.

SOLDIER #2 Some of them, yes.

MIKE What kind of weapons?

SOLDIER #2 Three-oh-three. And . . . er . . .

SOLDIER #1 Point two-two.

SOLDIER #2 Point two-two.

SOLDIER #1 SL . . .

SOLDIER #2 SL, and . . . er . . .

SOLDIER #1 MiG 58 . . .

SOLDIER #2 Yes, MiG 58 . . . and then, er . . . *(to Soldier #1)* what's the Russian MiG?

SOLDIER #1 SKS.

SOLDIER #2 *(to Mike)* SKS 47.

We cut to Emma and Brian still watching.

EMMA *(laughing)* They're unbelievable.

BRIAN Wait, Zig and Zag aren't finished yet.

The interview continues. Mike is in another location with the same two soldiers.

MIKE So those mountains are literally crawling with rebels?

SOLDIER #1 I don't know. *(both soldiers are confused)*

MIKE You see those mountains? There are rebels up there . . . lots of boom boom.

There is an obvious cut. Mike attempts to start the interview again.

MIKE Take seven . . . So those mountains are full of rebels?

SOLDIER #1 You said so . . .

There is another cut. Stu leans into shot and indicates visually 'Take eight'. This time Soldier #1 (who has obviously been coached) speaks first.

SOLDIER #1 Those mountains are full of rebels.

MIKE Are they armed?

SOLDIER #2 *(helpfully)* They are full of rebels.

Cut back to Emma and Brian still watching.

EMMA This is hilarious.

BRIAN I tell you what's hilarious. Mike isn't gonna lose his job – I am. Oh yeah, if we ever get to use this vision of huts, make sure we wipe the audio.

EMMA Why?

Brian plays the footage of the huts.

MIKE *(voice only)* So, Stu, what do you think of Brooke?

STU *(voice only)* Shut up, Mike. I'm rolling.

Brian spools forward on the video to show Mike and a so-called 'warrior rebel tribe'.

BRIAN This is an armed tribe of rebels. Help me out. Is that a weapon or a souvenir?

A 'tribesman' tries to sell a spear to Mike who looks interested in it in a news sense, then indicates to Stu to cut. He then attempts to barter for it.

EMMA Thommo, are you really surprised Mike hasn't come up with the goods?

BRIAN I am, actually, Em. Maybe he's a little out of his depth, but he's a half-decent reporter. We're being done over.

EMMA By who?

BRIAN PNG government, Defence Department, I dunno. Someone's not happy we're up there.

EMMA Can't we speak with the rebels?

BRIAN Speak with the rebels? Speak about killing, speak about mistreatment . . . Come on, Emma, are you deaf? We need vision. You're not listening.

EMMA *(seeing something on the screen)* Go back a bit.

BRIAN You see? You're not listening.

EMMA Just go back.

BRIAN What do you want to see? The kid with the toothpick or Chief Unintelligible?

EMMA The chopper (behind Mike) . . . It's an Iroquois.

BRIAN What?

EMMA An Iroquois. That's one of the choppers Australia donated.

BRIAN So?

EMMA They were donated on condition they were used purely for humanitarian purposes.

BRIAN *(he still hasn't got the point)* Yeah, so Mike doing a George Negus impersonation on it is a contravention of the agreement.

EMMA Thommo, that is a humanitarian chopper. There are machine guns on it.

Brian stops and takes a closer look.

BRIAN *(to Emma)* Will you marry me?

ONE WEEK LATER

SCENE 21

THE PRODUCTION OFFICE

It is the following Monday morning. Great deal of exuberance. Mike, Stu and Jase have obviously just arrived back from the airport. Mike is showing a spear to Marty. Emma is reading from the Australian.

EMMA This is from the *Australian.* 'Government Orders Bougainville Inquiry. Following the bombshell dropped by TV current affairs show Frontline last week concerning the misuse of defence funds, the government has appointed an independent committee to investigate the matter. The political damage caused has forced Defence Minister Senator Ray to review our aid policy to Papua New Guinea. Though unavailable for comment, army sources have expressed regret of the incident claiming that they had no knowledge of the brief given to them.'

STU Those rebels are good value. They can drink, can't they Jase? *(Jase nods)*

Mike and Marty are talking near Marty's desk.

MIKE *(showing Marty the pissy spear)* It is real. They usually put poison on the tip. I'm amazed I got it through customs.

MARTY Maybe the fact it's plastic . . .

MIKE Oh, Marty. That's what I wanted to ask you. Why did you want me to see the banana?

MARTY The banana?

MIKE In your top drawer. *(Marty looks confused)* This one. *(opens top drawer of Marty's desk)* You told me to look in your top drawer one day. *(realising it isn't there)* Where's it gone?

MARTY I ate it.

MIKE Well, what did it have to do with journalism?

MARTY Look behind, Mike. Further in. *(he pulls out a Walkley award)* It's a Walkley award.

MIKE You won a Walkley?

MARTY Now do you know what I'm talking about?

MIKE Ah! . . . I forgot why you told me to look.

MARTY (Don't worry about it.)

MIKE Marty, you shouldn't keep a Walkley award in your drawer. You'll scratch it. Look, it's got banana on it.

The rest of the staff are listening to Emma.

EMMA This is from the Melbourne *Age.* 'After a withering attack from the media and in particular Frontline's Mike Moore who broke the story, the Senator relented, admitting his government has been embarrassed over the chopper incident.'

DOMENICA How about this? 'Mike Moore is a man of courage and inspiration . . . '

MIKE Who wrote that?

DOMENICA School paper. The kids sent it in. 'Christian values which were developed at school . . . '

MIKE Sssshhhh.

DOMENICA Wow. I didn't know you wanted to be a priest.

BROOKE *(snatches paper from Emma)* Blah blah blah. I'm glad they mentioned who hosted the show. greed.

There is an awkward silence as Brooke exits.

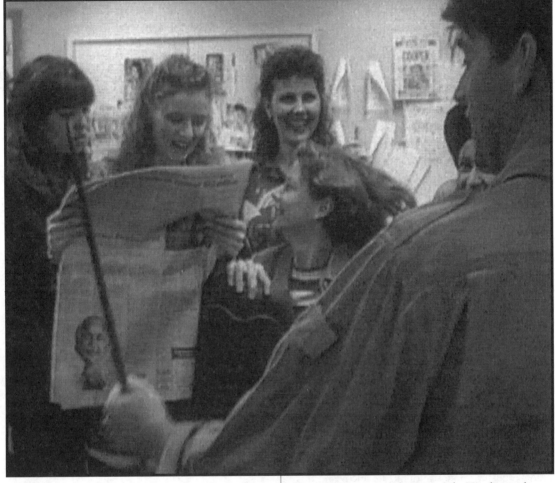

SCENE 22

BRIAN'S OFFICE

Brooke enters Brian's office.

BROOKE (So the network's) happy with last week, Brian?

BRIAN Stoked. We kicked arse. I'm telling you – you did a great job. Hit the mark with the viewers, execs are happy, (more importantly) sales department's over the moon. *(holding up sheet of paper)* You made these ratings.

BROOKE Thanks, Brian.

Brooke turns and leaves as Mike enters Brian's office.

MIKE You know she's barely said a word to me? She should be thanking me, Brian. She got a dream run thanks to my story.

BRIAN Mike. You did a great job. Hit the mark with the viewers, the execs are happy, (more importantly) the sales department's over the moon. *(holding up sheet)* You made these ratings.

Emma enters.

EMMA They're waiting for you in make-up, Mike.

MIKE Right.

Mike leaves. Emma remains in the doorway of Brian's office. She speaks as soon as Mike is out of earshot.

EMMA That's all right, Mike. No need to thank me. Any time I can help you out with a story . . .

BRIAN Emma, see these figures? *(holding up sheet)* You made them. Thanks.

EMMA Is that what you said to those two?

Brian is delighted with Emma's uncanny perceptiveness.

irony → tells them what he thinks they want to hear.

repitition of same sentance to suck up.

BRIAN Promise you will never leave me.

EMMA. Promise me a pay rise.

BRIAN I'm serious, Em. Saved my arse. You found the footage – it was a great get.

Shelley enters Brian's office.

SHELLEY Brian, Greg Evans is here to see you.

BRIAN *(puzzled)* (Greg Evans?)

Farmer enters, holding a bottle of champagne. He ignores Emma in the doorway and she leaves.

FARMER Gotta keep the guard up, Thommo.

BRIAN You're a bastard, Fez.

FARMER Congratulations, kid. These *(indicating ratings)* are sensational.

BRIAN Mmm.

FARMER You're not happy.

BRIAN It's Moore and Vandenberg. They shit me, Fez; worse than children. What's their problem? The show works, their faces are on the fucking screen. If they don't like it, they can bugger off. If they're happy, then shut up.

FARMER Come on, Brian. You've been around long enough. They just want a bit of credit for success.

BRIAN Then they're more deluded than I thought.

FARMER You're being too tough, mate.

BRIAN Bullshit. Mike still thinks he uncovered this whole story. *(indicating newspaper)*

FARMER *(pause)* He didn't?

BRIAN 'Course not. I was sitting here last Monday night, took one look at that helicopter and bang, I knew I'd made a great get . . .

Irony
- Emma underacknowledged hero. Doesnt recieve as much credit.

- Characters satirised.
- Everyone enjoys their ego being pampered.

Episode 7

We Ain't Got Dames

Day 1

SCENE 1

THE FRONTLINE STUDIO

Elliot Rhodes, the slightly balding, bow-tied satirist, is standing at an electric piano, singing a Gilbert and Sullivan-style song.

ELLIOT The UN said, 'What's going on here?
Commies with bombies is what we fear
No more reactors, let's make that clear
Or it's goodbye North Korea.

'Armageddon's getting near
Making bombs, that's what we hear
So let's kick him in the rear
And say goodbye North Korea.'

As Elliot winds up to what sounds like a finish, we reveal Mike Moore at his desk, listening to the song and trying to gauge whether or not it is funny. None of the crew appear to be laughing, as the floor manager counts down silently from five.

MIKE Ha, ha, ha. Elliot Rhodes, our Friday night funnyman, with the 'North Korean Konga'. He's a national treasure . . .

Day 4

SCENE 2

BRIAN'S OFFICE

contrast

Brian, Mike and Marty meet.

MIKE He's shithouse, Brian.

BRIAN Look, Mike, what's funny? What's not? I don't know. He's playing the piano, he's got the bow tie. It's just a way of ending the week on a feel-good note.

MIKE It's not even satirical. He just thinks if he rhymes 'Korea' with 'beer' he's making some sort of political point. wasnt listening

BRIAN Mike, we've been through this before. There's only one John Clarke.

MARTY Weren't you going to ring him?

BRIAN We've got a meeting today.

MARTY Great.

MIKE I'm not sure we should be poaching people from other stations.

BRIAN We poached you.

MIKE Sure, but . . .

MARTY See? It can backfire . . .

Emma walks in with several sheets of paper.

EMMA Breakdowns. Sorry they're late; photocopier's still busted.

BRIAN *(without even reading)* Women?

Emma motions 'thumbs down'.

BRIAN 24 to 39?

EMMA Down.

BRIAN 39 to 55?

Emma just nods.

BRIAN What the hell's going on?

MIKE I know someone who'd be good. The Irish guy.

BRIAN *(still reading breakdowns)* It's Melbourne . . . Sydney.

MIKE Brian, that Irish guy.

BRIAN Who?

MIKE Jimmy Owen. *(silence)* Jim – oin.

His suggestion is ignored.

BRIAN *(to Emma)* Phone Barb.

SCENE 3

THE PRODUCTION MEETING ROOM

Brian, Emma, Kate and all reporters meet with Barb. Mike has a notebook computer with him. People are just sitting down to start the meeting.

EMMA *(to Kate)* Cheryl Kernot's confirmed for Thursday.

KATE Live?

Emma nods 'yes'.

MARTY Nice laptop, Mike.

MIKE It's a notebook. Got all my research on it.

MARTY Gee, that must be a whole paragraph.

BRIAN OK, people, let's get started. I think most of you know Barb, network research supervisor. She's looked at why we're losing so many women.

BARB Thanks, Thommo. We spent yesterday running focus groups, all female. Lot of negatives here. *(reads)* Frontline is 'too blokey', 'too much sport', 'not friendly enough' . . .

Brian notices Marty not paying attention; he is reading the sports page of the newspaper.

Irony

BRIAN *(chastising him)* Marty!

Marty stops reading and pays attention as Barb continues.

BARB A lot of women felt the show has become a bit sleazy, tabloid, bullying . . .

MIKE *(joking)* Hate to see what they say about the host!

Without looking up Barb passes a sheet of paper to Mike. He goes pale as he begins to read.

BARB There seems to be a trend towards stories that are only of interest to men.

BRIAN Give 'em some examples.

BARB *(reading)* The topless cleaners, sport, all that foot-in-the-door stuff; it's too aggressive for a lot of female viewers. Remember we're up against a program presented by the former host of 'Midday'. Women love Ray.

MIKE *(looking up from his reading)* What's 'insipid' mean?

BARB And they don't want to spend *(reading)* 'a day with the Hell's Angels' or hear about industrial relations.

BRIAN *(Hang on)* what's blokey about industrial relations?

BARB Politics. (Your) female viewers are not interested (in politics).

MIKE Excuse me. This may be the difference between a commercial network and the ABC, but I find that comment a little . . .

BARB Sexist? Mike, I don't take any more comfort in these figures than you do. But the facts are, we sampled 220 women. What was the one thing they could tell us about our Prime Minister?

MIKE Um, he deregulated the banking sector? *(Barb shakes her head 'no')* He deposed Bob Hawke in a coup?

BROOKE (He) married an air hostess.

BARB *('clicking' to indicate she is correct)* Ninety-five per cent.

MIKE Is she an airline hostess? I though she was Dutch. But a lot of my women friends are interested in politics.

BROOKE Not at 6.30, Mike. Screaming kids; husband to feed . . .

MIKE But . . .

BARB If you are going to do politics, keep it simple. You mentioned an interview with Cheryl Kernot. What's she want to talk about?

EMMA The Print Media Inquiry.

BARB Forget it.

EMMA Sorry?

BARB Personalise the interview. How does she balance work and family? What's it like being a woman in Canberra? Other good areas in general are *(consulting notes)* the environment: cloth versus disposable nappies . . . Body image is big: liposuction, breast implants, anything on diets. You also rate well with celebrity profiles . . .

MARTY Hey Brooke – another day with Russell Crowe.

MIKE Barb, I've got a story here. I'll just bring up the folder . . . *(his computer beeps)* Hang on. *(it beeps again)* It's just . . . *(gives up on computer)* It's got direct appeal to women. Illegal textile factories in Australia employing migrant women, paying them below award wages . . .

BARB Uh-huh. *(she moves on)* Another area that researched well, not surprisingly, is romance. Love life, the art of kissing, older women and younger men.

MIKE *(to Brian)* They pay below award wages and . . .

BRIAN Mike, I think it's a little heavy. *(he appeals to Barb)*

BARB Way too heavy.

BRIAN Thanks, Barb. Can we get some copies of that? *(indicating her notes)*

EMMA AND KATE Photocopier's broken.

Shelley comes over to Mike. The meeting starts to break up.

SHELLEY Mike, phone call for you.

MIKE Hang on, I've just gotta power down.

His computer starts beeping again as he attempts to switch it off.

BRIAN *(checking watch)* I've gotta get going. *(to Barb)* Thanks, Barb. *(to Emma)* Are you right to speak with Elliot?

Emma nods unhappily. Mike continues to struggle with his computer.

MARTY I'll do it for you, Mike. *(he leans over and pulls out the power cord)*

Mike goes to take his phone call.

SCENE 4

THE PRODUCTION OFFICE

Elliot Rhodes enters the main office. A sympathetic silence falls over the staff as he walks in. Emma takes him aside to speak privately.

Cut to Emma and Elliot in meeting room.

EMMA You know the problem? The network thinks you're too clever. Your stuff's too sophisticated; it's going over our audience's head.

ELLIOT So I'm out.

EMMA No! You've been with us since . . . um . . .

ELLIOT Wally the Worker.

EMMA Since Wally. And we plan to keep using you, on a rotational basis.

ELLIOT Who'll be doing the spot this Friday?

EMMA That's up to Brian . . .

SCENE 5

A RESTAURANT

Brian and Farmer are speaking with two people we at first see only from behind. There are drinks on the table.

BRIAN . . . it doesn't have to be long. I mean, you know yourself – a lot of the stuff you do goes on a bit. Just something light and frothy to end the week on.

We reveal the other people are in fact John Clarke and Bryan Dawe.

FARMER We know what you're thinking. You're worried. 'Does our stuff have legs?' But if you come across to Frontline you'll get one of the best production teams in the country.

BRIAN Nine have crucified you guys as far as publicity goes. I've not seen a single promo.

FARMER You come across to us, we'll have you on the cover of *TV Week* tomorrow. And we've had an idea. Thommo?

BRIAN Those interviews you do? We thought we could take them to the next level and make you up to actually look like the guy you're impersonating. Well, what do you think?

John and Bryan are speechless.

SCENE 6

GEOFF'S OFFICE

MIKE I get this call. Head of ABC TV comedy.

GEOFF Wow.

MIKE Wants me for next week. World Series TV Debate.

GEOFF Fantastic. When is it?

MIKE They're taping tonight. I've gotta fly to Sydney after the show.

GEOFF Not much notice.

MIKE Someone else pulled out.

GEOFF Still, it's a big honour.

MIKE You bet it is. They get some smart people on that show.

GEOFF Andrew Denton.

MIKE He doesn't do it any more.

GEOFF Yeah, but the girl. Wendy Hughes.

MIKE Harmer. She's not doing this one. But the guy that hosts it is hosting it.

GEOFF Have you told Brian?

MIKE Bugger him. You know that sweat-shop story I've been working on for months?

GEOFF That's a winner.

MIKE 'Too heavy'.

GEOFF What?

MIKE You should have been at this meeting today, Geoff. So patronising to women. 'They don't understand politics'. 'They want stories on dieting'. It's so short-sighted.

GEOFF It's just like the time I tried introducing pollen counts into weekend weather.

MIKE I remember that.

GEOFF Said it was 'too technical' for the audience. Well, you know what happened next.

MIKE No, what happened?

GEOFF Everyone started doing them. If they'd just listen to us talent.

Mike and Geoff pause to consider the wisdom of these words.

GEOFF Anyway, do you need a hand with your speech tonight?

MIKE *(producing book)* All in here.

We see the title: 'The Macmillan Dictionary of Relevant Quotations'.

MIKE Book of quotations. Topic tonight: 'Money can't buy happiness'. I've looked up 'money'; have a listen. Katherine Mansfield: 'I must say I hate money, but it's the lack of it I hate most.'

Polite laughter from Geoff. Mike reads another quote.

MIKE 'Money can't buy happiness, but it buys such a good imitation it's often difficult to tell it from the real thing.'

More laughter from Geoff.

MIKE You want more? Some guy called Schopenhauer: 'Money is human happiness in the abstract; he, then, who is no longer capable of enjoying human happiness in the concrete devotes himself utterly to money.'

Geoff tries to laugh but can't hide his lack of understanding.

GEOFF I'm not sure about that one.

MIKE It's a quote.

GEOFF Oh, a quote!

MIKE Mate, this speech is written.

SCENE 7

MIKE'S OFFICE

Marty and Stu are playing with Mike's laptop.

STU No, it's Apple. Control panels . . . audio.

Shelley walks past with a pile of magazines.

SHELLEY Does Mike know you're playing with his computer?

MARTY Shelley, we are not 'playing'. We're modifying some of the settings.

SHELLEY Oh.

MARTY So you can change this 'beep' thing?

STU Yeah, any noise you like.

Shelley continues walking into Brian's office. We cut.

SCENE 8

BRIAN'S OFFICE

Brian, Emma and Kate are going through ideas for stories. Shelley walks in with a pile of magazines.

SHELLEY I found some *Cleos* and a *New Woman*. *Cosmo* doesn't come out till next week.

BRIAN Chuck 'em over . . .

He indicates where to leave the magazines. Shelley departs.

EMMA How's this? Dangerous dieting. Women who smoke to lose weight.

BRIAN Perfect.

KATE Pain-free childbirth?

BRIAN In. We got anything on women and their bodies and shit . . .

EMMA *(getting tape)* Hang on. Here's one we've had on the shelf . . .

She inserts tape and hits 'Play'. While this is happening, Mike enters carrying a tub of salad.

BRIAN Mike! Come in.

Mike enters and sits. Tape starts with '5, 4, 3, 2, 1' leader and then images of women's faces with a voice-over by Brooke.

BROOKE It's a case of Australian women literally dying of embarrassment. The pap smear.

Story cuts to close-up of hands being fitted with rubber gloves, and picking up surgical instrument.

BROOKE It should be as common as a trip to the dentist, but for many . . .

Brian mutes the story with his remote control.

BRIAN We don't need to see all that.

EMMA Brian! That's exactly what women want to . . .

BRIAN Yeah, but we've just lost our entire male audience. I'm at home eating my tea and you're shoving women's plumbing problems down . . .

MIKE I actually found it quite interesting.

EMMA Brian, don't you think this whole push to get female viewers is a little . . .

BRIAN A little . . . ? Come on, Em, say it. 'Cynical'?

EMMA Yeah.

BRIAN Cynical? Em, we're just trying to keep up with our opposition. Look at 'Real Life'. What was their first story this year? *(Emma gives an 'I dunno' shrug)* The announcement that Stan's wife had just had a baby. Probably induced it to coincide with the ratings. They're all chasing women, Em, and we can't be left behind.

KATE *(reading magazines)* Here's one. Doctor who molested one of his patients.

BRIAN That's good.

KATE Oh no. As seen on 'A Current Affair' last week.

BRIAN Nah, not the case specifically. I'm talking about the issue in general. 'How honest is your doctor?' 'Are women safe in the surgery?'

EMMA That's a good women's story.

KATE I'd watch it.

BRIAN 'Check-up or chat-up?' Give us a chance to do a re-enactment. Haven't had one of them for a while. Cut a promo, say it's a story . . .

EMMA ' . . . no woman can afford to miss'.

BRIAN Great. So that's Tuesday. Wednesday?

MIKE There's my sweat-shop story ready to go, if we're light on.

BRIAN Plenty there, Mike.

MIKE No, I'm just saying if we're light on. I mean, it doesn't have to be this week.

Shelley's voice is heard over the speaker-phone.

SHELLEY Roland Roccheccioli's at reception.

BRIAN *(to Emma)* Who?

EMMA The guy shooting Mike's new promo.

BRIAN Oh. Kate, would you . . . ?

Kate gets up and leaves to fetch Roland.

MIKE What's this about?

BRIAN We're gonna shoot a new promo, Mike. Feature you in a softer light. And *(to Emma)* who's this guy?

EMMA Roland Roccheccioli. He's a stylist – what they call an image consultant. He's gonna direct the promo.

BRIAN Is he . . . ?

EMMA Is he what?

BRIAN You know . . . *(limp wrist)*

EMMA Brian!

BRIAN I'm just asking. I mean, I hope he is. Women love poofs.

Kate enters with Roland. General introductions.

BRIAN Roland, we've got a problem with women. Nothing drastic, but they're starting to switch off. We want a new promo, national, that'll drag 'em back in. Something soft, stylish.

ROLAND You want to shoot it in the studio?

BRIAN Sure. Outside too if you want. But we wanna avoid that walking through town, waving at construction workers, Channel Nine shit.

EMMA Or Jennifer Keyte in a park.

BRIAN Somewhere between the two. Just make him look sort of warm and fuzzy. But not a poof. I want the women of Australia to fall in love with this guy.

EMMA Mike, you got a bit of salad on your (face) . . .

SCENE 9

THE PRODUCTION OFFICE

It is evening, after the show. The staff are having a drink.

BRIAN No, worse stuff-up than that. Must have been '74, 'This Day Tonight'. We'd organised a reunion for two sisters who hadn't seen each other since the war. Flew one in from Poland, the other from the States. It was gonna be the big on-camera reunion, lots of tears, usual crap. Turned out they bumped into each other in a transit lounge in Bangkok. Spent half the day together, got into an argument . . . By the time they hit the studio they weren't talking to each other.

General laughter. Mike appears with an overnight bag.

MARTY Hey, Mike, come and have a drink.

MIKE I've actually gotta get going.

MARTY Where you off to?

MIKE Oh, just out to dinner.

KATE I wish I had the money to go out to dinner.

MIKE Well, you know what they say. I hate money, but it's the lack of it I hate most.

There is mild laughter.

DOMENICA That's actually quite funny.

Mike gives himself a private thumbs up as he goes into his office and comes out with the computer.

BRIAN So what time are you shooting?

MIKE *(guiltily)* What?

BRIAN The promo with Roland.

MIKE Oh. Um, not till the afternoon.

BRIAN See you then.

MIKE Did I hear there's a production meeting at ten o'clock?

BRIAN Em?

EMMA No. I don't think so.

MIKE But . . . Oh, OK, if it's not on . . . See you for the promo shoot.

All call goodnight as Mike leaves.

BRIAN Who keeps telling him about our meetings?

SCENE 10

THE WORLD SERIES DEBATE IS BEING TAPED IN A THEATRE.

Tim Smith is just finishing his speech.

TIM And that is why I am proud to be a poor man.

He walks away from the podium to huge applause. Mike is seated with his team, applauding politely. Campbell McComas approaches the podium.

CAMPBELL Thank you, Tim. The first of our three stooges for the negative tonight. Next up, ladies and gentlemen, we have a speaker who you could say is at the very 'front line' of current affairs. It's his job to convince us that money can in fact buy happiness . . . not to mention certain members of the Queensland judiciary.

Laughter from the audience. Mike smiles confidently as he studies his notes.

CAMPBELL You know, I think it was the noted author Katherine Mansfield who once said, 'I must say I hate money, but it's the lack of it I hate most.'

Laughter from audience. Mike looks at his speech notes in horror

CAMPBELL Though no truer words have been spoken than by the man who said, 'Money can't buy happiness, but it buys such a good imitation it's often difficult to tell it from the real thing.'

Another horrified look from Mike.

CAMPBELL But the final word must surely go to Arthur Schopenhauer, who stated 'Money is human happiness in the abstract; he, then, who is no longer capable of enjoying human happiness in the concrete devotes himself utterly to money.'

More laughter. Mike slumps in despair. Irony

CAMPBELL Ladies and gentleman, you want more? I give you Mike Moore . . .

Day ⑤

SCENE 11

MIKE'S OFFICE

Mike is hunched over his computer, head in hands. Domenica appears at the door.

DOMENICA Mike . . . you all right?

MIKE *(looking up)* Yeah.

DOMENICA How was dinner?

MIKE Good.

DOMENICA Where'd you go? Hey, is this for your stories?

MIKE It's not just for the TV stuff. I'm actually writing a novel, but it's hush-hush.

DOMENICA Hush-hush.

MIKE This is the novel file, see, and if you press this key it tells you how many words you've written.

DOMENICA Wow, 113! What's 'Thes'?

MIKE Thesaurus. I'll show you how to get into it.

Mike hits a button and his computer makes a farting noise. He is mystified. Marty walks past heading for Brian's office.

MIKE Someone's tampered with this. Marty!

DOMENICA Is he in trouble?

SCENE 12

BRIAN'S OFFICE

Brian and Emma are meeting as Marty walks in.

BRIAN We are not having a ventriloquist on this show.

EMMA He's not just a ventriloquist, Brian. He's a satirist.

MARTY Friday night funnyman?

BRIAN We're still searching.

MARTY Didn't you have a meeting with John Clarke and Bryan Dawe?

BRIAN Didn't seem that keen.

MARTY You mention the make-up thing?

Brian nods 'yes'.

BRIAN I might have a chat with Bryan Dawe on his own.

MARTY You reckon he'll work as a solo act?

BRIAN Maybe. And if not, at least we've split the team.

EMMA So it's 'no' to the satirical ventriloquist?

MARTY You know who's a funny bloke? That guy who goes 'oi oi oi'.

EMMA Rodney Rude?

MARTY Nah, he goes 'aah' with the tongue. This bloke goes 'oi oi'. Looks like me. Had some piss-awful game show once on Channel Ten.

BRIAN Greg Evans?

MARTY No, woggy name. Sorrento . . . ?

BRIAN Maybe we go back to running footage of American baseballers getting hit in the nuts.

EMMA Brian . . .

BRIAN So find me another Friday night funnyman.

EMMA Or woman. I mean, we are chasing a female audience. It might help.

MARTY Great. That's what we need – a fat chick doing tampon jokes.

BRIAN Shut up, Marty. (*to Emma*) Good idea. See who you can find. (*he hears Mike's computer making farting noises*) What's that noise?

SCENE 13

THE PRODUCTION OFFICE

Emma walks in. Domenica, Shelley, Brooke and Kate are hanging around Domenica's desk watching something.

EMMA What's going on?

DOMENICA They're shooting Mike's new promo. Isn't it exciting?

Emma looks to where Roland is directing Mike. There is an attractive model seated at Emma's desk. Stu and Jase are the film crew.

EMMA Who's that?

DOMENICA I think it's supposed to be you.

ROLAND OK, quiet please. We'll go for a take. Ready, Mike?

Mike gives the thumbs up.

ROLAND Roll camera. Mark it. Action!

Mike saunters across to the desk, jacket slung casually over his shoulder. He reaches the desk, leans over the model and utters his soon-to-be-famous catchphrase.

MIKE Looks great. Edit it . . . there.

ROLAND Cut!

MIKE What's wrong?

ROLAND (You forgot) the leg!

Roland indicates that Mike was supposed to lift and lean on his leg, George Negus-style.

ROLAND Come on, one more take. We've gotta be at the beach in half an hour.

SCENE 14

THE PRODUCTION OFFICE

The staff are having another meeting with Barb.

BARB (*reading figures*) It's starting to turn. Women have been up for the last two nights.

General congratulations.

BARB Don't get too carried away. You're still down in the forty-plus demographic.

BRIAN What do they wanna see?

BARB Care to take a guess?

BROOKE Tonight on Frontline – meet the Queen Mum.

BARB Sad, but true.

MIKE Barb, our overall rating hasn't dropped, has it?

BARB No.

MIKE So who cares if our audience is made up of men or women?

BARB The advertisers care. It's a thing called TARP.

MIKE *(feigns understanding)* Oh yeah. Which is?

BARB Target audience rate per thousand. Advertisers choose programs not just for the number of people watching, but the type. A million kids watch 'Melrose Place' but none of them's gonna buy superannuation.

BRIAN And if we keep losing women, no-one's gonna buy perfume, or dunny cleaner, or margarine; stuff women buy.

EMMA You're such a man of the nineties . . .

BRIAN *(wrapping up the meeting)* Thanks, Barb.

People get up and start dispersing. Mike collars Brian privately.

MIKE Brian, my sweat-shop story . . .

BRIAN Mike . . .

MIKE I just don't buy that 'Women don't understand politics' crap. It's so patronising.

BRIAN Mike, name the best politically based current affairs programme in this country.

MIKE Well, 'Lateline'. I've got a lot of respect for Kerry O'Brien.

BRIAN And what does it rate?

MIKE I don't think ratings are necessarily . . .

BRIAN Three.

MIKE Three. Really?

BRIAN You rate five times that.

MIKE You wonder why he's so rude to me. *(getting back to the point)* But Brian, my story's main-stream. It's not even that political.

BRIAN Mike, I'll come clean with you. I think your story's great. If it was up to me, we'd run it tonight.

MIKE But . . .

BRIAN It's coming from upstairs. They think it's a bit heavy.

MIKE Oh, they are so . . . *(he can't think of the word)* I'm going to speak with Farmer, tell him . . .

BRIAN Mike, don't. I'll tell you what – let me take a look at the story.

MIKE Would you? Thanks, Brian.

Brian starts to walk off. Mike stops him again.

MIKE Oh, Brian, one more thing. Seeing you've been honest with me . . . I think I may have done something a little foolish last night. You know those ABC debates . . .

Mike starts to tell Brian the story. Brian looks pained.

Day 6

SCENE 15

BRIAN'S OFFICE

Brian is on the phone. He holds a TV guide.

BRIAN Look, I know it's late notice to drop the show, but we're just not happy with our host being seen in this light. I don't give a stuff how much you edit it . . . Listen, I am not trying to bully you . . . Can't you schedule something else tomorrow night? What about that Mr Bean thing; you'd have a few hundred of them on the shelf, wouldn't you? Well, fuck you! *(hangs up)* ABC arseholes.

We reveal Mike is in the office with Brian. He is wearing his on-air jacket and has tissues around the collar to protect it from make-up. Emma walks in with a tape.

EMMA Got a minute?

Emma inserts a tape in the player. Mike tries to take this opportunity to sneak off.

BRIAN Sit down!

We see a stylised re-enactment featuring a spunky doctor and an even spunkier female patient. The doctor approaches the patient.

DOCTOR I've just got to give you an examination.

WOMAN But doctor . . . What are you doing?

The picture goes into soft focus as a minor struggle ensues. We see a close-up of the woman's bra being undone.

MARTY *(voice only)* The GPs of Sleaze. It's a story no woman can afford to miss – tonight on Frontline.

Brian hits pause.

BRIAN What the hell is that?

EMMA It's supposed to be a re-enactment.

BRIAN Looks like a Coke commercial.

MIKE I found it chilling.

BRIAN Shut up. *(to Emma)* You think women will watch that story?

EMMA *(thinks)* Yeah.

BRIAN OK, get it on.

MIKE I can give the story a bit of a plug on AW.

BRIAN Um, don't worry about the radio today, Mike.

MIKE Has Neil cancelled?

BRIAN No, we just want to try something a little different.

SCENE 16

BROOKE IS ON AIR AT 3AW WITH NEIL MITCHELL.

NEIL Welcome to the studio, Brooke Vandenberg.

BROOKE Pleased to be here, Neil.

NEIL Now, what do we owe this to? Some sort of push to present the feminine side of Frontline?

BROOKE *(laughing this off)* No, Neil, Mike's simply tied up. But we've got a fascinating story tonight; it's the Queen Mum's forty-eighth year in public life.

Day

SCENE 17

THE EDIT SUITE

We start full frame on a packaged story, showing women working in a dimly lit, crowded factory.

MIKE *(voice only)* It could well be a scene from China or Korea, but this sweat shop is operating right here in Australia.

Cut to vision of factory exterior.

MIKE *(voice only)* Dalgarni Fabrics is just one of the dozens of clothing factories in this country employing illegal immigrants in unsafe conditions and paying them below award wages. *(cut to table of figures)* The Textile Industry Workers Union sets down minimum wage levels . . .

The story is stopped, the frame freezing. We reveal Brian, Mike and Hugh in the edit suite. Brian has stopped the tape.

BRIAN What's this story about?

MIKE What?

BRIAN Because five seconds in I completely lost consciousness. This is Mogadon.

MIKE Jesus, Brian. Hugh, what do you . . . ?
(Hugh feigns unconsciousness) I see, so we just can it, do we?

BRIAN No, but we're gonna have to re-edit. Pace it up.

MIKE *(indicating screen)* But that's lightning!

BRIAN Look, do you want this story to go to air?

MIKE Yes.

BRIAN Then leave it with Hugh and me.

MIKE OK.

Mike leaves. As he goes he removes a 'No smoking' sign pinned to the wall and hands it to Hugh as a way of drawing his attention to it. Hugh takes the sign and begins using it as an ashtray.

BRIAN *(to Hugh)* This needs major surgery.

HUGH Leave it with the doctor.

Brian leaves.

SCENE 18

THE PRODUCTION OFFICE

Everyone is standing around watching the monitor. Emma is cueing up a tape.

KATE Please, one more time!

EMMA *(looking around)* He's not around, is he?

BROOKE He's in make-up.

Everyone calls for another screening. Emma hits the remote. We cut in close to reveal they are watching Mike's promo.

The promo is played. We see Mike, jacket over shoulder, walking through the office (included is the line, 'Edit it . . . there'); Mike walking along the beach skipping a stone; Mike stopping to pick up a teddy bear and handing it to a young child in a pram being pushed by a mother; Mike playing guitar by an open fire, with the back of a woman's head in shot. The scene is accompanied by James Taylor's 'You've Got a Friend'.

VOICE-OVER In the world of current affairs, it's nice to know . . . you've got a friend.

MIKE *(voice only)* Sometimes I guess it's easy to get a little carried away with work. I love my work, but you've still gotta take time out to smell the roses . . .

VOICE-OVER Mike Moore, 6.30 weeknights on Frontline.

The promo ends to great cheers. Brian has entered during the screening.

BRIAN Well, what you do reckon? Are you in love with him, ladies?

KATE Head over heels.

MARTY And we've got a Friday night comedy spot.

SCENE 19

THE FRONTLINE STUDIO

Mike is at the desk just about to interview Cheryl Kernot.

MIKE Busy in the Senate?

CHERYL Still involved with the Fairfax inquiry. Have you read the report?

MIKE *(not convincing)* Yeah . . .

CHERYL Thought we might look at some of the ramifications tonight, especially the role of the Foreign Investment Review Board.

MIKE *(even less convincing)* Sure.

FLOOR MANAGER In five.

MIKE Here we go.

The floor manager counts down from five.

MIKE Good evening, I'm Mike Moore. Welcome to Frontline.

The opening titles run.

MIKE Well, they say it's a 'man's world'. But one woman who's made a name for herself in the male-heavy halls of Parliament House is Democrat leader Senator Cheryl Kernot. Senator Kernot joins us now. Senator Kernot, what's it like being one of the few women in Canberra?

CHERYL It can be difficult, I guess, but it's like any other job. You just get on with it.

MIKE How do you balance work and family?

CHERYL Well, I have a very understanding and supportive husband. Mind you, he has to be with the hours I've been working lately. The Fairfax Media Inquiry has revealed major flaws in the foreign investment . . .

MIKE Of course, it's not just your husband; you also have a daughter. Does she often come to Canberra with you?

CHERYL No, she's at school. As I was saying, the Foreign Investment Review Board . . .

MIKE You must have had mixed feelings when Ros Kelly resigned.

CHERYL *(mystified)* Ros Kelly?

MIKE Well, being a woman, a sister . . .

We cut to Cheryl's look of exasperation.

SCENE 20

THE MAKE-UP ROOM

Mike is having his make-up removed.

MIKE I mean, it was a tough interview. She was giving nothing.

Marty walks in with a TV guide.

MARTY Not to worry. We'll be able to 'edit it . . . there'. *(Mike looks mystified)* How many Mike Moores are there in this country?

MIKE Um, I think there was a New Zealand Prime Minister . . .

MARTY *(reading)* World Series Debating, 8.30 tonight on ABC TV. Featuring Tim Smith, Mike Moore . . .

MIKE Marty. I gotta ask you a favour on this one. Could you keep it quiet? Brian's a little 'thingy'.

MARTY *(in mock horror)* You've told him?

MIKE *(really worried)* Yeah, but I'm hoping he'll kind of forget about it . . .

SCENE 21

BRIAN'S OFFICE

Brian watches Mike on the debate in disbelief. He is drinking. We cut to vision of Mike at the podium in mid-speech.

MIKE Of course money can't buy everything. No-one said it could. It's impossible. That's why we've got credit cards for.

We cut away to the audience looking unamused, then cut back to Brian looking stunned.

Day 8

SCENE 22

THE PRODUCTION OFFICE

Mike arrives. The office is empty, except for Domenica.

DOMENICA Mike! You're in early.

MIKE I skipped gym. You see me on the debate last night?

DOMENICA That was very sneaky not telling us, Mike. My sister rang: 'Mike's on the telly, Mike's on the telly!'

MIKE How'd you think I went?

DOMENICA *(not convincing)* Good. Why did you repeat the quotes that the bald guy said? I mean, they were funnier the first time.

MIKE You know they edited a lot of my good stuff out . . . Is Brian in?

DOMENICA I think he's in the studio with Emma. *(she goes back to work)*

MIKE Oh. Got a big story tonight, Dom.

DOMENICA Really?

MIKE It's about the exploitation of women in our clothing factories. You should see the conditions these girls work under, for just about no money.

DOMENICA That's terrible.

MIKE Brian thought it was a bit 'heavy', but I convinced him it was an important issue for women.

DOMENICA Yeah, right. *(the phone rings)* Hello, Frontline. Domenica speaking. Hi, Assunta! Yeah, he was on the debate. Uh-huh . . . Oh, apparently they edited out a lot of his good stuff.

SCENE 23

THE FRONTLINE STUDIO

Brian and Emma are watching a female comedian audition.

COMEDIAN . . . so he killed her. Well, come on – she was asking for it; wearing those provocative shoes and daring to walk down the street at night. And she said 'no' which as any South Australian judge will tell you means 'yes please please please'. And the facial bruising – just look on it as 'foreplay'.

There is an awkward silence, broken only by Brian's forced laughter.

BRIAN Excellent! Very funny indeed.

EMMA That was great, Helen. Thanks for coming in. We'll get back to you.

The comedian leaves.

BRIAN That was excruciating.

Mike enters.

MIKE Who's the . . . ?

BRIAN We're looking for replacements for Elliot.

EMMA (*checking watch*) And we've got just under six hours.

MIKE Didn't you have a meeting with John Clarke and Barry Dawe?

BRIAN They weren't quite right.

MIKE I agree. He has never made me laugh. Doesn't even get the voices right.

EMMA I think we'll have to go with Elliot.

MIKE No! No!

BRIAN Emma, I've made a commitment to Mike . . . That bow-tied twerp will not be appearing on this show.

SCENE 24

THE MAKE-UP ROOM

Mike is in make-up. Emma runs through details of the show with him.

EMMA . . . we come out of the ad break with 'Young girls who binge-drink' – that's a straight 'Brooke Vandenberg reports'; then there's your fashion story.

MIKE It's not a fashion story. It's about below award-wage payments in the textile industry.

EMMA (*not entirely sure*) Right.

Brian pokes his head in on the way to the control room.

BRIAN Set to go?

MIKE Sure. (*Brian starts to leave*) Oh Brian, how does the sweat-shop story look now?

BRIAN Come up 100 per cent.

MIKE Thanks for backing me on it.

BRIAN I did tell you there'd be a re-edit.

MIKE Oh yeah, 'pace it up'. You kept the factory shots?

BRIAN (*thinks*) Yes.

SCENE 25

THE FRONTLINE STUDIO

Mike is at his desk. A story is just winding up. The floor manager calls.

FLOOR MANAGER Five to go.

BROOKE (*voice only*) . . . to stop these young girls literally drowning in drink. Brooke Vandenberg, Frontline.

MIKE Mmm, it's a worrying trend. Well, they say 'Clothes maketh the man', but in Australia's fiercely competitive fashion industry, it's women who maketh the clothes. Here's a Frontline exclusive . . .

We cut full frame to the monitor, showing the same 'sweat shop' factory footage as used in the original story.

BROOKE (*voice only*) It could well be a scene from Paris or Rome, but this clothing factory is operating right here in Australia.

File footage of fashion spokesperson. We cut to standard catwalk shots of models parading. Music grabs from David Bowie's 'Fashion'.

Cut to Mike watching his 're-edited' story completely changed into a fashion report.

MIKE What the . . . ? Where's Brian?

Mike gets up from his desk. We see him head over to Brian, who has come into the studio to placate his star.

MIKE (*angrily*) What have you done to my story?

BRIAN We kept the factory shots.

MIKE You've turned it into an ad for Sportsgirl! You've massacred my story.

BRIAN You almost massacred your career last night.

MIKE Oh, so it's about the debate, is it? I didn't ask your permission, Brian, because I knew you'd say 'no'. I knew you wouldn't listen to me. You never listen to me.

BRIAN I do, Mike.

MIKE About the only thing I've suggested this week (that) you actually agreed with was getting rid of Elliot Rhodes.

We see Emma rush into the studio with an electric piano and table, followed by Elliot Rhodes.

EMMA Mike, here's the intro. *(hands over paper)* It's the 'Recession Rap'.

ELLIOT *(smiling, to Mike)* Yo, bro!

Episode 8

The Art of Gentle Persuasion

Day ❶

SCENE 1

BRIAN'S OFFICE

Brian and Emma are meeting. Brian reads from the newspaper.

BRIAN 'The semi-nude performances, known as "tabletop dancing", are now commonplace in the city, with twelve venues in operation . . . ' Geez, some of these girls are gorgeous; you seen them? 'With no existing regulations against them, more are expected to open in the near future.'

EMMA *(under her breath)* Something to look forward to.

BRIAN Geez, I'd love to do a story.

Emma gives him a 'look'.

EMMA It's tabloid and sleazy. It's not worth doing.

BRIAN Emma, it's tabloid and sleazy: that's why it's worth doing.

EMMA It's an excuse to show nudity.

BRIAN Exactly . . . Hey, let's not be coy about it. Everyone likes a bit of flesh. I didn't see you complaining during the Manpower story.

EMMA *(protesting)* We can't be tabloid.

BRIAN No, we can't *appear* to be tabloid, so we do it for the right reasons.

EMMA Which are . . . ?

BRIAN Hang on, hang on, give us a second . . . um . . . Right. Of course. The moral thing . . . community outrage.

EMMA What outrage?

BRIAN The community outrage.

EMMA Where?

BRIAN In the community.

EMMA I don't know of any . . .

BRIAN Oh, if you don't see that you've misread the mood of this town.

EMMA I'm sorry.

BRIAN We're being forced to live on the streets of sleaze. It's a moral issue. This is where we need Mike's self-righteous streak – takes the mozz off it. *(picks up the paper)* Geez, they are beautiful.

EMMA One small problem.

BRIAN What?

Emma points to a photo of Mike on the noticeboard.

EMMA Allow me to quote the scriptures according to Mike. *(she takes the article from the noticeboard)* 'I think viewers will be pleased by the new Frontline this year. No more hidden cameras, foot-in-the-door and most of all no more of the titillation and nudity of other current affairs shows.'

BRIAN Why did he say that?

EMMA You wrote it for him. He won't do this story.

BRIAN Oh, he will . . .

EMMA Hmm.

BRIAN . . . with the art of gentle persuasion. Start chasing interviews.

Kate enters in a hurry with a fax.

KATE *(handing over fax)* Just in.

BRIAN Crocodile attack.

KATE This morning. A woman, up in Kakadu – in a dinghy with her husband and kids, fell out . . .

EMMA Oh my God . . .

KATE They witnessed the whole thing.

BRIAN Where are they now?

KATE Flying back this afternoon.

Emma is still in empathetic shock.

BRIAN Get Marty onto it.

EMMA Brian! It's just happened. He'll be in shock.

BRIAN That's right. We gotta hurry.

SCENE 2

BROOKE IS IN HER BATHROOM TALKING ON THE PHONE.

BROOKE Are you sure? Are you sure? Are you sure . . . ? Definitely. I better go: I'm on the mobile. Thanks for letting me know. *(she hangs up)* My life is about to fall apart.

SCENE 3

THE PRODUCTION OFFICE

Kate is on the phone. Brian is staring at the whiteboard.

KATE *(hanging up)* Brian?

BRIAN What?

KATE The crocodile man. Not talking.

BRIAN What?

KATE Spoke to his brother. He's home but he's refusing all interview requests.

BRIAN Did you offer him anything?

KATE Not interested. Too distressed.

BRIAN Shit. You got his address?

KATE He's not talking to anyone.

BRIAN Marty? See what you can get.

KATE (But) he said 'no' . . .

MARTY *(leaving)* Hey – leave it to the pros.

As Marty leaves, Mike enters listening to a portable CD player.

DOMENICA Hi, Mike.

MIKE *(shouts)* Morning, Domenica. *(takes off headphones)* Sorry, had the CD up a bit loud.

DOMENICA CD? Give us a look. Who's Ottmar Liebert?

MIKE A wonderful guitarist from Europe.

DOMENICA Oh, he's the guy from Roxette.

MIKE He may well be.

Mike shows Domenica his new CD player.

BRIAN *(to Mike)* Got a minute, mate?

Mike follows Brian into his office. Domenica hums the guitar riff from 'She's Got the Look'. Mike enters Brian's office. Brian shuts the door.

SCENE 4

BRIAN'S OFFICE

BRIAN *(holding the pamphlet)* You know anything about tabletop dancing?

MIKE Oh, only what I read in the paper.

BRIAN Look, I'm no prude, but this is a bloody disgrace.

MIKE Absolutely.

BRIAN It's spreading, too. Twelfth venue's about to open. It's like McDonald's.

MIKE Sorry – is this new to you, Brian?

BRIAN *(pointing out the window)* I didn't know it was a plague.

MIKE I know. There was an article in the paper today saying exactly what you're saying.

BRIAN *(slightly holding paper)* Really?

MIKE The treatment of women, and of course the links to sexual violence.

BRIAN I wish we could do a story. Expose those venues for what they are.

MIKE Yeah. You're right, but of course we can't, 'cause the audience'd think we're being sleazy.

They laugh together.

BRIAN The irony. There's no way Marty'd pull it off. He looks a little . . .

MIKE I know what you mean, but it's a good story.

BRIAN Maybe I could get Brooke to . . . Nuh. I don't know.

MIKE Brian . . . Brian. *(points to himself in smug triumph)* Me. I'll do it.

BRIAN You?

MIKE Absolutely. The story needs to be done.

BRIAN It's going to be a tough exposé. You'd have to go inside, film this stuff.

MIKE Sure.

BRIAN Ever been to one of these places?

MIKE No. Well, a mate's bucks party – but I didn't watch.

BRIAN I reckon we show what it's really like. *(clicks finger and points)* Actually film the girls dancing . . .

MIKE Interview one of 'em. Find out about the drugs, prostitution. A real exposé.

BRIAN Yeah, but the dancing's the main thing.

MIKE OK. I'll get started.

Emma enters.

BRIAN Get Emma to help you.

MIKE Em, we're doing a story on tabletop dancing. Could you do some research?

EMMA *(to Brian)* You're unbelievable.

SCENE 5

A SUBURBAN STREET

Stu and Marty are sitting in a car outside a home with a piece of paper in their hands. Stu is actually reading the paper.

STU Jesus, poor husband. It sounds like the perfect family . . . This ain't pleasant.

MARTY No. And to think we could be interviewing a tabletop dancer.

STU Why don't we just knock on the grass? Tell Brian he wasn't home.

MARTY If we don't do the interview, someone else will, and I get my arse kicked. Now what's the number?

STU Six. Or is it an eight?

MARTY Great.

SCENE 6

A STREET LOCATION

Mike is standing in the street with a microphone doing vox pops.

MIKE Is sleaze taking over the neighbourhood?

WOMAN What do you mean?

MIKE The tabletop dancing.

WOMAN Where?

MIKE *(pointing)* In that hotel.

WOMAN (Oh, I) didn't know it was going on.

MIKE Are you outraged?

WOMAN 'Bout what?

MIKE Thanks for your time.

The woman wanders off. Mike goes over to Emma and crew.

MIKE This is hard work.

EMMA We've got plenty of time.

MIKE Don't these people realise it's becoming the . . .

EMMA Streets of sleaze?

MIKE These places are springing up like . . .

EMMA McDonald's.

MIKE Like McDonald's. Hang on, here we go.

SCENE 7

THE FRONT DOOR OF A HOUSE

Marty, Stu and Jase are at the door of number 76. A man opens the door.

MARTY Hello. I'm Martin di Stasio from Frontline. I'm very sorry to hear of your wife's death.

The man's wife appears beside him.

WIFE What is it, Des?

MARTY *(to Stu)* So that was an eight.

SCENE 8

MIKE IS OUT ON THE STREET SPEAKING TO OLD PEOPLE.

MIKE *(pointing)* In there.

OLD GUY Where?

MIKE There, in the pub. *(he gets totally frustrated and starts turning the old guy around in an aggressive manner)* That big thing in front of your face.

OLD GUY What about it?

MIKE There are half-naked women dancing on tables in there.

OLD GUY Wonderful!

He starts to go in, but Mike stops him.

MIKE Let me explain again. This neighbourhood is being turned into a porn centre. It'll become known as the suburb of sex. Aren't you angry about that?

OLD GUY No, I don't live here.

The old guy wanders off. Mike comes over to Emma.

MIKE This is hopeless. He's the tenth person.

EMMA Maybe we're in the wrong spot.

SCENE 9

THE DOOR OF ANOTHER SUBURBAN HOUSE

Marty and the crew are at the door of the victim's house. The door opens.

MARTY Mr Ramar, I'm sorry to disturb you at a time like this.

RAMAR I'm not speaking to anyone. That has been made very clear.

MARTY We just wanted to ask . . .

RAMAR I'm sorry, gentlemen. Please, you'll have to leave.

He goes to close the door.

MARTY Fine, I understand. I'm sorry to have troubled you.

RAMAR That's all right.

MARTY *(on a human level)* We actually didn't want to come. I'm extremely sorry for the intrusion. Needless to say you have our deepest sympathies.

RAMAR Thank you.

MARTY Let's leave this man in peace . . .

He goes to leave but stops with an afterthought.

MARTY Oh, would you mind if I called my producer to tell him the story's off (and) make sure you're not bothered by anyone else from our office?

RAMAR No, I think I'd appreciate that.

As the man walks into the house Marty turns to Stu and Jase and tells them to roll. He points at Mr Ramar as if to say, 'Film him'.

In the house, Marty picks up the phone and dials no-one.

MARTY *(indicating a photograph next to the phone)* Is this your wife?

RAMAR Yes.

Marty looks sensitively at the photo.

MARTY *(into the phone)* Brian, thanks . . . *(to Mr Ramar)* Why didn't you want to talk to anyone?

RAMAR It's a very tragic thing, both for myself and my children. I think we have the right to grieve in private. *(cut to tape rolling)* It was a shocking way for her to die. I want her to be remembered for what she was, not how she died. I owe that to our children.

A child's voice calls out.

RAMAR Don't worry, Sarah. I'm still here.

Mr Ramar leaves to attend to his obviously distressed child. Marty slides out one of the photos of Mrs Ramar and pockets it.

SCENE 10

THE PRODUCTION OFFICE

Brian is looking at the whiteboard.

BRIAN I want a profile on someone who's been through this before. I know – that family who lost their two kids a few years back. Get Brooke on to it.

DOMENICA Brooke's not coming in till later.

BRIAN Why?

DOMENICA *(shrugs shoulders)* Dunno, but she didn't sound well.

SCENE 11

A NEW STREET LOCATION

Mike is vox popping a woman.

WOMAN It's sickening. These young girls – a lot of them are on drugs. It encourages immorality. I'm absolutely against it.

MIKE Thank you very much.

We reveal that Mike and the crew are now taping in front of a church.

SCENE 12

BRIAN'S OFFICE

Marty and Brian are viewing footage of Mr Ramar.

MARTY It's not long.

BRIAN You done well, mate.

MARTY Thanks, mate.

BRIAN It's a credit to you.

MARTY How'd you go with the other stuff?

BRIAN Got some file footage of crocs – I think it's from an old Jack Absalom doco.

MARTY What about an expert?

BRIAN *(calling)* Kate, how we go with the croc expert?

Kate comes to the door with a clipboard.

KATE Having a little difficulty. Aren't that many around. I've got a zoologist specialising in reptile . . .

BRIAN No scientists.

KATE There's Ron and Valerie Taylor . . .

MARTY Sharks.

KATE Or Vic Hislop.

Marty hums the Jaws theme.

BRIAN *(to Kate)* Get someone.

SCENE 13

INSIDE A HOTEL

Mike is at a hotel where tabletop dancing is conducted. There is a very attractive semi-clad woman on the table behind him, dancing provocatively. We see the scene through the perspective of the camera.

MIKE Am I full frame?

He obviously isn't.

CAMERAMAN Yep.

MIKE All right, take three . . . It's these porn palaces that have families fuming and guys going gaga.

EMMA That's fine. *(calls to the dancer)* That's fine, thanks.

MIKE OK. Let's get this interview out of the way. *(under his breath, to Emma)* Here comes some rocket science.

Katrina approaches, having finished dancing for the camera.

KATRINA How was that?

MIKE Fine.

KATRINA I was a little nervous, I'll have to admit.

MIKE Why's that?

KATRINA I'm afraid I'm a bit of a Mike Moore fan. Where do you want me to sit?

The camera operator takes Katrina over to interview position and begins setting up. Mike is flattered, uncomfortable and awkward all at the same time.

MIKE Lovely girl.

EMMA *(looking at clipboard)* Mike, these questions.

MIKE Yeah?

EMMA 'Are you a prostitute?' 'How much of your salary goes on drugs?' It's a little heavy.

MIKE Hey! We've decided to do an exposé here. It's not a grubby little excuse to show naked women.

EMMA I know that.

MIKE It's an exposé.

CAMERAMAN Set to go.

Mike takes a seat and starts the interview.

MIKE Katrina, you've been a tabletop dancer for how long?

KATRINA Eighteen months.

MIKE You enjoy your work?

KATRINA I love it. I see myself as a businesswoman. I market my looks in the same way as a Cindy Crawford or an Elle Macpherson.

Mike nods in agreement, lost in love. Emma has to prompt him to move on to the next question.

EMMA Mike? Streets of sleaze . . .

MIKE People say you're turning this city into the streets of sleaze.

KATRINA Well, that's just silly.

MIKE Sure, maybe they're being prudish . . . But it's said there's a link between explicit exhibitionism and violence against women.

KATRINA Well, that seems silly too. Oppression has been found to lead to crime, not liberation.

MIKE Good answer.

KATRINA Did you think? I'm flattered.

MIKE I did. That's an answer of an expert.

KATRINA Why, thank you.

MIKE Only saying the truth.

KATRINA You're so sweet.

SCENE 14

THE PRODUCTION OFFICE

KATE OK, the zoo bloke's said yes.

BRIAN Great. When Brooke gets in, tell her to go out there . . .

KATE She's called. Not coming in at all.

BRIAN Is she OK?

DOMENICA She's sick. She's in bed.

BRIAN Anything serious?

MARTY Probably just a footballer.

BRIAN OK – the zoo bloke goes live tonight with Mike.

Emma returns with a tape.

EMMA Well, that was an enlightening day.

BRIAN How'd you go?

EMMA *(handing him tape)* We got outraged citizens, interview with someone from Women Against Pornography . . . What else? Oh that's right, forty minutes of half-naked women.

BRIAN Great. Where's Mike?

EMMA Stayed on to do some more research.

Brian gives Emma a look as if he can't believe it's true. Emma shakes her head and walks off.

SCENE 15

THE FRONTLINE STUDIO

On the screen we see the story running.

MR RAMAR I still have three children to worry about. That's my major concern now.

Cut back to Mike in the studio.

MIKE Certainly tragic stuff. Well, joining us now is deadly aquatic animal expert Noel Cronin. Noel, we had reports that only an arm was found. Is that typical of crocs?

NOEL Not really. They normally eat everything. They take a person, then drown them first.

MIKE So what you're saying is that Mr Ramar would have watched his wife taken while she was still alive?

NOEL Most definitely.

MIKE And that while he and the children were standing shocked above, she was drowning in the mouth of a croc below?

NOEL That's the way it would have happened.

MIKE Our hearts certainly go out to the Ramar family.

SCENE 16

THE PRODUCTION OFFICE

Brian and Mike walk in after the show.

MIKE I was very moved by that Mr Ramar. Very tragic story.

BRIAN You handled it well, Mike.

MIKE It was good of him to speak with us. That stuff with Noel Cronin was a bit gruesome.

BRIAN I didn't know he would go into all that gory detail. *(changing topic)* So how'd you go with the tabletop dancing story?

MIKE I think we've got some good stuff. There's definitely community outrage out there in the . . . community.

BRIAN Absolutely.

SHELLEY Brian, Mr Ramar's on the line.

BRIAN I'll take it in there. *(indicates his office)* Mike, good show. You head off.

MIKE Give him my best. *(to Emma)* He's a lovely and decent man, that John Ramar. You can only wish him the best.

SCENE 17

BRIAN'S OFFICE

Brian is talking on the phone.

BRIAN Well, I have no reason to doubt the word of my most experienced reporter. You were answering questions from a reporter with a film crew, who you invited into your house – of course you were being recorded . . . I don't think there's any need to do that. What conditions? All right, yes, I do give you a total assurance we won't play those pictures again.

He hangs up. Emma enters.

BRIAN I didn't tell Marty to do it.

EMMA Come on, Brian, you want to wash your hands just like that. You knew he was going to get what you wanted.

BRIAN It's a legitimate technique.

EMMA God, Brian. He's just lost his wife, he's got three young children, he said he wanted to be left alone. Why can't we just leave him alone?

BRIAN We're only showing . . .

EMMA Why do we have to splash his grief all over the screens?

BRIAN We're only showing what people want.

EMMA Oh, how convenient. People want snuff movies – do we give them that?

BRIAN We're all voyeurs at heart. You can't deny that.

EMMA Yeah, when it comes to Luke Perry's hideaway.

BRIAN It's a fine line, Emma.

EMMA It's not a fine line. It's a fucking big line. That's just the bullshit we spin. It's not a fine line, Brian.

BRIAN Any time you don't want to be part of this just let me know. But in the meantime you do the job – your job. Clear?

She nods.

BRIAN Thank you.

Day ②

SCENE 18

THE PRODUCTION OFFICE

Brian is reading the ratings.

BRIAN Won the night everywhere. Sensational stuff.

MARTY Why does any story involving a crocodile attract an audience?

BRIAN I dunno, don't care, but we do a follow-up tonight. 'Life before the killer croc: a grieving husband remembers'.

KATE He's not going to talk to us again.

BRIAN Doesn't need to. Marty, cover the funeral today. We'll use the footage and overlay it with some sound bites you haven't used from yesterday's tape.

EMMA You told Mr Ramar you weren't going to show any more.

BRIAN I said I wasn't going to show any more vision. We can still play the sound. Em, just cut a promo for Mike's tabletop dancing story. Depending on what Marty gets it may be our lead for tonight. And . . .

Brooke walks in with sunglasses on. Everyone looks at her.

BROOKE Have you got a moment, Brian?

SCENE 19

BRIAN'S OFFICE

BRIAN Did you actually go out with this guy?

BROOKE Four years ago, for six months, and we both wanted to break up.

BRIAN Then how can their front cover be 'How Brooke Broke My Heart'?

BROOKE I don't know.

BRIAN And it comes out tomorrow.

BROOKE Uh-huh.

BRIAN Those bastards. That magazine is a rag – tabloid crap.

BROOKE He could have said anything.

BRIAN What do you mean? Is there anything grubby?

BROOKE No, it was just a normal relationship.

BRIAN Bastards. They think they have the right to splash your private life across the . . .

BROOKE I'm devastated. *(she starts to cry)*

BRIAN Relax, relax. The first thing we do is say nothing.

BROOKE But what if . . . ?

BRIAN Nothing. Remember this: it always blows over if you shut up. Don't make the mistake.

BROOKE Jesus.

BRIAN I'll ring Jan.

SCENE 20

MARTY, STU AND JASE ARE PARKED OPPOSITE A CHURCH.

MARTY Geez, how long's this funeral taking? Sure we can't sneak in with a camera?

STU What, hidden in a wreath? We'll get the shot from here.

SCENE 21

BRIAN'S OFFICE

JAN I can't believe it. This is your private life. There's grief involved – always is. The insensitivity of it all.

BRIAN What can we do?

JAN The first thing we do is say nothing.

BRIAN I told her that.

JAN It's only the poor poppets in the public that respond.

BROOKE We can't stop it?

JAN AND BRIAN No.

BROOKE So we don't do anything.

BRIAN Oh, we'll kick 'em up the arse. Farmer's stopped their ads going to air, and the big boy's going to throw some weight around at the board level.

JAN And that little cretin won't get another story from this place.

BROOKE Well, that helps me.

JAN Don't panic. All we need is a counterbalance – something else about you.

BRIAN Like some charity thing.

JAN Yes . . . your trip to Ethiopia.

BROOKE That's already been done.

JAN You're returning.

BROOKE (quickly) I'm not going back.

JAN No . . . But we say you are in the future. You see, my dear – subtly, without appearing to, we have to emphasise the caring Brooke.

BRIAN Good, Jan.

JAN Then he's the bastard. We're the ones that care.

SCENE 22

THE FUNERAL

There is an army of journos outside the church as the coffin emerges. Stu, Marty and Jase are amongst them.

SCENE 23

GEOFF'S OFFICE

GEOFF So how'd you go yesterday? With the strippers.

MIKE They're not really strippers, Geoff.

GEOFF No?

MIKE More businesswomen. Very smart.

GEOFF Is it a real exposé?

MIKE (thinks) In a controlled way. You see the show last night?

GEOFF That crocodile must have been big.

MIKE Scary animals. You see the interview we did with the husband?

GEOFF Very sad. Seeing your wife die in front of . . .

MIKE I thought it was a great honour that he chose to speak exclusively with Frontline.

GEOFF That's 'cause people know you care. I reckon half of your job is a community service.

MIKE I tend to think that.

GEOFF Mike, I heard that the guy didn't know he was being filmed.

MIKE Oh no, no, Brian wouldn't allow that . . . (thinks) Who told you that?

SCENE 24

BRIAN'S OFFICE

Brian and Marty are looking at the footage of the funeral. We see Mr Ramar and his children emerging from the church behind the coffin. They are moving in slow motion. We hear Mr Ramar's voice from the original interview.

MR RAMAR (voice only) It's a very tragic thing, both for myself and my children . . .

MARTY There wasn't much footage so we had to slo-mo it.

BRIAN It still works.

Mike enters.

MIKE Brian, got a moment?

BRIAN (handing tape to Marty) Sure. Cut a promo.

Marty leaves with tape.

MIKE That interview with Mr Ramar last night.

BRIAN You see the ratings? We killed, Mike.

MIKE Someone told me he didn't know he was being filmed.

BRIAN I'll be honest, Mike. It's not a practice I approve of. I didn't know Marty had done it, but I spoke to Mr Ramar after the show.

MIKE I know he was angry.

BRIAN He understood our position. And I gave him an assurance that the footage would not be used again.

MIKE Well, you can't do much more than that.

SCENE 25

THE FRONTLINE STUDIO

Cut to the show that night. Full frame on the telly, with voice-over and music.

MR RAMAR *(voice only)* I just want to grieve in private.

Music ends.

MIKE Let's hope everyone grants him that wish. A moving story by Martin di Stasio. *(changing tone of voice)* And tomorrow night, I go behind the scenes in the great dirty dancing debate.

Quick grabs of the tabletop dancers accompanied by the song 'Let's Talk About Sex'.

MIKE Tough job. *(realises there's more on autocue)* And also tomorrow night, Brooke Vandenberg's lifetime love affair with the children of Africa. See you then. *(off air)* When did that get added?

Day

SCENE 26

NEIL MITCHELL IS INTERVIEWING MR RAMAR ON 3AW.

NEIL How would you describe the media coverage of this tragedy, in particular the Frontline story that aired last night?

RAMAR It's a self-seeking departure from common decency. It was a barbaric exploitation of a situation that any feeling human being knew required sensitivity and understanding.

SCENE 27

THE PRODUCTION OFFICE

We hear Ramar's voice coming out of Domenica's radio.

RAMAR *(voice only)* They came into my house, secretly filmed their invasion of my grief. I'm just . . . I'm sorry, Neil. *(he breaks down)*

NEIL *(voice only)* We'll leave it there. John Ramar. Back after the break.

Widen to reveal everyone listening. Domenica turns the radio down.

MARTY Well, when he breaks his silence he certainly breaks his silence.

DOMENICA The poor man.

EMMA Exactly.

Brian bursts from his office holding ratings.

BRIAN Won the night.

General glee. Brian sees Emma looking unhappy and follows her into the kitchen.

BRIAN You still got a problem?

EMMA Yes I do. That poor, poor man. We stamp all over his grief, use it for what it's worth then say it's tragic, like we feel for him. We don't feel for him. We just say that so we don't look like bastards. Well, someone's going to catch on one day. We are bastards. We make people victims. We're the crocs.

Emma goes to leave.

BRIAN Emma, that's a fine speech . . . but you're still here.

EMMA Maybe I'm not.

Emma storms out towards the loos.

Cut back to reception where Brooke walks in and is greeted by Mike, who comes out from his office holding a magazine.

MIKE I'm shocked. Words fail me. I feel for you. That little sleazebag – I'd like to see if he's been to Ethiopia.

BROOKE Thanks, Mike.

MIKE Doesn't anyone have any ethics? I can't believe the double standards of some people.

He sees something off camera which turns out to be the tabletop dancer, Katrina.

MIKE Katrina.

KATRINA You said lunch any day.

MIKE And today's a great day.

Brooke walks over past Domenica, who is deep in reading the magazine.

DOMENICA Brooke, I just gotta say that is terrible.

BROOKE Thanks, Dom.

DOMENICA *(reading)* You were on your way to Port Douglas and the car broke down. It ruined your holiday.

MARTY He comes across well, Brooke. And he wrote poetry. How'd you let him slip through your fingers?

BROOKE Listen, Marty. That might work fine with Mike, but don't try your smartarse shit on me.

Brooke goes to her desk.

STU *(to Marty)* You gonna do the rest of the jokes?

MARTY Nah. I've already been to one funeral this week.

SCENE 28

OUTSIDE WOMEN'S TOILET

Emma emerges.

EMMA Forget it, Brian.

Brian emerges from the door.

BRIAN Hear me out.

EMMA Forget it.

BRIAN He can come on the show.

EMMA I told you forget it.

BRIAN Hey listen, you talk about ethics. You say we've got none. Well, all right, he can come on this show – our show – and say whatever he wants. There.

EMMA Whatever he wants.

BRIAN Whatever. The way he's been treated, what Marty did, whatever. He can go us on our own program.

Emma pauses.

EMMA Live?

BRIAN Live.

EMMA This isn't more gentle persuasion, is it?

BRIAN Jesus, Em, it ain't like I want this.

EMMA All right. I'll ring him.

SCENE 29

BRIAN'S OFFICE

Marty walks in.

MARTY I heard a rumour that John Ramar's going us on our own program.

BRIAN Tonight.

MARTY Brian!

BRIAN Wear it, Marty. It doesn't matter. Even if we lose we win. It doesn't matter what he says about us. People are going to watch it. He's responding – he's making the story last. Three nights now!

MARTY He's no idiot, Thommo.

BRIAN If he nails us we acknowledge it, say he's made a fair point, maybe we did overstep the mark, and we've recognised our mistakes. *(Marty smiles at this)* But we've still got the ratings.

Jan and Brooke appear at the door and Jan asks in actions, 'Got a minute?' Marty leaves and walks past Emma, who is a little smug now and just finishing her phone conversation with Ramar.

EMMA Mr Ramar is on the show tonight.

MARTY I know.

EMMA He'll have a few interesting things to say.

MARTY We'll wear it. As Brian says, the main thing is to get a third night out of the story.

Marty walks off leaving Emma with the realisation that Brian has 'done her' again. She looks down and with deep anger mouths the word 'bastard'.

Brooke, Jan and Brian are in Brian's office. Jan has a stack of fax papers in her hand.

JAN *(reading)* 'He's a bastard.' 'When did he go to Ethiopia?' 'I'm not buying that magazine again, but I'll keep watching Frontline.' We have been flooded with calls and faxes.

BRIAN Thank God we didn't respond.

JAN The journos are so sympathetic they all want to do a story on the return trip of the caring Brooke.

BROOKE But I'm not going.

JAN No, of course not. Now let's get this show on the road.

BRIAN Well done, Jan.

JAN It's all just gentle persuasion.

Brooke and Jan leave. The shot picks up Emma sitting at her desk putting the phone down. Looking worried, she then walks into Brian's office. Brian can see by the look on her face that something's not right.

BRIAN What?

EMMA Brian, 'Real Life' have offered John Ramar money.

BRIAN What?

Brian takes his glasses off and looks up at Emma. There are many conflicting emotions: a combination of victory over Emma's bleeding heart and defeat at the hands of Ramar. Brian possibly even yells.

BRIAN How much?

EMMA Fifteen grand.

BRIAN Now everyone wants him. The money-grabbing . . . So much for *(imitating Emma)* 'the poor man, the poor man'. He's not going to be poor.

EMMA All right, all right.

BRIAN We gotta have him . . . Offer him twenty-five. (I suppose this makes you happy?)

The question is unanswered.

SCENE 30

THE FRONTLINE STUDIO

On that night's show Ramar is being interviewed by Mike.

RAMAR It's an absolute obscenity.

MIKE With all due respect, you're a public figure.

RAMAR I'm not. The only public statements I made were in response to the vulture-like manner in which my family's tragedy was preyed upon. It was covered in the sort of lurid and unnecessary detail that you knew would hurt, and for you to ape sympathy is the height of hypocrisy.

MIKE Well, I'm afraid we're out of time. Again, Mr Ramar, our sympathy to you and your family. *(cut to single shot of Mike)* Coming up after the break on Frontline, we turn the tables on some dirty dancing.

We hear audio 'I'm Too Sexy'. Mr Ramar gets up and leaves without speaking to anyone. Brian comes over to Mike.

MIKE I don't know why I'm the recipient of all that. I've demonstrated my principles, I don't seek advantage, I stick to my guns.

We catch a glimpse of Katrina waving at Mike. She is excited to be in the studio.

SCENE 31

THE STUDIO CORRIDOR

Emma chases Mr Ramar as he leaves.

EMMA Mr Ramar, I'd like to wish you all the best.

Ramar is at first not sure how to take this. But then he assesses it as the first genuine emotion he's had from the media.

RAMAR Thank you.

EMMA And this is for you.

She hands over the cheque. He looks mystified, obviously knowing nothing about the money.

RAMAR What's this?

EMMA It's something for the kids.

RAMAR Twenty-five thousand! But how . . . ?

EMMA Let's just call it the 'art of gentle persuasion'.

Ramar makes eye contact with Emma. He gives the half-smile of one who isn't sure how it came about, but who knows that it came about through someone who was, in the end, genuine.

Episode 9
The Invisible Man

Day ❶

SCENE 1

A CLOTHES STORE CHANGE ROOM

We see a woman undressing as she tries on a blouse. She stuffs another blouse into her handbag, clearly stealing it. We tilt up to reveal a small hidden camera recording the event.

Day ❷

SCENE 2

THE PRODUCTION OFFICE

STU How much?

MARTY You wouldn't do it.

STU How much?

MARTY *(calculating)* You'd have to sneak into the foyer, at night, and unscrew it from the wall . . . Fifty bucks.

Stu and Jase produce a framed photo of Mike they had hidden behind the desk.

MARTY *(reaching for wallet)* You bastards. *(laughing)* He is gonna freak.

STU You reckon he'll notice?

MARTY Have you seen Mike walk into the building?

Marty demonstrates Mike's look.

STU Better hide it, Jase.

Mike arrives.

DOMENICA Hi, Mike!

MIKE Morning, Domenica. Stu, Marty.

STU AND MARTY Mike.

Mike walks into Brian's office.

STU Reckon he's noticed?

MARTY Watch the blinds.

The blinds on Brian's window are shut.

SCENE 3

BRIAN'S OFFICE

MIKE It is missing.

BRIAN Probably just been taken down for cleaning.

MIKE There's only one reason your photo gets taken down. *(he makes a throat-cutting gesture)*

BRIAN Mike, I'll find out about it.

MIKE It's not just the photo, Brian. Take a look at this.

Mike hands Brian a newspaper.

BRIAN Where?

MIKE *(pointing)* There!

BRIAN It's Brooke at some film premiere.

MIKE *City Slickers II*. Take a look at the shoulder next to her. Mine!

BRIAN So?

MIKE They cropped me out!

BRIAN So Brooke looks better in a dress.

MIKE Brian, my profile is not high enough. I'm either getting edged out, not invited, taken down – I may as well be invisible. I host a national current affairs show. When's the last time you saw a photo or an interview with me?

BRIAN Um . . . you did that *Who* magazine the other day.

MIKE It was five weeks ago! Where is it?

BRIAN All right. I'll speak to Jan.

Emma opens the door to let Brian know a production meeting is due to start.

EMMA Brian, are you right to . . . ?

She sees that Mike is in Brian's office.

BRIAN To what?

EMMA To . . .

KATE *(calls)* Production meeting!

EMMA To go to the production meeting.

MIKE Is there a meeting? Great.

Mike heads out. Emma looks apologetically at Brian.

SCENE 4

THE PRODUCTION OFFICE

Everyone is gathered for the meeting. Brian comes out of his office followed by Mike. Marty is opening his mail.

MARTY Woo-hoo! I may be a little busy this weekend. The Coca-Cola Celebrity Golf Pro-Am.

EMMA You must be the last person in this building to have got an invite.

MARTY Oh really? You got one, Em? No, of course – you're not a celebrity. Mind you, if you'd like to caddy . . .

Brian joins the group. Mike takes Marty's invite and has a look during the meeting.

BRIAN OK, let's get started. Jesus, what's with these rundowns?

EMMA AND KATE Photocopier's busted.

BRIAN What have we got for tonight?

EMMA *(checking list)* Good piece from London on Fergie and Prince Andrew. Rumours of a reconciliation.

MIKE I thought we were cutting down on royal stories.

BRIAN We'll tie this one to the republican debate. It won't look like a royal story. Brooke, how's the shoplifting piece going?

BROOKE Unbelievable. We've had the camera in place for two days and we've already caught on tape seventeen shoplifters.

EMMA Alleged shoplifters.

BROOKE There's nothing 'alleged' about these shy petals. We've caught them red-handed.

BRIAN That's our lead then for tomorrow night. Em, get a promo cut.

Brian gets up and heads back to his office. The meeting disperses. Mike follows Shelley over to her desk and speaks in slightly hushed tones.

MIKE Shelley, is my mail in?

SHELLEY It's in your pigeonhole, Mike.

MIKE I didn't receive anything about a celebrity golf tournament, did I?

SCENE 5

THE EDIT SUITE

Brooke, Stu, Jase and Hugh are viewing tapes from the clothes change room. A woman is trying on a top. Emma enters.

EMMA What's with the audience?

MARTY Just keen to help with the story.

STU Does she show her tits?

BROOKE Not this one. Spool forward, Hugh.

EMMA *(protesting)* She's almost nude.

BROOKE It's a changing room, Emma.

EMMA We can't show this.

BROOKE What's your problem? We got permission from the shop in writing.

EMMA And permission from the women? They would die if they knew they were about to be shown on national TV.

BROOKE Should have thought about that before they broke the law.

EMMA That's bullshit, Brooke.

STU AND BOYS Tits!

All the boys lean in to look at another woman remove her bra. Emma looks disgusted. Hugh has an asthma attack.

SCENE 6

GEOFF'S OFFICE

Geoff and Mike meet.

MIKE Brian's keen for me to do some more publicity. Lift the profile.

GEOFF Well, you are the front man. And for the front man your profile's very low.

MIKE Oh, I don't know. You know how many times I was recognised in the supermarket yesterday?

GEOFF Ten?

MIKE *(pause)* Twice. But it's a lot.

GEOFF It sure is a lot.

MIKE I mean it's a pain in the arse, but you gotta do it. Appearances, promos, interviews . . .

GEOFF Hey, when's the *Who* thing out?

MIKE Pretty soon.

GEOFF 'Cause I hate all that publicity stuff too. I said to the news director the day I started here: I'm a TV personality five nights a week, and I'm a private person the other two. That's why I said 'no' to this weekend.

MIKE What's this weekend?

GEOFF The celebrity golf day.

MIKE Oh yeah. I said 'no' too.

SCENE 7

BRIAN'S OFFICE

Marty, Emma, Brooke and Brian are watching more footage of a woman changing, accompanied by Brooke's voice-over.

BROOKE *(voice only)* . . . but the last laugh is on these light-fingered ladies, with in-store security now ensuring . . .

Brian hits the mute button. The story continues on screen.

BRIAN Sensational!

EMMA Brian! I thought public humiliation went out in the Middle Ages.

BRIAN They've broken the law, Emma.

EMMA Then report them to the police.

BRIAN Oh, that's brilliant.

MARTY We could put a wipe over their norks. Or what are those digital effect things . . . ?

EMMA *(protesting)* Marty, can you imagine how humiliating it would be for a woman to know her breasts had been seen by half the country?

MARTY Brooke, what's it like?

Brooke thumps Marty.

EMMA If you're not going to take this seriously . . .

BRIAN Emma, these women have broken the law, therefore they forfeit their rights.

EMMA That's not true. If someone breaks into your house, you don't have the right to shoot them. The penalty for shoplifting, if proved, is about 100 bucks. Not complete humiliation.

BROOKE Were you in the debating team?

Emma ignores this comment.

EMMA And even if we do show only the girls who were shoplifting – allegedly – what about all those girls who just got changed without stealing a thing? What happens to the footage of them?

BRIAN I can guarantee that it will not go to air.

Emma leaves Brian's office.

MARTY But we can still keep it for the Christmas tape?

BRIAN Oh yeah.

SCENE 8

THE PRODUCTION MEETING ROOM

Jan, Mike, Brooke and Marty meet.

JAN So that's the *Australian Women's Weekly*. It will be a double-page spread. You'll probably need three outfits.

MARTY Rules me out.

JAN *(ignoring him)* That's Brooke. Three-thirty Tuesday. Now, Qantas want to do an interview for their in-flight magazine.

Mike acts as if he's about to agree to the interview.

JAN *(oblivious of him)* And Brooke, that's on the phone. The 'Talk Show' on SBS are keen for . . .

MIKE I'm happy to do that.

JAN They did ask for . . . I'll put it to them. *(she starts to pack up)* So Martin, don't forget they'll be phoning this afternoon.

MIKE Anything else for me?

JAN Oh, Mike, you're far too busy.

MIKE No, no. Anything else. Just to take the load off.

JAN *(flicking through her file)* Well of course there are all those silly requests: Celebrity Stars in the Bath, Why I Wear What I Wear . . . You wouldn't want to do one of those.

MIKE No. Well, maybe one.

JAN Well, what about this? *Herald-Sun* Celebrity Chefs. Just a photo in the kitchen. They'll credit the show. It has to be this afternoon.

MIKE Great.

JAN I should just clear it with Brian.

MARTY *(slyly)* He's in a network meeting.

MIKE I spoke to Brian earlier. He's very keen on me lifting the old profile. Come on, Jan, it's just a photo . . .

Day

SCENE 9

BRIAN'S OFFICE

Brian is bawling Mike out. Jan is also present.

BRIAN What the hell were you thinking?

MIKE They said they wouldn't use it!

BRIAN Right.

Brian holds up a copy of the Herald-Sun. *It is open on a photo of Mike wearing a chef's hat, lying across his kitchen bench. The caption reads 'What's Cookin', Mike?'*

BRIAN 'Just one more shot to finish the film. We won't use it; we'll send it to you for a laugh.'

MIKE That's what they said!

BRIAN Come on, Mike. You've been around too long to fall for that sort of crap.

MIKE It's publicity.

BRIAN So is getting arrested.

JAN I blame myself, Brian. I should have been there.

BRIAN Mike, there are people out there, like game-show hosts, who will do anything to get in the paper. They're professional self-publicists. But you're a current affairs host. You've got an image to protect.

MIKE I've gotta have some sort of profile. I mean you let it all drop and next thing you know you're not invited to a celebrity golf day.

BRIAN You've got a profile! Everyone knows Mike Moore. You've just done an article in *Who* . . .

MIKE It's still not out.

JAN They promised me this week, Mike.

MIKE *(depressed)* Oh well, at least I've got that to look forward to.

BRIAN *(softening)* Come on, tiger. Better get ready for that promo.

MIKE Sure.

Mike turns to leave. He stops and reaches for the newspaper.

MIKE Can I take . . . ?

BRIAN No!

Mike leaves, shutting the door behind him. He goes out into the production office, where nearly everyone is wearing a chef's hat.

DOMENICA I'm not wearing one, Mike.

SCENE 10

BRIAN'S OFFICE

Back in Brian's office, Jan and Brian continue to discuss Mike.

BRIAN What am I going to do with him?

JAN He wants more profile.

BRIAN Can't we get him an interview?

JAN We push. But they're just not interested. Mike's sort of . . .

BRIAN I know.

JAN Even *Who* was on condition they also spoke to Brooke.

BRIAN Can you find him something quickly?

Jan goes to leave.

BRIAN Oh, and Jan . . . no photos.

SCENE 11

THE FRONTLINE STUDIO

Mike is at the studio desk, recording a promo.

MIKE Tonight on Frontline, we lift the lid on some light-fingered ladies who make shopping a steal.

We roll a five-second grab of a woman undressing. Cut back to Mike.

MIKE That's an exclusive, tonight on Frontline.

SCENE 12

MIKE'S OFFICE

Mike is pasting the photo of himself in the chef's hat into a well-used scrapbook. Domenica pokes her head in the door.

DOMENICA Jan on line one, Mike.

MIKE Thanks, Dom. Oh, any word on . . . ?

DOMENICA The celebrity golf day? They still haven't rung back. And I spoke to someone from *Who* – the article should be out today.

MIKE Thanks.

Mike hits the speaker-phone.

MIKE Jan?

JAN *(voice only)* Mike darling, I'm in a terrible spot. The *Age* have been at me for ages to interview you, and I've been fending them off.

MIKE Don't fend.

JAN Any chance of this afternoon?

MIKE I'll check.

Mike calls Domenica.

MIKE Dom, am I clear this afternoon?

DOMENICA Yeah.

MIKE Good.

DOMENICA You're clear every . . .

MIKE *(cuts off Domenica)* Thanks. *(into phone)* OK, Jan, no probs.

SCENE 13

BRIAN'S OFFICE

Emma and Brian meet.

BRIAN You honestly want me to drop the best story we've had since Elle Macpherson went starkers in *Playboy*?

EMMA Yes.

BRIAN What's wrong with it?

EMMA When you go into a changing room or a toilet or a doctor's surgery there is an assumption of privacy – whether you're doing something illegal or not. I thought we'd grown out of this hidden camera obsession.

BRIAN This is different.

EMMA How?

BRIAN Do you know how much shoplifting costs this country?

EMMA No.

BRIAN Well find out – we'll use it in the intro. Look Em, how is this different from a police speed camera?

EMMA One – the average driver is not naked. Two – speed camera photos are not broadcast on national television. Three – police are ultimately responsible to an elected government; we are responsible to no-one. Four – their existence is publicised by road signs. Five – you want me to go on?

BRIAN Is five the last?

EMMA No.

BRIAN Can I get a coffee?

SCENE 14

MIKE'S OFFICE

Mike is being interviewed by a journo.

JOURNO Right, so that was when you were in Perth doing the '7.30 Report', and then you went to Kalgoorlie.

MIKE That's right.

JOURNO So . . . hang on, what else did Jan say? Oh, apparently you fly aeroplanes.

MIKE No, but I'm thinking of learning.

JOURNO So you spent quite some time in Asia?

MIKE Yeah, a holiday. Three weeks.

JOURNO Um . . . I'm trying to think of an angle for this story.

MIKE What about me – the host of Frontline?

JOURNO What's this scuba-diving thing?

MIKE Oh, that's . . .

JOURNO *(spots Brooke outside in the production office)* Ah, Brooke's here! I thought Jan said . . . Could I just meet Brooke?

MIKE Sure.

Mike gets up. The journo grabs a tape recorder and hides it in his pocket. Mike introduces him to Brooke.

JOURNO I'm just interviewing Mike.

BROOKE Great.

JOURNO Your celeb profiles are going well.

MIKE They're all right, aren't they . . .

JOURNO Mike, do you mind if we just take a breather at this moment?

MIKE *(pause)* Good idea. Ten minutes. *(he walks away towards Brian's office)*

JOURNO *(to Brooke)* What are they like to interview? Are they all pleasant people?

BROOKE Well, just between you and me . . .

SCENE 15

BRIAN'S OFFICE

Mike enters.

MIKE Got a minute, Brian?

BRIAN Sure. Aren't you doing an interview?

MIKE Just taking a break. Brian, I've been thinking about this shoplifting story. Did we sort out the whole deal on the hidden camera?

BRIAN All fine.

MIKE Because Emma was saying to the girls earlier . . . I mean, I don't think she fully understands the whole issue.

BRIAN All right, Mike. A hidden camera in a changing room, a police hidden speed camera – can you tell me one difference between the two?

MIKE *(thinks)* Can't think of one.

BRIAN Well, there's your answer.

MIKE Oh yeah! One's outdoors, one's in.

BRIAN *(pause)* That's one more than Emma could think of.

MIKE Well, she's green.

We follow Mike out into the production office. Brooke and the journo have disappeared.

MIKE Hey Dom, where did they go?

DOMENICA They just went out for a coffee.

Domenica is going through the mail. She pulls out a Who magazine.

DOMENICA Mike! Look what's arrived – 'Fronting Frontline'.

Mike tries to act uninterested. He goes into his office. Domenica follows.

DOMENICA Aren't you going to read it? *(she is reading the article)*

MIKE I don't read articles about me as a rule. Not interested. What's it like, Dom? Just a general gist . . . Dom?

DOMENICA Why's there a photo of Brooke?

MIKE *(looking over her shoulder)* Oh, and her fucking dog!

Mike storms out.

DOMENICA *(calls)* Shall I tell your weatherman friend you're coming?

MIKE *(shouts)* Geoff! His name's Geoff!

SCENE 16

GEOFF'S OFFICE

Mike is reading from the article.

MIKE 'The key to Frontline's success is that Mike Moore is less of a star than the show he fronts. Unlike other current affairs programs where the host rules supreme, Mike Moore plays the role of invisible man.'

GEOFF That's very complimentary.

MIKE But 'invisible man' is a bit much. I'm one of the biggest celebrities in this country. I mean, I don't want to be.

GEOFF You know what this is?

MIKE The Tall Poppy Syndrome.

GEOFF *(pause)* Yeah, sort of.

MIKE What do I do?

GEOFF Well, if you're really upset . . . blanket ban on publicity. Tell 'em you're not doing any more interviews, appearances, promos – that's it for Mike Moore.

MIKE Wouldn't I love to do that. Can't. Sake of the show. I've got to have a profile.

GEOFF I reckon you can.

MIKE No, I can't. Not an option.

SCENE 17
BRIAN'S OFFICE

Jan and Brian meet. Brian is reading the Who *article.*

BRIAN Good article.

JAN Lovely.

BRIAN Only one problem. 'Moore plays the role of invisible man'.

JAN I know. I'm on the case.

Jan removes artwork for billboards from her folder.

JAN I think this might just help. We're putting these billboards up all over town.

BRIAN Great. *(reads)* 'Who gives you Moore current affairs?' *(he looks concerned)*

JAN What's wrong?

BRIAN Dangerous asking a question on a billboard.

JAN They'll be up high. I've also organised some more interviews . . .

BRIAN I think he's a little 'interview-shy' at the moment.

JAN All right, what about a charity angle?

BRIAN *(interested)* Yeah . . .

JAN Of course, he already sponsors a child.

BRIAN He never told me that.

JAN He doesn't know. We do it automatically at this network.

BRIAN This Africa stuff – it's a bit . . .

JAN Yes, I know. There is a telethon on this weekend in Perth, for, um . . . what's the one when you shake?

BRIAN Whatever. Mike could go to that. It's in Perth. No-one's gonna see it.

JAN They did actually ask for Brooke.

BRIAN You could swing them around.

SCENE 18
THE KITCHEN

Stu is sticking up a video freeze-frame image of one of the girls changing. Marty is looking in the fridge as Emma enters.

MARTY Is there any milk?

Emma pulls out a carton of Rev.

EMMA What's this?

MARTY Girls' milk. I want real stuff.

Marty sees the Who *picture of Brooke and her dog on the fridge.*

MARTY I can take one bitch, but two?

Marty exits with his coffee. He sees Stu putting up the poster.

MARTY Very nice.

Emma notices the poster.

EMMA What is that?

STU Hugh gave it to us. It's from Brooke's story.

EMMA I know where it's from. Take it down, Stu.

STU Oh come on, Em . . .

EMMA Stu!

Stu takes it down. Brooke enters to get a coffee.

STU Great tits. You really offended?

EMMA Yes.

BROOKE *(under her breath)* 'Jealous' might be more the word.

Brooke walks off. Emma restrains herself from stabbing her with a butter knife.

STU Any objections if I put it in the blokes' dunny?

EMMA *(walking away)* You can flush it down the dunny for all I care.

We follow Emma back out into the production office. Mike is seated, being given a neck massage by Shelley and Domenica.

SHELLEY How's that?

MIKE Fantastic.

Marty walks across and pretends to sit on Mike.

MARTY Sorry, mate, didn't see you there. It's like you're invisible . . .

DOMENICA Marty! He's all tensed up again.

Brian emerges from his office holding a fax.

BRIAN Mike, you got a moment?

Mike gets up and follows Brian into his office.

SCENE 19

BRIAN'S OFFICE

BRIAN You're probably not interested, but they'd freak if they could get you.

MIKE What?

BRIAN Oh, telethon this weekend in Perth. I'll tell 'em you're busy.

MIKE *(eagerly)* Brian, I'm happy to help out. I mean, if it's a good cause.

BRIAN Oh yeah.

MIKE What's it for?

BRIAN *(shakes)* Oh, what am I thinking? You've got a celebrity golf day.

MIKE I reckon I can get out of that.

SCENE 20

THE FRONTLINE STUDIO

MIKE Hi, welcome to Frontline. I'm Mike Moore.

The opening titles run.

MIKE It's a sorry statistic, but each year Australian shops are watching just under 300 million dollars' worth of merchandise literally walking out the door.

We see footage of shoplifters being led into court and general shop footage.

BROOKE *(voice only)* Although the culprits call themselves 'petty thieves', shoplifting is costing Australian business big bikkies. But as we found out, one shop is about to hit back . . .

We see vision of a woman changing in a cubicle.

Day

SCENE 21

THE PRODUCTION OFFICE

Domenica is answering the phone.

DOMENICA Good morning, Frontline. Thank you, I'll pass those comments on. Good morning, Frontline. Right, I'll pass those comments on.

Brian arrives. Between calls Domenica passes a clipboard to him.

DOMENICA Good morning, Frontline. No, we don't screen 'The House of Elliot'. Good morning, Frontline . . .

Mike is standing beside Domenica and intercepts Brian. They walk and talk en route through the office to the kitchen.

MIKE Brian, they've been phoning all morning. Brooke has really got us into hot water.

BRIAN *(reading clipboard)* Yep.

MIKE With complaints.

BRIAN Yep.

MIKE Aren't you worried?

BRIAN Mike, they're watching.

MIKE *(reads)* 'I'll never watch Frontline again.'

BRIAN They're the ones who always tune in, hoping to be outraged. *(to Brooke, who is at her desk)* Ratings?

BROOKE *(reads from a fax)* Twenty-eight, twenty-seven . . .

BRIAN You've done it again, babe.

MIKE Brian! If that's how you get ratings . . .

BROOKE Any time you have difficulties with a story, Mike, just hand it to me.

MIKE What if they dob us into the Australian Broadcasting Authority?

BRIAN *(making himself a coffee)* Won't happen.

MIKE But . . .

BRIAN The Broadcasting Authority is a myth. To get a complaint heard you've gotta write to us – not phone, write. Rules out 70 per cent of the population. We've got sixty days to respond, which we'll definitely let go by. By that time these galahs won't even remember what they were originally complaining about and the ABA can't do a thing. Self-regulation is a joy, Michael.

Brian sees the photo of Brooke on the fridge.

BRIAN Wait till Marty sees this. Has he done the bitch joke?

STU *(entering kitchen)* Yes.

Mike and Brian walk back through the office.

MIKE It's good to see that everyone can have a laugh. But I've got to go on the radio in less than an hour and defend this story. I'd like to see Brooke handle that assignment.

BRIAN So would I.

MARTY So would I.

BRIAN Brooke, you happy to do the radio spot?

BROOKE Love to.

MIKE I didn't mean literally, Brian . . .

SCENE 22

BROOKE IS ON THE RADIO AT 3AW WITH NEIL MITCHELL.

NEIL *(reasonably worked up)* How could you possibly justify it?

BROOKE The fact is, Neil, those women were breaking the law. And when you break the law you forfeit certain rights. Like the right to privacy.

NEIL I see. And the right to a fair trial? And the right to dignity? And the right to life?

BROOKE Wait a minute, Neil. If you're not doing anything wrong you have nothing to fear. I don't see what the problem is. And I'd do a story like this again without hesitation.

SCENE 23

A CITY HIGHWAY

Mike drives by a Frontline billboard to see that it's been vandalised.

SCENE 24

THE PRODUCTION OFFICE

Marty is practising his golf putting. He putts a ball onto a scale version of a billboard with Mike's head cut out lying on the floor.

MARTY So, Brooke, you want to team up with me this Saturday?

BROOKE I'm busy.

MARTY What are you up to?

BROOKE If you must know, I'm doing a charity function.

MARTY Wow.

BROOKE I happen to have received an invitation from *(reading)* 'the Australian Fashion Industry to take part in a celebrity fashion parade to raise money for osteoporosis'.

MARTY And you're giving up a weekend to do this, for free?

BROOKE I'm a humanitarian, Marty.

EMMA And she gets to keep the outfit.

BROOKE Oh really? I didn't know that.

Mike arrives.

DOMENICA Hi, Mike. How was gym?

MIKE *(whispers)* Phone Jan. Another one of my billboards has been . . .

DOMENICA What does it say this time?

MARTY Hey, Mike. You wanna caddy for me tomorrow?

MIKE I'm off to Perth. Got a telethon.

MARTY What's it for?

MIKE Um . . . kids.

MARTY With what?

MIKE Is Brian in? *(he heads towards Brian's office)*

MARTY *(quietly, to Stu)* Where was it you hid Mike's photo?

STU Same place I hid his invitation to the Golf Pro-Am.

SCENE 25

THE FRONTLINE STUDIO

Mike is at his desk. Elliot Rhodes is winding up another zinger.

ELLIOT Don't get in a tizzie
Just leave it to Lizzie
Doing the Buckingham blues.
Oh yeah!

MIKE Ha ha. Elliot Rhodes with perhaps our new republican national anthem – 'The Buckingham Blues'. Well, that's about it for tonight. Join us next week on Frontline when we meet the accountant dubbed 'Mr Dodgy'.

We hear some audio about 'Mr Dodgy'.

MIKE That's Monday. Until then, have a great weekend.

Mike leans back and loosens his tie as Emma comes over. Brian also comes over.

BRIAN Good show, tiger. All set for the telethon?

EMMA Here's your ticket, Mike.

MIKE Yep.

BRIAN Have fun. And don't let 'em make you do anything you're not comfortable with.

MIKE Brian . . . (don't treat me like a kid).

Mike starts walking off.

EMMA See you Monday.

BRIAN And don't sit next to Agro.

SCENE 26

OUTSIDE THE STUDIO

Mike gets into a taxi.

DRIVER So you work for TV?

MIKE Yeah.

DRIVER What do you do?

MIKE It's a show called Frontline.

DRIVER Oh yeah. And what do you do on it?

MIKE *(pause)* I'm the host. How long have you been in the country for?

DRIVER Eighteen years.

Mike slumps back in his seat.

Day

SCENE 27

THE FRONTLINE OFFICE

Marty, Emma and the office staff are working. Stu enters with a tape.

STU Gold! I've got gold!

EMMA Not more of those women . . .

STU *(putting the tape in)* Anyone know what Mike got up to on the weekend?

KATE He went to Perth for a telethon.

Stu smiles knowingly as the tape starts. We see a typical telethon panel (the cause is nerve deafness). It starts on a single shot of Pete Smith.

PETE *(on screen)* Welcome back. And time to welcome some new faces to the panel. From 'A Country Practice', Jane Hall. *(pissy applause)* From the Triple M network, Ed Phillips. Good to have you along.

ED Great to be here.

PETE Also football legend Tim Watson, and from the Logie Hall of Fame, Mr Bud Tingwell.

We cut back to the office staff watching this scene.

EMMA Where's Mike?

STU Wait for it.

We cut back to the telethon on screen.

PETE But before we get stuck into a few more donations, it's time for some music. In a light we haven't quite seen before, Frontline host Mike Moore and 'Tears in Heaven'.

The last few words of this introduction are drowned out by disbelieving gasps from the Frontline office staff. On screen we cut to Mike performing 'Tears in Heaven'.

SCENE 28

THE PRODUCTION OFFICE

It is later. Emma, Marty and the general office staff are working. Mike enters without looking up. They all start humming 'Tears in Heaven'. Brian's voice is heard from within his office.

BRIAN Mike!

SCENE 29

THE PRODUCTION OFFICE

Some time later, Emma goes through the rundown with Mike.

EMMA We throw straight to the shonky accountant, no changes . . .

MIKE Brian still pissed off at me?

EMMA It's not just you, Mike. It's this whole billboard thing.

MIKE How many have been vandalised now?

EMMA Seventeen confirmed.

MIKE There's only nineteen. Didn't we have security?

MARTY They're our prime suspects.

Brooke enters in her new outfit. General whistles.

BROOKE It's not a bad look. You should have seen me up on the catwalk.

KATE And they gave you that to keep?

BROOKE In return for giving myself, Kate. It was a charity event.

MIKE All I got was yelled at by Brian.

BROOKE I didn't make a fool of myself, Mike.

Domenica comes over with a newspaper.

DOMENICA Hey, the *Age* is here.

MIKE Oh, my interview. What's it like, Dom?

DOMENICA Oh . . . different.

MIKE In what way?

DOMENICA It's about Brooke.

MIKE What? I gave up my time for this guy.

BROOKE What? I never gave an interview. *(looks)* That sneaky bastard recorded me. Oh my God, look what I said!

MIKE Thank God I haven't been quoted out of context.

MARTY Haven't been quoted at all.

BROOKE That is so unprofessional – taping someone without their knowledge.

EMMA Thank God we're above that, Brooke.

BROOKE Don't start, Emma.

KATE 'A Current Affair' promo!

Those in the office gather around the monitor. Brian emerges from the kitchen area. The audio is turned up.

We see on the monitor shots of a woman getting undressed in a changing room, shot on hidden camera.

VOICE-OVER She's the peeping Tom reporter who's about to get a taste of her own medicine. That's tonight on 'A Current Affair'.

The woman is revealed to be Brooke. She is trying on her new outfit. Cut back to the staff watching enthralled.

BROOKE Oh Jesus.

EMMA Relax. You weren't doing anything illegal. You've got nothing to worry about.

On the screen, Brooke continues to undress . . .

EVERYONE Tits!

Smaller Fish to Fry

Day ❶

SCENE 1

BRIAN'S OFFICE

Open on a scene from a Frontline story. We see a fridge repairman shot on hidden camera. He is reaching into a fridge.

MARTY *(voice only)* . . . he reaches in and replaces one light bulb.

Cut to a close-up of a bill.

MARTY *(voice only)* And the bill for this thirty-second task? Eighty-seven dollars plus parts.

Cut to Stuart Littlemore.

STUART Yet another easy target for Mike Moore and the team at Frontline: the refrigerator repairman – public enemy number one. Oh, how very brave of you. Ever wonder why current affairs programs never go after the big fish? I do. Goodnight.

Brian, Marty and Mike are watching this on television.

MIKE Well?

BRIAN Well what?

MIKE He makes an interesting point.

BRIAN You made us sit through that just to . . . ? What does that wanker know about current affairs?

MARTY Too much for my liking.

BRIAN Oh, don't you start.

MIKE He's got a point. We hammer these guys – trick the little saps and ruin them – but we're not bagging the big fish.

BRIAN (Hey), do you know how much that fridge bloke ripped them off?

MIKE Eighty-seven dollars!

BRIAN Yeah, but you multiply that by 100.

MARTY (It's only) eighty-seven hundred.

BRIAN By a thousand.

MARTY Eighty-seven thousand.

BRIAN Whose side are you on? OK, we'll let those rip-off merchants get away with it.

MIKE No, but . . .

BRIAN But what?

DOMENICA *(appears at the door)* Mike, phone call.

MIKE Who is it?

DOMENICA (A) Bob Foster.

BRIAN What's that hack want?

MIKE *(to Domenica)* I'll call him back. *(to Brian)* He's not a hack.

MARTY Second-rate investigative journalist who screwed up and can't get a gig.

MIKE But he used to write great articles.

BRIAN Why won't anyone hire him?

Mike moves to the window so that he has his back to camera.

MIKE Maybe they're scared. I mean, you only get hired these days if you're a spineless lapdog.

Marty goes to speak and Brian gestures that he'll kill him if he opens his mouth.

SCENE 2

THE KITCHEN

Emma walks into the kitchen where Brooke is making coffee. She is studying a milk carton with extraordinary care.

EMMA You right?

BROOKE What's 157 divided by seven?

EMMA Counting calories?

BROOKE Renegotiation time. Gotta look the best. How do I look?

EMMA Increasingly like the child I sponsor.

BROOKE *(slightly taken aback by her wit)* How'd you go with Michael Hutchence?

EMMA Nuh. Initial interest and then things went downhill.

BROOKE Did you tell them it was me?

EMMA Yeah, just before things went downhill.

BROOKE *(looks her up and down)* And to what do we owe this new-found cockiness?

EMMA Think I may have a better interview. The Prime Minister's department rang back. He's a possibility.

BROOKE (*stunned*) Yi-yi-yi.

Emma and Brooke walk out of the kitchen and into the main office as a production meeting gets under way.

BRIAN OK, what have we got for this week?

MARTY Running out of people to nail. Dom had an idea for drycleaners.

BRIAN What are they doing wrong?

DOMENICA Well, it didn't happen to me, but Morena – who's Assunta's second cousin because their fathers are . . .

MARTY Dom . . . (get to the point).

DOMENICA Well she took a jacket along and accidentally left fifty dollars in the pocket and when she went to pick it up it was gone. The money, not the jacket.

MARTY I thought we could try a little test. Leave some money and if it goes missing walk in with a camera.

BRIAN Get onto it.

BROOKE Under-age smoking (is another good area). You know, people selling cigarettes to kids.

BRIAN (*excited*) We get some thirteen-year-olds, wire 'em up with a hidden camera and see if we can't get someone to sell 'em smokes.

EMMA (Brian), that's entrapment.

BRIAN No, it's called current affairs. Get a thirteen-year-old. Actually, I've got one – Damien.

KATE Your son's fifteen.

BRIAN Is he? Oh well, hire someone. Brooke – any word on that Michael rock star bloke?

BROOKE Might have someone a little bigger. Em?

EMMA Prime Minister's department have said he's a possibility.

General excitement.

MIKE (*to Brooke*) You'll be able to ask him about all that stuff Hawke said.

BROOKE (*not that interested*) Oh, yeah.

EMMA We have to work the questions out, Mike.

MIKE I'd be happy to help.

BRIAN (*standing*) I think we're done.

The meeting winds up.

SCENE 3

MIKE'S OFFICE

Mike is in his office calling Bob.

MIKE It's Mike Moore. Is Bob Foster there?

BOB (*voice only*) Speaking . . . Thanks for ringing back. Did you see 'Media Watch' last night?

MIKE Ah . . . I caught a little of it.

BOB How'd you like to go after a big fish?

MIKE What have you got?

BOB Can you be in the Hyatt lobby by twelve?

MIKE Sure. What name are you travelling under?

BOB (*pause*) Bob Foster.

SCENE 4

THE PRODUCTION OFFICE

Emma and Brooke are at Brooke's workstation. Brooke is eating a carrot.

BROOKE I still don't get it. When will they say yes?

EMMA Not for a few days. They just wanna make sure we'll ask the Prime Minister the sort of questions he's comfortable with, that you won't raise any inappropriate issues.

BROOKE I hate politics. Don't know anything about it.

EMMA Which, believe it or not, is your competitive advantage.

BROOKE So when will they say yes?

EMMA When they're absolutely sure the interview's going to be a puff piece.

SCENE 5

A CITY STREET

Mike and Bob are walking.

MIKE So you no longer write for any paper?

BOB I write for them; they just don't publish it. Comes from treading on too many toes.

MIKE Yeah, I know the feeling.

BOB I doubt it.

MIKE Bob, we do big stories on Frontline.

BOB Shonky fridge repairmen.

MIKE You're saying he's not guilty?

BOB Oh, he's guilty, but he's a distraction.

MIKE Hang on. Do you know how much that guy ripped people off?

BOB Probably about eighty bucks.

MIKE Yeah, but you multiply that . . . *(pauses to think)* by a million.

BOB Why?

MIKE *(confidently)* Forget it.

BOB He's an easy target. Typical. You don't go after the big fish.

MIKE That's not quite true.

BOB Name one.

MIKE Alan Bond.

Bob laughs.

BOB Yeah, when he was outta money, outta friends and in jail. Easy target.

MIKE Skase.

BOB Outta friends and outta the country.

MIKE Bjelke-Petersen.

BOB Outta his mind. All easy targets when they're down and out. When are you gonna go after people while they're actually doing the damage, when it matters?

MIKE Why don't you?

BOB Can't get a gig. You see, I . . .

MIKE Screwed up?

BOB Yeah . . . or was set up. I've never been quite sure. You want a real story?

MIKE Yes!

BOB (All right), follow me . . .

They have arrived at Bob's car, a beaten-up Mazda. Bob notices Mike staring at it.

BOB Crusading doesn't pay.

MIKE I thought that was crime.

BOB Oh, no. Crime pays beautifully.

Bob gets into his car. Mike activates the security alarm on his Subaru parked opposite.

SCENE 6

BRIAN'S OFFICE

Jan walks into Brian's office.

JAN Hello, Brian. Is Michael about?

BRIAN Gone to lunch. *(indicates desk)* That's why I'm getting some work done.

JAN Could you tell him we're shooting the Christmas messages the day after tomorrow?

BRIAN Jesus. *(looks at his watch)* It's October.

JAN I know. We're running late.

BRIAN The dreaded season of renegotiation begins.

JAN You'll be signed up!

BRIAN Yeah *(points out to the office)*, but I've gotta put up with all the antics.

JAN Try being in my shoes. Everyone wants more profile so they can up the ante. They drive me mad.

BRIAN Geez, you could have some fun if you wanted to.

JAN I'm sorry?

BRIAN *(aping Jan)* More profile? I don't think there's much point, poppet.

JAN *(laughing but aghast)* Brian!

BRIAN *(still aping her)* An article about you, now. Seems rather a waste really.

JAN Don't tempt me, Brian. *(still laughing, she turns to leave)* Oh, that (impersonation) is very good. Who *is* that?

SCENE 7

BOB'S HOUSE

Mike and Bob are sitting around the dinner table of Bob's house. Mike studies a manila folder full of documents.

MIKE I thought all this dodgy bank stuff was over.

BOB Nuh, there are still dud loans everywhere, technically referred to as 'non-performing'.

MIKE That's not a crime.

BOB No, but the way they were approved was.

MIKE So why is the bank still operating?

BOB Certain things have been covered up.

MIKE Why?

BOB Half the networks are on borrowed money from them. Major players involved, government connections – you can join the dots.

MIKE *(nods, and then)* Can you join them for me?

BOB You won't get very far with this.

MIKE Look, I may be at a commercial network but no-one's ever told me to pull a story.

BOB And they never will. No-one ever gets told directly they can't do a story. But as if your network owner's likes and dislikes are not known to the people working for him . . .

MIKE Yeah, but there's . . .

BOB And it's not just your boss. How many stories have you done on Packer?

MIKE Not many.

BOB How many?

MIKE None.

BOB That's not many. Conrad Black?

MIKE Nuh.

BOB Thank God for 'Four Corners'.

Day 2

SCENE 8

A SHOPPING STREET

Marty, Stu and Jase are in a parked car opposite a drycleaner's. Stu is preparing his camera, loading tape.

STU When did they say your jacket would be ready?

MARTY *(checking watch)* About ten minutes from now.

STU And if the money is missing?

MARTY We walk in with the camera and have a little 'chat'.

STU Jesus, will Hugh bloody well . . . ? *(showing tape)* Look at that.

MARTY What?

STU He's recycling old tape stock but he doesn't label 'em. Can't tell the difference between the used and the blanks.

MARTY How I love techo talk.

STU You gotta label tapes, mate, or things go missing.

MARTY Guess that's why I keep losing my home videos.

STU Label 'em. 'Porn' isn't that hard to spell. P.O.R.N.

SCENE 9

BRIAN'S OFFICE

Brian is looking at the manila folder with Mike.

BRIAN It's pretty amazing stuff.

MIKE *(excitedly)* Massive cover-up. Just about the biggest merchant bank in this country.

BRIAN Where'd you get this stuff?

MIKE I'm afraid I can't reveal my sources.

BRIAN Bob Foster?

Mike gives him a 'How did you know?' look.

BRIAN *(pointing to folder)* (His) name's on the folder.

MIKE There's been a cover-up, Brian. And half the media in this country are involved.

BRIAN A lot of facts and figures . . .

MIKE (It's) the sort of story we should be doing.

BRIAN Absolutely.

MIKE I'll get straight onto it.

BRIAN Just hold on a second, tiger. Let's not go in half-cocked. Let me check around first. We don't want to blow it.

MIKE I guess.

BRIAN Let's just keep it on the backburner for a day or two.

MIKE OK.

SCENE 10

A SHOPPING STREET

Stu and Jase wait in the car. Marty approaches with his jacket in a plastic drycleaner's wrapper. Stu winds down the window.

STU Is the money gone?

MARTY Yep. And so is our drycleaner.

STU Let's nail him.

Stu and Jase get out of the car. Marty straightens his tie for an on-camera confrontation.

SCENE 11

NEAR THE OFFICE TOILETS

Emma runs into Brooke as she's entering the toilets.

BROOKE Any word from the Lodge?

EMMA They'll tell us in a day or two.

BROOKE What's the vibe?

EMMA Good. They're pretty happy you're taking a soft line. Um . . . Michael Hutchence's people called back. They're happy to do it now.

BROOKE See if they'll do it first thing in the New Year.

EMMA You could still fit it in this year.

BROOKE Nuh. I want to finish with the Prime Minister and start again with a bang.

EMMA Aren't you even slightly tempted to make it a hard-hitting interview?

BROOKE No, I just want the interview. You get the big interviews – you get ahead. You don't get ahead by pissing people off. So what if this is all about popularity and appearances?

EMMA For who?

BROOKE For both of us. You can't burn the big ones; it gets around. And anyway I'm not an experienced political journalist. If I go in half-cocked, I'm doing everyone a disservice. I've got a better chance of revealing things by concentrating on the personal side.

EMMA That sounds like a reasonable explanation.

BROOKE That's why I use it all the time.

SCENE 12

MIKE'S OFFICE

MIKE *(into the speaker-phone)* Is that Traveller?

BOB *(voice only)* Mike, there's no need for code names.

MIKE Oh, that's a pity. Anyway, the story's a goer.

BOB Have you spoken to anyone on the list?

MIKE Not yet. Brian's holding off for . . .

BOB Mike, did he say to put it on the backburner?

MIKE Yeah, but he's running it past a few people.

BOB No, he's not.

MIKE Traveller, he said . . .

BOB I'll bet you it's buried in his desk. And mate – this is just the start.

Mike is a little perplexed.

SCENE 13

BRIAN'S OFFICE

Mike runs around to Brian's office and pulls open the bottom drawer of his desk. He finds the file is just where he was told it would be. Emma walks in.

EMMA Brian . . . Oh.

MIKE Em. Um . . . do you know where the um . . . ? I was looking for the . .

He makes some indeterminate movements with his hands.

EMMA The paper clips?

MIKE No, the um . . . You know . . . *(more movements)*

EMMA Staples.

MIKE No. Oh, you know, the um . . . *(pretending to remember suddenly)* Oh, I know where they are.

He walks out the door with the folder in his hand.

SCENE 14

THE EDIT SUITE

Marty, Stu and Hugh are editing a story.

MARTY OK, I've got the voice-over on one. Where's the vision?

HUGH *(searching)* It's around here somewhere . . .

STU *(exasperated)* Would you label these tapes?

HUGH *(finding tape)* Here it is.

STU That was in the 'recycle' box!

Hugh inserts the tape and hits play. We see a hand-held shot of Marty walking into a drycleaner's with his jacket.

MARTY Excuse me. Martin di Stasio – Frontline. When I left this jacket here two hours ago it had fifty dollars in the pocket. Can you tell me where the money's gone?

The drycleaner looks confused. Marty stops the tape.

MARTY I think there's something there. *(to Hugh)* You right to cut a promo?

Hugh nods. Marty and Stu get up to leave.

STU And label the tape!

SCENE 15

NEAR THE KITCHEN

Mike is walking down the corridor to the kitchen.

MIKE Brian! Brian?

Brian comes out of the toilet.

MIKE Brian, how's it coming along?

BRIAN What?

MIKE The bank story.

BRIAN Great. There's a lot of stuff in there.

MIKE What are you doing?

BRIAN Oh, I've given it to a few contacts to see if they can't flesh out a few things.

MIKE You've given it to a few contacts.

BRIAN Yeah.

MIKE Then how come it was still in your desk?

He shows the folder from behind his back.

BRIAN Come into the office, Mike.

SCENE 16

BRIAN'S OFFICE

BRIAN Mate, I want to nail the big stories as much as you, but fraud's a difficult beast.

MIKE *(angrily)* Brian, these people have ripped off millions.

BRIAN But when you divide that by the number of customers, it's not much.

MIKE You just don't want to do it.

BRIAN Wait a sec . . .

MIKE You're just fobbing me off.

BRIAN Hey (listen mate, watch yourself), when have I backed away from something that'll get us ratings?

Mike gives slight acknowledgement.

MIKE Sorry.

BRIAN We've got three minutes to do a story; five if it involves nudity.

MIKE I can do this story in three.

BRIAN Another problem. Fraud doesn't give you vision. A whole bunch of hand shots flicking through documents – it looks like you're televising an audit.

MIKE Stories don't get bigger than this.

BRIAN You've gotta make it work for telly. Vision.

MIKE And then you'll run it?

BRIAN Every night for a week.

SCENE 17

THE FRONTLINE STUDIO

An unseen story is just ending.

FLOOR MANAGER In five . . .

MIKE Mmm, Brooke Vandenberg there with the lighter side of parent-teacher nights. Coming up after the break, the drycleaner who's cleaning you up.

We see a brief teaser from the drycleaner story, featuring Marty walking in on him.

SCENE 18

THE STATIONERY ROOM

Mike is in the stationery cupboard stealing a sheet of copy paper. Domenica walks in and startles him.

DOMENICA Oh, it's you, Mike!

MIKE *(embarrassed)* Sorry, Domenica. I was just grabbing some paper for home.

DOMENICA That's OK, Mike. Everyone takes stationery.

MIKE *(conspiratorially)* I might just grab an extra.

DOMENICA Sure. It was a good show tonight.

MIKE Yeah?

DOMENICA Yeah. *(pause)* You look really good on camera.

MIKE Thank you.

DOMENICA I kinda like you off camera, too.

Mike is a little taken aback but Domenica is looking straight at him. The pause is broken by them leaning into each other about to kiss.

DOMENICA Sorry.

MIKE Don't be. *(he goes to kiss again)*

DOMENICA This is stupid. I better go, Mike.

MIKE Not yet.

DOMENICA I better go.

MIKE Domenica . . . *(he grabs for her)*

DOMENICA Mike, I have to go.

She wrestles out and we see Brian is at the door. Domenica scurries away.

MIKE She started . . .

BRIAN Mike, she's been keen on you from the moment you walked in the door.

MIKE She was . . .

BRIAN Forget it. I'm off. See you tomorrow.

MIKE Sure. Oh, and Brian . . . *(referring to Domenica)* Nothing happened.

Brian nods and leaves.

Day ❸

SCENE 19

A PARK

Mike and Bob Foster are walking through the park. Mike is in an overcoat and looking over his shoulder.

BOB It's not a John Grisham novel. We could have met in your office.

MIKE Hey, I'm just trying to protect you.

BOB So your boss wants vision?

MIKE Says we can't run the story without it; too boring.

BOB Well, I had a word to my informant . . .

MIKE Who was . . . ?

BOB A senior administrative officer with the bank. Turns out he was more streetwise than I thought.

MIKE What do you mean?

BOB A few months back he set up a home video camera in his office and secretly filmed the managing director discussing the whole box and dice.

MIKE *(excitedly)* And he's got a tape of this?

BOB *(pulling a Hi-8 tape from his coat)* No, you do.

MIKE *(looks at the tape)* Fantastic.

BOB Let me give you a warning. A lot of people won't like this.

MIKE I won't give in.

BOB Your job could be on the line.

MIKE They won't sack me for this.

BOB No. They'll find something else.

SCENE 20

THE FRONTLINE MEETING ROOM

Brooke and Emma and two minders in suits are sitting around the meeting room table. One of the minders is examining a sheet of questions. There is a long pause as Brooke and Emma eye the men nervously.

MINDER This question here.

BROOKE I think we can drop that.

MINDER OK, sure. As long as you're happy.

BROOKE Absolutely.

The minder crosses out the question with a black texta.

MINDER I mean, obviously the Prime Minister is happy to canvass any issue, but . . .

EMMA We just felt like a distraction . . .

MINDER And the 'Labor in Power' stuff.

BROOKE What do you think?

MINDER Oh, you can ask whatever you want.

BROOKE AND EMMA It's gone.

MINDER Yeah. *(crosses it off immediately)* As long as you're happy.

BROOKE Sure.

MINDER Where were you thinking of doing the interview?

EMMA Er, wherever. In the studio here?

MINDER *(slightly cuts her off)* Did you think about on the lawn at the Lodge? A more casual sort of environment . . .

BROOKE That would be even better.

MINDER As long as you're happy. You do whatever you want.

SCENE 21

BRIAN'S OFFICE

Brian and Mike are in Brian's office. Mike is holding the tape. He has just told Brian the story.

BRIAN *(excited)* It's unbelievable.

MIKE And we've got it all. *(waves the folder)*

BRIAN Now I know how Woodward and Bernstein felt. *(Mike agrees, but unconvincingly, and then pauses)* They broke Watergate.

MIKE Oh, yeah.

BRIAN I better speak to Fez. *(points upstairs)* They'll have to know about this.

MIKE *(making his way to the door)* Of course.

BRIAN And get that down to Hugh.

MIKE *(calls)* Kate.

Kate takes the tape, and as she rushes off Stu calls after her.

STU Make sure he labels it.

SCENE 22

THE EDIT SUITE

Marty and Hugh are editing a story.

MARTY OK, let's take a look.

Hugh hits 'Play'. We see vision of several council workers at a road site taking a smoko.

MARTY *(as voice-over)* Council regulations require these workers to take a ten-minute tea break. Well, it's now 10.15 . . . *(dissolve)* 10.25 . . . Back to work, fellas . . . *(dissolve)* 10.40 – still no action. *(dissolve)* At last! Ten fifty-three.

Marty stops the tape.

HUGH What happens to these guys?

MARTY These guys? Nothin'; they're council workers.

HUGH But the other blokes – the fridge guy and the cigarette bloke.

MARTY They go bust.

HUGH It ruins 'em?

MARTY If you get caught, there's no special privileges.

Kate enters with a Hi-8 tape.

KATE *(urgently)* Brian wants you to hang onto this. I think it's important.

Hugh takes the tape and throws it on top of a pile of other tapes. Kate leaves as he and Marty get back to work.

MARTY You gonna label that?

HUGH Label what?

SCENE 23
BRIAN'S OFFICE

Brian is walking towards his office.

SHELLEY *(calls)* Brian, Ian Farmer on one.

Brian goes into his office and presses a button on his speaker-phone.

BRIAN Fez, you see the tape?

FARMER *(voice only)* Great. Unbelievable.

BRIAN We run it?

FARMER Absolutely . . . If legal clear it.

BRIAN I thought they cleared it.

FARMER A few aspects have become a bit hazy.

BRIAN Is everyone behind it?

FARMER You got 100 per cent support. It's just that we've gotta be careful.

BRIAN Careful?

FARMER Take some time to check a few facts . . . We can't hammer this guy because of one piece of footage.

BRIAN There's a fair bit in there.

FARMER Sure, but let's not forget we have the courts to decide these things as well.

Understanding gradually dawns on Brian. He changes the subject.

BRIAN We still on for Thursday?

FARMER Might have to postpone that, mate.

BRIAN *(pause)* Sorry?

FARMER Nothing serious. They'll sign you again. They're just . . . you know.

BRIAN Sure.

FARMER Keep your nose clean for the next couple of weeks, and . . . you know.

SCENE 24
GEOFF'S OFFICE

MIKE I mean, it's incredible. It's like Woodford and Redford.

GEOFF Who?

MIKE The guys who cracked Watergate.

GEOFF Oh. Mate, you deserve this. A big story.

MIKE Makes a change from nailing refrigerator repairmen.

GEOFF And there's no problem with you doing it?

MIKE Brian's speaking to Farmer right now. Shouldn't be any problems . . .

SCENE 25
BRIAN'S OFFICE

Mike and Brian meet.

MIKE What sort of problems?

BRIAN Now, don't get excited. We just have to tread carefully; maybe just hold things over for a bit.

MIKE But it's the biggest story we've had this year.

BRIAN And it's going ahead. There's just a few legal things to clear up.

MIKE They have been cleared up.

BRIAN A few other people may be implicated.

MIKE Because they're guilty.

BRIAN Let's just take some time to check the facts. We don't want to ruin these people because of one piece of footage.

MIKE I see.

BRIAN Hey, let's not forget we have the courts to decide these things as well.

MIKE Let me clear something up. I know what's happening.

BRIAN Listen, mate . . .

MIKE No, you listen. Either this story goes public, or I go public.

Mike goes to leave. Brian calls after him. Mike turns and look back.

BRIAN Be careful, mate.

SCENE 26
THE FRONTLINE STUDIO

Mike is at the desk winding up the show.

MIKE Well, that's about it for the show. Join us tomorrow night when we look at the so-called injured workers who can still bend over backwards if the price is right.

We show vision shot from across the road of a pensioner shuffling along the street. She stops, looks around, then bends to pick up some money lying on the footpath.

Cut back to Mike.

MIKE That's tomorrow night, on Frontline.

The lights fade and closing music runs.

MIKE *(sarcastically)* Well, that should send shock waves through the underworld.

Emma walks across to Mike.

MIKE What are you doing in shot?

EMMA Brian thinks it looks good for a member of the crew to walk over and sort of have a chat as the show finishes.

Day

SCENE 27
THE PRODUCTION OFFICE

Mike heads into the office in a deflated mood. Shelley is sitting at Domenica's desk.

SHELLEY Oh, Mike . . .

MIKE Where's Dom?

SHELLEY Brian gave her the day off. Mike, you're wanted . . . *(she motions upstairs)*

MIKE Farmer?

SHELLEY *(shakes head)* Managing Director.

MIKE Caville?

SCENE 28
FARMER'S OFFICE

Mike is in Farmer's office. Caville is just finishing introductions to two lawyers.

CAVILLE Anyway (let's sit down). How are you, Mike?

MIKE Fine.

CAVILLE Just borrowed Ian's office for the afternoon.

MIKE How long are you down for?

CAVILLE Go back tonight.

MIKE Short trip.

CAVILLE Been here for a few days already. Had a few sitcoms to axe. *(slight laugh)*

MIKE Uh-huh. What can I . . . ?

CAVILLE Mike, I never enjoy these conversations.

MIKE The story . . . Bob, we have rock-solid evidence. I think we should run it.

CAVILLE Story? What story?

MIKE The loans scandal. With the bank.

CAVILLE I don't want to talk about some bank. I've got a highly paid current affairs host who could be up on a sexual harassment charge.

Mike looks stunned.

SCENE 29
BRIAN'S OFFICE

Cut straight to Mike and Brian in the middle of a quarrel.

BRIAN Mate, I only said what I saw – you struggling with Domenica and her upset.

MIKE Hang on.

BRIAN Mate, I don't think there's anything in it, but I have a duty to all my staff.

MIKE I know what's happening, Brian. It won't work.

BRIAN Mike, let me give you a hypothetical. A hypothetical, you understand.

MIKE About a current affairs host?

BRIAN A highly paid one. Good car, nice home . . . and let's say it got out that he was caught stealing.

MIKE *(he can't believe this)* Paper?

BRIAN Theft's theft. And he was caught rifling through someone's desk, and there was a question of sexual harassment. If all that got out, even if there wasn't much in it, the damage to his reputation . . . And let's say . . .

MIKE His contract was up for renewal.

BRIAN This is a hypothetical, you understand.

MIKE Sure.

BRIAN That fellow's got a lot to lose, wouldn't you say?

MIKE And if that fellow dropped a certain story?

BRIAN There's no linkage, Mike.

MIKE I thought we were still in a hypothetical. Forget it.

BRIAN Mate, you've got a lot to lose.

MIKE *(bitterly)* Excuse me, I have to record a Christmas message.

SCENE 30

THE FRONTLINE STUDIO

Brooke is standing in front of a decorated Christmas tree in her on-air gear and a Santa hat. Emma hurries in and finds her.

JAN Just keep it warm and fuzzy, Brooke.

EMMA Sorry, Jan. Can I interrupt?

JAN Darling, I've got forty-three to do . . . Quickly, Brooke.

Stu bursts in with a Hi-8 tape.

STU Has anyone seen Brian?

JAN No. Can we please get on with this?

Stu exits.

EMMA Brooke, the PM's department rang. It's a no.

BROOKE What? Why?

EMMA They got cold feet. *(drops her voice)* Apparently this story of Mike's . . . Someone's had a word in their ear.

BROOKE Jesus!

JAN Darling, can this wait?

MIKE *(entering)* Are you ready for me, Jan?

BROOKE You fucknuckle. You blew my interview with the Prime Minister!

MIKE What?

BROOKE Apparently he got wind of your stupid story and pulled the plug, you dumb bastard.

JAN *(trying to restore calm)* Brooke, would you please . . . ?

BROOKE *(calmly, smiling to camera)* Hi. I'm Brooke Vandenberg from Frontline and I'd like to wish you and yours a very merry Christmas and a happy new year. *(to Mike)* You're an arsehole, Mike. *(she storms out)*

MIKE *(stunned)* Do you want me to do mine?

JAN I don't think there's much point, darling.

SCENE 31

GEOFF'S OFFICE

Mike is in Geoff's office showing him some papers.

GEOFF What do I reckon? I reckon it's a fantastic story.

MIKE Yeah.

GEOFF A lot of people are going to be unhappy about this.

MIKE Yeah.

GEOFF You've really put your neck on the line.

MIKE Uh-huh.

GEOFF And I respect you for that.

MIKE Really?

GEOFF Yeah. Well, you've got so much to lose.

MIKE Geoff, I'm thinking of pulling the story.

GEOFF Wow.

MIKE I don't want to.

GEOFF Of course not. You're on the verge of exposing a major financial scandal.

MIKE Exactly. And that's why I reckon we gotta *(thinks)* wait till we have a few more facts. Sort out the legal problems . . . We've gotta be careful about ruining people on the basis of one piece of footage.

GEOFF Absolutely.

MIKE And anyway we've still got the courts to decide these things.

GEOFF Gee . . . Brian'll be disappointed.

SCENE 32

THE STUDIO CORRIDOR

Mike walks down the corridor outside the studio. Stu is holding a tape and speaking to Brian.

BRIAN He what?

STU I just found out.

MIKE *(subdued)* Brian, can I have a word with you?

BRIAN Mate, I know you're not going to believe this, but Hughie thinks he's taped over the bank bloke.

Mike is stunned.

BRIAN It's gone. There's no way we can run the story.

MIKE That's terrific . . . that you told me.

BRIAN Mate, I had nothing to . . .

STU I'm sorry, Mike. Hughie's hunting for it but I'm pretty sure it was on this one.

MIKE You know how much I wanted . . .

BRIAN I know, mate. We can go and look.

MIKE No, no, the story's dead. I'm just saying . . .

BRIAN I know, mate.

EMMA *(approaching them)* Can someone tell me are we running the bank story tonight?

MIKE It's not going ahead.

EMMA Thanks for letting me know. *(walks off modifying her clipboard)* Oh, and that Bob Foster's outside.

Mike braces himself and walks out to meet Bob. Brian stops him.

BRIAN And Mike, it turns out Domenica never even wanted to report that thing.

SCENE 33

OUTSIDE THE BUILDING

Mike walks up to Bob.

BOB Are they running it?

MIKE Can't, Bob.

BOB I thought that would happen.

MIKE Bob, the tape's gone.

BOB Bullshit.

MIKE I'm telling you they can't find it. They're pretty sure they taped over it.

BOB You're bullshitting me. You've just got cold feet.

MIKE Listen, Bob. I threatened to walk over that story. I put everything on the line to see that it went to air.

BOB This is straight?

MIKE It was going to air tonight, or I walked.

BOB And it's gone.

MIKE There's nothing we can do about it.

Hugh bursts outside with a tape in his hand.

HUGH Found it!

Episode 12
Judge and Jury

Day 1

SCENE 1

THE PRODUCTION OFFICE

Kate is on the phone.

KATE . . . and we were wondering if we could speak to you about your husband's death and the . . . I understand, but yes, if we could just . . . *(the phone is obviously hung up in her ear)* I hate Mondays.

Marty comes over.

MARTY Story?

KATE Brian makes me write down all the car crash and accident people over the weekend and then I've got to ring their families and try and talk them into an interview.

MARTY Yeah?

KATE Well, it's not easy, Marty. They're upset and I feel terrible, then Brian yells at me . . .

MARTY *(cutting her off)* What did you say to that lady just then?

KATE I asked if we could talk about her husband's death.

MARTY Nah. You don't ask for an interview, you tell 'em. This is TV – we're like the cops as far as they're concerned. You gotta make it sound like we're doing them the favour. You see? Here, give us your list.

Kate passes Marty her list.

MARTY Who's next?

KATE Mr Connell.

MARTY Nah, go for a wog – they always talk. Let's try this 'Zitas'. Mrs?

Kate nods.

MARTY *(dialling)* Watch and learn. What's the . . . ?

KATE Her three-year-old son drowned in a neighbour's pool.

Marty waits for the phone to be answered.

MARTY *(concerned tone)* Hello, Mrs Zitas? Martin di Stasio here, Frontline. I'm terribly sorry to hear about your son and we wouldn't normally disturb you in this time of grief, but we feel it's vital that something is done about the whole issue of pool fencing, and you're in a position to do this, Mrs Zitas. I think it's the least we can do, as a tribute to . . .

Gestures frantically to Kate for her clipboard. She points to name.

MARTY . . . Simon. Yes, I do think it'll make a difference. Of course, it's entirely up to you and I think people would understand if you didn't want to raise awareness of the dangers. Mike Moore himself has pushed for this issue to be addressed. Um . . . yeah. What about tomorrow? Well, after the funeral. About two o'clock? See you then. Oh, and if anyone else rings from the press, I'd just give them a blanket 'no'. You're already doing more than enough. OK, see you tomorrow at two. *(hangs up)* They're expecting us at two.

KATE *(a little shell-shocked)* Thanks.

MARTY I might be able to do it, if I'm not *(loudly)* stuck at the zoo!

EMMA Sorry, Marty.

MARTY No, it's a fascinating story you've organised for me, Em. Tenth anniversary of the zoo's butterfly enclosure.

EMMA It's a slow news day.

MARTY And you couldn't send Brooke?

EMMA She's out already.

MARTY What about Mike?

SCENE 2

BRIAN'S OFFICE

Mike, Brian and Jan meet.

MIKE No, Jan, don't try and sweet-talk me.

JAN She's a fascinating girl. She's been to Africa with World Vision.

MIKE She's an actress in one of this network's soap operas.

JAN Drama series, darling.

MIKE And you're trying to convince me it's a legitimate interview. Not gonna fall for it, Jan. I made it absolutely clear when I left the ABC that I would not be involved in cheap cross-promotional stunts. You wanna flog a book, or an album, or some TV series – don't expect Mike Moore to lend his name.

BRIAN You don't want to do it?

MIKE I don't want to do it.

BRIAN (to Jan) Inform Miss D-Cup her services will not be required.

Jan leaves.

MIKE (backtracking) I mean, I don't wanna sound precious or anything.

BRIAN Mike, you're absolutely right.

Brian leaves his office, followed by Mike. Brian goes over to Kate.

BRIAN How'd you go?

KATE Got a 'yes' from the drowning family, 'yes' from the car crash mum and a 'maybe' from the bashed guy's wife provided he's well enough to speak.

BRIAN (surprised) All three? Well done.

Kate looks suitably proud.

SCENE 3

THE BUTTERFLY ENCLOSURE AT THE ZOO

Marty, Stu and Jase look bored as they wait next to the camera. A curator stands by, ready to be interviewed.

MARTY Twenty-one years as a journalist. You'd think I'd be beyond this zoo stuff.

STU At least it's not a baby orang-utan.

MARTY Geez, I've done a few of those stories. (to the curator) Just be a few more seconds. (to Stu) What's the hold-up?

STU They're just finding a place to plug the lights into. We had to get an extension cord and . . .

A voice from off calls 'OK'. Stu waves back.

STU Set to go.

Marty brings the curator over into position.

MARTY (to curator) We'll just mention it's the tenth anniversary, talk a bit about the rare species you've got here . . . It'll only take a few minutes. Where are the butterflies?

CURATOR They're camouflaged.

MARTY Oh, great. But they'll fly around?

CURATOR Oh, yeah.

MARTY (to Stu) Set to go.

STU (calls) Lights!

The lights are switched on. Marty starts the interview.

MARTY Christine, how long have you been curator here at the butterfly enclosure?

Before this question is really finished both Marty and the curator are distracted by the sound of butterflies frying as they become attracted to the lights.

CURATOR Shit!

MARTY The lights! Turn 'em off!

STU (calls) Turn off the power. No, off!

SCENE 4

BRIAN'S OFFICE

Brian is yelling at Marty, Stu and Jase. He refers to a fax.

BRIAN 'The orange lacewing butterfly. Previously twenty in the world. Now two.'

MARTY Brian . . .

BRIAN No, no – there's more. 'As of five o'clock yesterday there were only four known specimens of the speckled Bogong moth. As of today, formally extinct.'

MARTY How are we supposed to know moths are attracted . . . (defeated) to light?

Stu and Jase snigger. Brooke comes to the door with a piece of paper.

BRIAN *(to Brooke)* What have you got?

BROOKE Phone number of a woman who claims she was raped by her parish priest.

BRIAN She spoken to anyone else?

Brooke shakes her head 'no'.

BRIAN Let's get an interview. *(he takes the number and walks out into the production office)* Em, got a possible lead here – woman raped by a priest. Want an interview.

EMMA Has the priest been charged?

BRIAN No idea. Let's get the interview.

KATE I'll do it.

Emma looks surprised at Kate's eagerness. Brian hands Kate the paper, and she dials.

BRIAN Make sure it's an exclusive.

Kate gives a 'Yeah, yeah, I know' expression as she dials.

KATE Hello, is that Dominique? *(concerned voice)* Dominique, it's Kate Preston here from Frontline; Brooke Vandenberg passed on your name. We're running a series on survivors of sexual abuse within the church *(Brian gives her the thumbs up)* and we were wondering if we could tape a short interview with you. Well, right now, if it's poss . . . Great. I'll just get your address.

Brian punches the air in excitement. Emma's phone rings and she answers it. Kate hangs up and hands a piece of paper to Brooke.

KATE *(smugly)* She's expecting you now. Exclusive.

BROOKE On my way.

Emma beckons Brian over. Mike approaches with a cup of coffee.

EMMA *(hand over phone)* Do we want to speak with Shirley Strachan about Skyhooks' new single?

BRIAN Mike?

MIKE Sounds like a another plug to me, Brian.

BRIAN *(to Emma)* Mr Moore has spoken. No.

Mike looks chuffed as Emma speaks into the phone, 'We're a little full this week . . .'

MIKE Thanks, Brian.

SCENE 5

JAN'S OFFICE

Jan and Brian meet.

BRIAN How bad is this?

JAN I've spoken to the zoo. They're a little upset, but we'll hose it down. Offer to do a story next time a baby monkey is born. *(makes a written note)* Actually, that would make a good piece for our weatherman.

BRIAN Mike's mate?

JAN Have you seen his latest proposal?

BRIAN No.

JAN *(handing Brian a folder)* Wants me to push a one-hour documentary on the urban fox. Check the title. *(Brian looks at the folder and winces)* 'Fox, Lies and Videotape'. This might distract him. What I really wanted to speak to you about is . . .

Jan holds up a photo of Shirley Strachan.

BRIAN Shirley Strachan.

JAN His band have got a new single out. Wants to come on the show and promote it.

BRIAN (That's right), they rang earlier. Mike knocked it back. Does not want his precious journalistic image to be compromised by cheap plugs.

JAN This one's not so cheap. Network's keen to speak with Mr Strachan about a lifestyles program for next year.

BRIAN Doesn't he already do one, on . . . ?

JAN It's about home maintenance; he does the carpentry segment. We're thinking of a series based solely on carpentry, called 'Wooden It Be Lovely'.

BRIAN I prefer the weatherman's title.

JAN Whatever. Mr Strachan's manager has let it be known that some favourable publicity for his new single might help sweeten the deal.

BRIAN Can I give it to Brooke? Profile piece . . .

Jan is shaking her head 'no'.

BRIAN Why?

JAN Apparently Shirl and our Brooke are no longer on speaking terms.

BRIAN They didn't . . .

Jan nods 'Yes, they did'.

BRIAN I knew her standards were low, but . . .

JAN (Think you can talk) Mike (into it)?

BRIAN (thinks) I'll try. But right now he's going through one of those 'serious' phases.

SCENE 6

THE PRODUCTION OFFICE

Marty stands next to Emma as she is on the phone. He speaks out loud to himself.

MARTY No, don't worry about Marty. His story count doesn't matter. Just as long as Brooke's got the big interviews.

Mike approaches with a can of flyspray and begins spraying.

MARTY You right?

MIKE Just thought I saw another butterfly. *(he bursts out laughing)*

MARTY Here's one.

Marty thumps Mike's arm with a rolled-up newspaper.

MIKE (angrily) Ow! I was doing a clever joke and you were just violent.

Emma hangs up and hands Marty a piece of paper.

EMMA Thank me later.

MARTY The reptile cage have an anniversary?

EMMA (ignoring his sarcasm) Two brothers from Sandringham saved a yacht crew from drowning last night.

MARTY Uh-huh.

EMMA They're heroes! It's a big story.

MARTY Did they then have sex with a nun or . . . ?

EMMA (trying to take back paper) If you don't want the story . . .

MARTY Nah, nah, I'll take it. Interview exclusive?

EMMA For a cost.

MARTY How much?

EMMA They want two slabs of beer.

MARTY Classy blokes.

EMMA And they said 'not light'.

MARTY Very classy blokes.

Brooke enters with a tape, followed by Stu and Jase. Brian enters after meeting with Jan.

BRIAN How'd you go?

BROOKE Good. Spoke to the victim, and her psychiatrist. Lot of tears; names the priest.

BRIAN You speak with him?

BROOKE Refused an interview.

BRIAN Shit. Did you get any vision?

BROOKE It's a little dark.

Brooke puts the tape in and hits 'Play'. On the office monitor we see vision of a priest in a confessional box, obviously shot by a hidden camera.

EMMA *(in disbelief)* You took a hidden camera into confession?

MARTY It's all right, Em – she went back in and got his forgiveness.

Brooke notices Brian's look of disbelief.

BROOKE What?

Brian gives her a 'You've gone too far' look.

BROOKE So we're not going to use it?

BRIAN Maybe in the promo. But I'd still like an interview.

BROOKE He refused.

BRIAN 'Course he did. He's guilty.

KATE Let me try.

EMMA *(protesting)* Kate!

KATE Well, we should hear his side of the story.

BRIAN Exactly.

Brooke hands Kate a piece of paper.

BROOKE His number.

Kate dials.

MARTY *(to Brooke)* Is there an audio track to this confession?

BROOKE Not that you'll be hearing.

BRIAN We should cut a promo right away. 'Priest or Pervert'.

MARTY I don't wanna sound like Emma here . . .

BRIAN (All right), you think of something better. Beginning with 'P'. 'Priest or . . . '

KATE *(on phone)* Hello, is that Father Croft? Kate Preston from Frontline. Yes, that's right. *(seriously)* Father, I realise you don't wish to be interviewed but those disturbing allegations made by one of your parishioners . . . we're concerned about airing them without giving you a right to reply. Of course . . . Well, to be honest we seriously doubt this woman's claims and if you could speak with us it would be an opportunity to clear your name. Then we could probably forget the whole story . . . This afternoon? *(she gives thumbs up)* That would be wonderful. *(hangs up)* Got him!

General jubilation.

MARTY Jase, Stu – got a story.

BROOKE I need them, Marty.

STU We gotta go with Brooke.

MARTY You wimps.

BRIAN *(to Marty)* Get another crew, Marty. This is big. *(to Shelley)* Is Mike . . . ?

Brian indicates Mike's office. Shelley nods that he is in there. Brian goes to the door of the office and looks in.

BRIAN Got a moment, mate?

MIKE Sure.

Brian enters and shuts the door.

SCENE 7

MIKE'S OFFICE

BRIAN Mike, got a story. A bit political . . .

MIKE *(condescending)* Brian, you seem to forget back at the ABC I was a political reporter.

BRIAN The PSA have just . . .

MIKE Who?

BRIAN Prices Surveillance Authority.

MIKE Yeah, yeah (I knew that).

BRIAN They've just released a report saying we pay too much for CDs.

MIKE True. Bought 'The Best of Enya' last week. How much do you think it cost?

BRIAN Forty bucks?

MIKE (pause) Twenty-eight bucks.

BRIAN It's still a lot. I thought we could look into it. Maybe do an interview with someone from the Prices Surveillance Authority and, say, get a few local musicians in.

MIKE Sort of a debate?

BRIAN Yeah.

MIKE Sounds a great idea.

BRIAN You able to pre-record something tomorrow arvo?

MIKE (thinks) I'll skip gym. No problems.

Brian starts to leave.

MIKE Might go do a bit of research. Have you got a copy of the report?

BRIAN The . . . ?

MIKE The Prices Surveillance Authority report. PSA.

BRIAN Track one down.

Brian leaves Mike's office. He passes Emma's desk.

BRIAN Get back to Shirley Strachan's people. Tell 'em we can do an interview tomorrow afternoon. Oh, and get one of those old budget reports. You know, the really thick ones. Stick a new front on it that says 'Prices Surveillance Authority' and give it to Mike.

EMMA Won't he read it?

BRIAN Won't get past the front page.

SCENE 8

A SUBURBAN PARK WITH GLIMPSES OF THE BAY IN BACKGROUND

Marty is seated on a director's chair as his freelance crew set up for a shot. The two brothers, Barney and Wally, are also seated, drinking heavily from their beer. We see a few empties on the ground.

MARTY (to crew) How much longer, fellas?

CAMERAMAN Couple of secs.

BARNEY It's me first time on telly.

MARTY Really?

CAMERAMAN Set to go.

MARTY (clearly relieved) All right. (to brothers) What was your feeling when you first saw the yacht?

WALLY Hang on. I need to take a slash.

SCENE 9

THE EDIT SUITE

We open on a suburban lounge room. Brooke is interviewing a middle-aged Catholic priest.

PRIEST I first met Dominique fifteen years ago. She attended mass with her parents, helped with flowers, organised activities . . .

BROOKE So you spent quite a bit of time with her?

PRIEST Yes, it seemed her home life wasn't quite . . .

BROOKE She claims you had sex with her.

PRIEST I'm stunned by that claim.

BROOKE (sternly) Father, did you sleep with Dominique?

PRIEST No. The very notion – it's . . .

The tape is paused. We widen to reveal Brooke and Hugh viewing it in the edit suite.

BROOKE He answers too quickly. Too confident. We need a pause.

HUGH Easy.

BROOKE Can you do it?

HUGH Chuck in a cutaway and I'll shift the audio back.

BROOKE Sure.

Hugh is already re-spooling the tape.

BROOKE Anything that makes it look like he's thinking about the question.

We run the last part of the interview again.

BROOKE (on screen) Father, did you sleep with Dominique?

We cut to a shot on screen of Brooke waiting for the answer, then back to the priest.

PRIEST No.

Cut back to the edit suite. Brooke and Hugh look pleased.

SCENE 10

THE PARK

Marty is trying to get an interview out of the even drunker two brothers. They sit quite 'formally'.

MARTY OK, take nine . . . When did you realise the yacht was sinking?

Wally burps and both brothers start laughing hysterically. Marty looks decidedly unhappy.

SCENE 11

BRIAN'S OFFICE

Brooke and Brian are looking at photos. The first shows Father Croft with one arm around Dominique and the other around her mother.

BROOKE This was taken at a youth mass. That's Dominique and her mum.

BRIAN Yeah, with the mum there it looks a bit . . . innocent.

BROOKE We thought about 'adjusting' the shot to highlight just the two of them.

Brooke produces a cropped version of the first shot showing just Father Croft and Dominique.

BRIAN That's a much better shot.

SCENE 12

GEOFF'S OFFICE

Geoff is watching a video of himself presenting the weather. He mouths along with the dialogue. Mike enters.

MIKE Geoff.

Geoff switches off the tape.

GEOFF Hi, Mike.

MIKE *(impressed)* Your attention to detail is staggering, Geoffrey.

GEOFF You don't stay a weatherman for twelve years without it, Mike.

MIKE Hey, (I'm) doing a big political story.

GEOFF Really?

MIKE Brian comes into my office this morning – shuts the door – and says he wants me to handle it.

GEOFF Because back at the ABC . . .

MIKE I did political stuff all the time! It's a great issue – are we paying too much for CDs?

GEOFF (unconvincing) Yeah.

MIKE Wants me to chair a debate.

GEOFF Fantastic! You deserve this, Mike.

MIKE So how'd you go with your doco?

GEOFF I gave Jan the submission to pass on. (indicates upstairs) She's always been behind the idea.

MIKE Urban foxes? It's a winner!

GEOFF And I came up with a title.

MIKE What?

GEOFF 'Fox, Lies and Videotape'.

MIKE Fantastic! 'Cause that film title . . . It's a twist; it's clever. (changing topic) Hey, you hear what I did to Marty this morning?

GEOFF No, what?

MIKE I snuck up behind him with a tin of flyspray and pretended to spray butterflies.

They both laugh.

MIKE 'Cause you heard what happened at the zoo?

GEOFF No, what?

MIKE Well, he killed all these butterflies.

GEOFF Really? That's terrible.

MIKE No, but the joke was . . .

GEOFF How many died?

MIKE But the point is . . .

SCENE 13

A FRONTLINE PROMO

The promo uses footage of the priest taken on the hidden camera. He has a black strip over his eyes which 'peels off' partially at the end of the promo.

VOICE-OVER Tonight on Frontline, we reveal the parish priest alleged to have sexually abused one of his flock. 'Wolves in Priests' Clothing' – that's tonight on Frontline.

SCENE 14

THE KITCHEN

Emma is putting her lunch into the microwave as Marty eats from a generic box of chips. He reads the side of the box.

MARTY What actually concerns me about these is that it says 'cheese flavour', but cheese is not actually listed as an ingredient.

Brooke enters.

MARTY How's the priest story looking?

BROOKE Not bad.

MARTY Saw the promo. 'Wolves in Priests' Clothing' . . . ?

BROOKE It was Brian.

EMMA He wanted 'Priests or Paedophiles'.

MARTY Is the guy actually guilty?

BROOKE She reckons he is.

MARTY But the sexual abuse. It was fifteen years ago.

BROOKE We spoke to her psychiatrist. He's done a lot of work with unlocking hidden memories. She'd forgotten the whole rape.

EMMA How do you forget a rape?

BROOKE You don't 'forget' it – you block it out. There's some technical term.

MARTY Bullshit?

BROOKE Hey, what is this? An inquisition?

EMMA Well, we are accusing this man tonight, on national television. We've gotta be sure he's guilty.

BROOKE He is.

EMMA Then why haven't the cops charged . . . ?

BROOKE Look, these guys are creeps. They prey on young girls. You wanna let them off the hook?

MARTY But we can't set ourselves up as judge and jury . . .

BROOKE (understanding dawns) Are you both Catholic?

Marty and Emma look at each other. Neither owns up.

BROOKE *(leaving with coffee)* Well, that explains everything.

EMMA *(to Marty)* Are you?

MARTY *(picking up tape)* Lapsed. In fact, right now I've gotta go to confession and beg forgiveness. *(leaving)* Bless me, Brian, for I have sinned . . .

SCENE 15

BRIAN'S OFFICE

Marty and Brian are viewing a tape.

BRIAN How'd you go?

MARTY Not bad. There was a bit of language.

BRIAN No worries. We beep it out.

We see footage of an overturned boat, people being brought ashore in blankets, etc.

MARTY *(voice only)* When a small yacht overturned in the icy waters of Bass Strait last night, it could have spelt the end for its skipper and crew. But they were rescued – plucked from the raging seas by two very unlikely heroes.

We cut to our bayside location. The two brothers are being interviewed by Marty. They both sip beer (although some attempt to cut around this has been made). All their expletives are beeped.

MARTY *(on screen)* What happened last night?

BARNEY Jesus, it was fair pissin' down and Wally here says, 'Fucking come over to the fucking window.' I come over and he says, 'Fucking look out there.' I says, 'I can't see a fucking thing.'

They both laugh.

WALLY You're a blind bastard.

BARNEY Well, fuck me, if I don't look again and there's this fucking boat. It's rolled over and I nearly shit meself.

WALLY So we get the fucking dinghy out. It weighs a fuckin' ton, and it's still pissin' down.

BARNEY Fuckin' pourin'. We sail out . . .

Brian stops the tape.

BRIAN Well, you've had a big day, haven't you?

Marty can say nothing.

BRIAN This is a disaster.

MARTY You should have seen the takes we rejected.

SCENE 16

THE FRONTLINE STUDIO

Mike is at his desk, playing with his chair height.

MIKE Brian, this is a little high. Am I too high?

BRIAN Looks good, Mike.

MIKE I just think . . .

FLOOR MANAGER Five to go.

Mike fiddles with the chair height lever one more time, causing the seat to drop absurdly low. He manages to present the show's intro by leaning on his forearms.

MIKE Hi, thanks for joining us. I'm Mike Moore – welcome to Frontline.

The opening titles run. We see a flurry of activity as Brian, Emma and various crew unsuccessfully attempt to raise Mike's chair. They run out of shot just in time.

MIKE First up tonight, the Catholic Church has long preached the need for sexual morality. But as Brooke Vandenberg reports, it's not always a case of 'Practise what you preach'.

We open with exterior shot of church spire, organ music running and Brooke's voice-over.

BROOKE *(voice only)* St Mark's is your typical Catholic church. Each Sunday its congregation gathers to practise their faith. But for one young parishioner many years ago, this faith was shattered.

The shot of the church spire is pulled out of focus. We cut to an interview with a woman in her twenties, in a standard lounge room location.

DOMINIQUE He would come up to me in the church after mass and just start talking. He was very kind. Then it started.

SCENE 17

THE PRODUCTION OFFICE

It is later that night. Everyone sits around having a post-show drink.

DOMENICA I reckon he was really creepy. He had creepy eyes.

KATE I reckon he did it.

MARTY What is this? Open season on priests?

KATE I'm sure he did it.

EMMA Kate, what if he didn't?

BROOKE (bored) Here we go.

EMMA What if this Dominique woman was lying? Or just wrong?

BROOKE She went to a psychiatrist, all right? He brought out these repressed memories.

DOMENICA I've read about that. This woman, in America, remembered she was, like, touched and stuff by her dad when she was eight, and she didn't remember it until she went to this psychiatrist twenty years later and then she remembered!

EMMA And then it was discovered it never actually happened and this so-called psychiatrist planted the whole thing in her head.

DOMENICA I don't remember that bit.

BRIAN I'm lost. Don't you women hate these sex creeps?

EMMA I've got no more sympathy for paedophiles than you do, but we can't set ourselves up as judge and jury.

BRIAN Yeah, yeah, 'judge and jury'. What are the other clichés here, people?

KATE 'Trial by media'.

BRIAN Thank you, Kate.

KATE 'Playing God'.

BRIAN Another beauty. The fact is, current affairs shows have to play judge and jury because the courts in this country are too bloody weak.

EMMA We've just destroyed a man's reputation on the unchallenged testimony of a psychotic woman.

BROOKE How do you know she's psychotic?

EMMA How do you know she's not? At least a court would have examined the issue. And spoken to a few more witnesses.

BROOKE We tried interviewing some other parishioners, but you know these micks . . .

MARTY Hey, lay off the micks.

BRIAN How many Catholics do we have here?

Emma, Marty, Domenica and Jase put up their hands.

BRIAN Christ! It's the Last Supper.

SHELLEY Brian – phone call. Shirley Strachan's manager.

Brian gets up to take the call in his office. Mike enters the production office with a TV Week.

MIKE Ah, Marty. Just doing the *TV Week* crossword. Twelve down. 'Popular man at the Frontline'. Five letters.

MARTY Idiot?

MIKE It begins with 'M'. And it's not Marty. Oh, hang on, it is. Shit . . .

Mike returns to his office, scribbling out answers. Brian beckons Emma across.

BRIAN Interview with Shirley Strachan's confirmed. Get some questions up.

EMMA What's he talking about?

BRIAN His new single.

EMMA I thought Mike didn't want cheap plugs on the show.

BRIAN Network politics.

EMMA Wouldn't it be easier to get Brooke to do the interview?

BRIAN (putting on coat) Apparently Mr Strachan and our Brooke are not on speaking terms.

EMMA (disgusted) You're kidding! She's unstoppable.

BRIAN You wanna lift?

EMMA I'm right.

BRIAN I could drop you at mass . . .

Emma flings a magazine at Brian as he departs.

Day

SCENE 18

THE PRODUCTION OFFICE

Marty takes a chocolate bar from the WWF stand and walks off.

KATE Hey, Marty!

MARTY What?

KATE You're supposed to pay for them.

MARTY So a few pandas cark it. What do I care?

EMMA *(passing)* Won't be the first endangered species you've wiped out this week.

MARTY *(pointing metal tube at her)* Hey – you sent me there.

EMMA *(referring to tube)* What's that?

MARTY It's a small piece of Mike's chair. I don't know how it fell off . . .

KATE AND EMMA Marty!

DOMENICA Mike's on the radio!

Domenica turns up her radio. We hear Mike's opening words before cutting to the next scene.

SCENE 19

MIKE IS ON THE RADIO AT 3AW WITH NEIL MITCHELL.

MIKE There's community concern, Neil, especially from women who themselves have been victims of this sort of abuse.

NEIL Sure, but there's just as much concern about the way current affairs shows set themselves up as judge and jury.

We cut to Brian and other staff listening in the production office.

BRIAN What's with this 'judge and jury' thing?

Cut back to 3AW studios.

NEIL All right, let's see what our listeners think. Call 696 1278 if you approved of the Frontline story last night. *(pause)* Switchboard's looking pretty dead.

We cut to the phone. One line flashes.

NEIL Oh, we've got a caller. Hello?

RHONDA *(voice only)* It's Rhonda here, Neil. I was a victim of sexual abuse myself from a priest several years ago and I thought the story on Frontline was good.

Cut back to the production office. Domenica is on the phone, with Brian standing next to her.

DOMENICA . . . really, really good.

NEIL *(voice only)* You don't think it was a little one-sided?

Domenica looks helplessly at Brian. He shakes his head 'no'.

DOMENICA No.

MIKE *(voice only)* Thanks, Rhonda. We felt it was our duty to left the veil of silence that for too long has been covering this whole issue.

DOMENICA That's . . . really good.

SCENE 20

BRIAN'S OFFICE

EMMA Shirl should be here at two.

BRIAN What about Mike?

EMMA On his way. That was a tough radio interview.

BRIAN He handled it.

EMMA But maybe we should speak to them about it. I mean, we do them a big favour sending Mike in every week . . .

BRIAN Hey . . . (come on). That's not a favour.

EMMA Isn't it?

BRIAN It's a paid spot. We just dress it up as an interview.

EMMA So it's really a plug for our show?

BRIAN Only Mike doesn't know that. He thinks he's their 'current affairs commentator'.

Brooke calls out to Brian and waves a newspaper.

BROOKE Brian!

BRIAN Not the butterfly thing?

Brooke reads from the paper, loud enough for the rest of the office to hear as well. Brian comes out as she reads.

BROOKE 'Church Denies Sex Claim. Following a report last night on television current affairs program Frontline . . . '

Cheers from office.

BROOKE ' . . . the Catholic Church has moved quickly to deny claims that one of its priests, Father Michael Croft, sexually molested a female parishioner some fifteen years ago.'

General congratulations to Brooke and Kate. Brooke hands the paper over to Brian.

BROOKE Half a page. With his photo.

Mike returns from his radio spot.

DOMENICA Hi, Mike! We're in the paper!

MIKE *(interested)* Is it about me?

DOMENICA No – Brooke.

MIKE *(less interested)* Oh. *(he spots Brian)* Oh, Brian!

Mike follows Brian into Brian's office.

MIKE I want to speak to you about my spot on AW. Did you hear it?

BRIAN I missed it.

MIKE He really got stuck into me. Were we wrong to screen that priest story?

BRIAN I think it would have been wrong *not* to screen it, Mike. We get a plea for help from some woman, cops have turned their backs, courts don't wanna know – who's she gonna come to?

MIKE *(agreeing completely)* Us.

BRIAN Exactly.

MIKE Yet I'm attacked on air. I mean, I'm doing that radio station a favour. I'm their current affairs commentator, and they ambush me.

BRIAN I'll speak to them, Mike.

MIKE I think you should, because I've got a good mind to withdraw my services . . .

BRIAN OK, Mike. In the meantime, you better get down to make-up.

MIKE *(remembering)* Oh, the debate. I'll just get my research. Very interesting report, Brian.

Mike leaves Brian's office. We follow him out into the production office.

DOMENICA Kate, Father Croft's on the phone.

The office falls silent. Kate picks up her phone.

KATE *(worried, to Domenica)* Is he angry?

DOMENICA He just sounds weird.

SCENE 21

THE FRONTLINE STUDIO

Mike prepares to pre-record an interview with Shirley Strachan.

MIKE You know my all-time favourite Skyhooks song?

SHIRL What?

MIKE 'Jump in My Car'.

SHIRL Right.

Mike spots Brian, who has just entered. He gets up and goes over to him.

MIKE *(to Shirl)* If you could just excuse me for a tick. Brian!

BRIAN What is it?

MIKE *(urgently, under his breath)* Where's the guy from the Prices Surveillance Authority?

BRIAN Isn't he here?

MIKE No!

BRIAN Bloody Emma.

MIKE And the musicians . . . There's only Shirley Strachan.

BRIAN Shit. We'll just have to make do.

MIKE *(desperately)* But it's not a debate any more. It's just an interview. *(Brian shrugs helplessly)* I've done all this research.

BRIAN And we don't want to waste that. We'll get the Prices Surveillance guy in next week.

MIKE OK.

BRIAN But while Shirl's here, what are we gonna do with him? We don't want to look like idiots.

MIKE Of course not.

BRIAN I mean, if he had a new single out or something . . .

MIKE He has!

BRIAN No! It's a bit of an ask, but do you think you can fly it?

MIKE Yeah, all right. Leave it with me.

Mike walks over to Shirl as the floor manager counts down from five.

MIKE Joining us now on Frontline, a man who's gone from living in the seventies to swinging a hammer in the nineties – Skyhooks lead singer, Shirley Strachan. And Shirl, tell us about the new single . . .

SCENE 22

THE PRODUCTION OFFICE

Mike enters, singing 'Women in Uniform'.

MIKE Hi, Dom.

DOMENICA *(subdued)* Mike.

MIKE What's up, Dom? *(really worried)* We haven't been axed? *(Domenica shakes her head 'no')* Oh my God. Me?

DOMENICA Our priest just committed suicide.

MIKE Thank God! *(realising what he has just heard)* What?

Mike goes into Brian's office, where Brian, Brooke Emma and Kate sit in silence.

MIKE Brian, I just heard. I gotta say I felt uncomfortable about this story all along.

BRIAN Mike . . .

MIKE So it was Brooke's story that caused it?

BROOKE If you ask me, it proves he was guilty.

EMMA What?

BROOKE Why else would you . . . (commit suicide)?

BRIAN Whatever, we do a follow-up tonight. Get her in for a pre-record.

EMMA Brian, It's 5.15 . . .

BRIAN Bugger it. Live to air. 'The victim left behind'. Kate, get the woman on. *(Kate looks blank)* Kate?

BROOKE *(getting up)* I'll do it.

SCENE 23

THE FRONTLINE STUDIO

Mike is being made up at his desk. Dominique sits in the guest's chair. There are last-minute preparations.

MIKE Certainly glad you could make it with such short notice.

DOMINIQUE *(smiling nervously)* My therapist said it would be a good idea. The more I talk about these incidents the more I neutralise the effects.

MIKE Right.

FLOOR MANAGER Five to go. Four, three, two . . .

MIKE Good evening, I'm Mike Moore. Welcome to Frontline.

The opening titles run.

MIKE Last night on the show we brought you the story of Dominique Prendergast, a woman who fifteen years ago was sexually abused by her parish priest. Well, this afternoon the man responsible for destroying Dominique's life, Father Michael Croft, committed suicide. Was it guilt, or a final plea for forgiveness? We'll never know, but it's cold comfort for the victim he's left behind. *(cut to wide shot)* Dominique, thanks for joining us.

DOMINIQUE Thank you.

MIKE Are you saddened to hear of Father Croft's death?

DOMINIQUE Yes, but I'll never forgive him for what he's done.

MIKE Fifteen years is a long time. You still remember the incident clearly?

DOMINIQUE I remember them all.

MIKE How do you mean 'them all'? You were sexually assaulted on more than one occasion?

Dominique nods 'yes'.

MIKE By Father Croft?

DOMINIQUE Not just him. I was raped by aliens. They impregnated me.

We hastily cut to a single shot of Mike.

MIKE We'll leave that interview there.

DOMINIQUE *(loudly, off screen)* No-one believes me, but it's true.

MIKE *(on screen)* And coming up after the break, Shirley Strachan talks about Skyhooks' latest single.

We cut to wide shot of the studio as they go to a break. Mike collapses on his desk.

DOMINIQUE I had Shirl's baby, too.

Bruno Lawrence

Most of us at Frontline had only known Bruno Lawrence for a year before he died, so we can't offer many insights into his early career. When we came to know him he'd achieved something of a rare balance. Bruno pursued his twin loves of acting and music, while spending the remaining time in an isolated town on New Zealand's North Island with his wife, Veronica, five children and an equal number of grandchildren.

We saw him as the product of all his work and struggles, possessing a warmth that was almost spiritual. It doesn't suit Bruno to list his films and miniseries coldly as a measure of his worth. To be sure, it is an impressive list: *Spotswood*, *Rikki & Pete*, *Smash Palace* and *The Delinquents*, to name four of twenty-five. His musical talent is usually mentioned as a footnote, but this was probably Bruno's first love and many would argue his greatest skill. An original member of Max Merritt and the Meteors, he played in bands throughout his acting life.

While Bruno was a legend in his native New Zealand, he had more of a cult following here, with a band of devotees that would mention his name in the same manner as a secret holiday destination. That band included many who championed his cause, such as directors Mark Joffe and Geoff Murphy, and musical historian Glenn A. Baker.

We were lucky to have one of that band in our group. In the midst of casting Frontline, Santo Cilauro said he'd love to have Bruno Lawrence play the executive producer. I can't remember what moved into the Frontline offices first: Bruno, his golf clubs or his drum kit. I'm pretty sure it was the drum kit.

Everyone loved Bruno and for good reason. Warm, generous and easygoing, he couldn't have been more supportive of the project or more complimentary of the scripts. His weekly ritual of losing his glasses before read-through, then squinting and struggling over the thirty pages like a five-year-old reading Dr Seuss, was followed next day by the most brilliant performances you would ever see.

It would be misleading to imply Bruno spent inordinate amounts of time in the angst-ridden

searches for elusive performance dimensions. He was a relaxed actor who knew great performances come from the souls of deeply emotional people.

We all miss him terribly. I can only guess what it is like for those who have known and loved him longer.

After the final day of Frontline, we went to the Nightcat for drinks. Towards the evening's end I said: 'Frontline was a fun experience, wasn't it?' It was unintentionally glib. Bruno leant across the table, gave me a warm smile and said: 'Mate, it was a lot more than that. It was really special.' I suspect he'd made a lot of projects special over the years.

And there he was in summary, sitting in a jazz club, having spent that day acting and planning golf for the next, with one arm around Veronica and the other tapping in time and being warm and generous to people he'd only recently met. As the jazz singer reeled off another vocal riff, Bruno yelled to all around in typically generous delight: 'Isn't she fantastic!' Yes, Bruno, and so were you.

Rob Sitch, on behalf of the Frontline team

Lawrie Zion interviews Mike Moore

On the eve of Frontline's new series, I interviewed the host of the show, Mike Moore, in his office at studio headquarters.

LZ: How do you feel about Frontline this year?

MM: I'm glad Peter Luck filled in for me over the Frontline summer edition but I'm keen to start back. What I'm proudest of is that last year we never dropped our standards, although others did, and we won't this year. We realise of course that we made mistakes last year: our set wasn't blue enough; my profile wasn't high enough.

LZ: With Stan out of the way, how do you feel?

MM: With Mercer in Sydney and Singer in Melbourne there's a bevy of new players and they're all moving targets – but I don't look over my shoulder.

LZ: How do you feel about the way the media has covered the Hugh Grant incident?

MM: He's a public figure. The allegations have been made by the police – we're only reporting it. Does that make any sense? Poor bloke. I interviewed him once you know, while he was filming *Sirens*.

LZ: Are there any other issues you'd like to see Frontline covering?

MM: I'd like to get to the bottom of this whole current account business, because quite frankly it doesn't make sense to a lot of Australians. It does to me of course, I mean I understand fully, in the position I'm in, sitting behind the desk, seeing the world through the teleprompter and the autocue machine.

LZ: Would you like to do more stories in the field this year?

MM: I started life as a reporter, but every time I go and do a field story, Stuart Littlemore thinks it's 'attack Mike Moore week' – and he thinks that just because he's accurate he can say whatever he wants.

LZ: Does anything ever get you down about your own life?

MM: I can't say, because a current affairs host isn't meant to talk about things like that. I like people to guess what's in my head – and as my old EP used to say, 'Mike, I bet nobody ever could.'

LZ: So how do you feel about Frontline's former Executive Producer?

MM: I liked Brian, but I found I played him like a harp at the annual SAPS convention – I could manipulate him, and I don't think that's good for the show. We need someone strong. Don't get me wrong – Brian and I were friends. We could look each other in the eye and talk openly, and that's why I can be frank now.

LZ: What happened to him?

MM: Well, I only got the official line – that he's gone on a holiday due to stress – but I'm pretty sure he got sacked.

LZ: What do you think of Brian's replacement, Sam Murphy?

MM: Sam has a very impressive track record. He was one of the real big-hitters at Channel Nine and we enticed him across. When it came to deciding who should get the job, they obviously respect my opinion – in fact so much that they didn't ask me for it.

LZ: So will Frontline change as a show in 1995?

MM: I think that they want to utilise my skills more. I'm also having a lot more holidays this year. My pet project is getting up a series of my interviews.

LZ: Who have been your favourite interviewees?

MM: Elle Macpherson – she's charming. Paul Keating – well, he would be one of my favourites if I'd interviewed him. We're obviously too tough for him.

Lawrie Zion interviews Brooke Vandenberg

I interview Brooke Vandenberg, at her insistence, in the Frontline boardroom, and she begins by asking me how long I'll need to speak with her because she has to go soon, before correcting herself (for the one and only time) with the line 'Actually, no, you're a journalist.'

I then tell her I've just been on the phone to Harry M. Miller, who has confessed that he would rather manage her career than Mike Moore's, and ask her how she feels about it.

BV: I believe I'm a far more viable and marketable product than Mike Moore – I see my role expanding beyond current affairs in Australia. With all his talk about Jana Wendt going to '60 Minutes' in America, I think Harry M. Miller should get in quick – because I've already had preliminary discussions with the network. They've seen tapes of mine, and I think they're looking for someone a bit younger than Jana. Also Jana's a bit private and guarded, whereas I'm prepared to be as open as necessary.

LZ: So who do you admire?

BV: Margaret Thatcher and Princess Diana.

LZ: Do you think there's still a lot of sexism in the industry?

BV: Yes, I'm not stupid. I realise I've only got about ten years left in this business.

LZ: What would you do then?

At this point Frontline's art director, Carrie Kennedy (sister of Jane), walks into the room, which she is setting up for an early morning shoot. Brooke quickly becomes distracted and irritable at the intrusion, and apologises to me about the production girl's behaviour: 'Just an "Excuse me, Brooke" would have been polite.' She then answers the question.

BV: My life will not be in this country then. I also think that there's not enough money to be made in Australia – someone of my profile should be on millions and I'm not. Look at Katie Couric. She'd be on millions.

LZ: Who would you like to interview this year?

BV: Bill Clinton. In fact our Washington bureau is working on it. He's most interested in Australian women, and in fact Australia as a country. I've sent tapes over to him, and I'm pretty confident of getting an interview. I'd also like to get Hugh Grant, especially because I totally sympathise with him. As for that dreadful Liz girl, what's she got to complain about? She still has that six-million-dollar Estée Lauder contract. I hear she's a bit tarty anyway.

LZ: Where would you interview Hugh Grant?

BV: I get so sad for journalists like you who want twee answers like 'in a white BMW'. I'd just take him somewhere like Lorne where he could relax over a weekend – I wouldn't rush into the interview. And you know what? I wouldn't even dwell on that nasty incident. I'd concentrate on the whole man and try to find out what makes him tick.

LZ: Frontline's being promoted as 'One Big Family' this year – how do you feel about that?

BV: Look, we do these network promos every year, and every year it's a different theme – I didn't even know what the theme was until you reminded me. I guess I'm happy with it as long as I don't have to shake hands with that weatherman.

LZ: There have been rumours of some staffing changes looming at Frontline. Are you worried?

BV: No, as long as I can be on camera, I don't care what happens.

LZ: If you weren't a reporter what would you do?

BV: I'd be an actress, playing roles like Meg Ryan's in *Sleepless in Seattle* or Sandra Bullock's in *Speed*. But I'm not prepared to do things like train in one of those amateur theatre groups just so I can get a start in that profession.

LZ: Is it true you once applied for a cadetship with Triple J's current affairs team?

BV: No, I don't like Triple J – I like those 70s and 80s stations like TT FM which play songs I can sing along to. I'm actually a very good singer.

Episode 1
One Big Family

Day ❶

SCENE I

THE PRODUCTION OFFICE

Gloomy atmosphere. Marty is reading a newspaper.

MARTY Jesus. It's even in the financial section. Anyone see the financial section?

Everyone looks up.

MARTY *(reads)* 'Growing Concern over Network's Plight'.

BROOKE Do we get a mention?

MARTY 'Amongst the programs rumoured to be under scrutiny are the teen soapie "Sunshine Cove", the infotainment show "You and Your Family" and the ailing current affairs program "Frontline".'

General annoyance from office.

MIKE 'Ailing' – that's a bit rich.

BROOKE How long's he been up there?

EMMA Two hours.

STU Could be a good sign. (I mean), if they were going to sack him they'd do it pretty quick.

KATE I reckon if they sack Brian we should all resign! What do you reckon?

There is little positive reaction to this suggestion.

EMMA Let's just see what happens first.

MARTY *(to Shelley)* Did you get the personal stuff off his computer?

Shelley waves a floppy disk. The phone rings.

DOMENICA Hello, Frontline – One Big Family.

BROOKE That is driving me insane.

EMMA You should see the promo they've got planned.

BROOKE *(incredulous)* One Big Family?

MIKE *(excited)* I think it sounds terrific. When do we shoot it?

MARTY When we know who's still in the family.

MIKE Come on, Marty. You're such a pessimist.

Caville enters with two security guards.

DOMENICA Morning, Mr Caville.

CAVILLE Pam.

DOMENICA Dom.

CAVILLE *(failing to notice correction)* I come bearing glad tidings. No doubt you've been hearing all sorts of rumours regarding Frontline over the past few months. Well, I'm pleased to announce that Frontline will be continuing *(cheering from staff)* with this network's complete support. Obviously we've had to make some adjustments.

MARTY Brian?

CAVILLE He was one of the adjustments. *(silence from staff)* He says to say goodbye.

Caville points the two guards in the direction of Brian's office. They go in and start packing up gear. The phone rings.

DOMENICA Hello, Frontline – One Big Family.

CAVILLE We both felt the sooner this matter was resolved the better for all concerned.

The security guards emerge from Brian's office carrying a computer and box of files.

CAVILLE Were there any extra files belonging to that computer?

No-one responds.

CAVILLE *(to Emma)* Brian tells me you're more than capable of holding the fort down here?

Emma nods blankly.

CAVILLE *(turning to leave)* I think this is the start of an exciting new era for the network family. Some exciting changes in store. Oh, Mike – we need to talk.

MIKE *(gestures towards his own office)* Sure . . .

CAVILLE Why don't we make it upstairs?

Caville leaves, accompanied by Mike.

MARTY Shall we get Mike's files off his computer? *(everyone glares at him)* (I mean), there could be some important games there . . .

SCENE 2

CAVILLE'S OFFICE

Mike and Caville meet upstairs. Two silent colleagues sit with Caville.

CAVILLE Mike, how much influence would you say you've had over Frontline in the past two years?

MIKE Oh, phew! An enormous amount. Brian and I worked hand in hand, we were a team . . .

CAVILLE *(disappointed)* Is that right?

MIKE *(sensing he's said the wrong thing)* But we were separate. When I said 'enormous', (I meant) enormous in the sense I put in a big effort, he put in a big effort, but it was a separate effort.

CAVILLE *(searches Mike's face)* And it was very much a case of Brian taking responsibility?

MIKE Yeah. And I disagreed with a lot of things he did.

CAVILLE Good. I'm glad you say that. Because we haven't been happy with the direction the show's been taking of late. But now we've fixed that situation and we want you to know you have this network's 100 per cent support.

MIKE Thanks, Mr Caville.

CAVILLE *(indicating the meeting is over)* So carry on with the good work.

He points to the door. Mike gets up and exits. After he has gone Caville turns to one of his colleagues.

CAVILLE And Neil Mercer said no?

COLLEAGUE Everyone on the list said no.

SCENE 3

THE PRODUCTION OFFICE

SHELLEY I'm really going to miss him.

KATE We all will. I know, why don't we organise a dinner? To really say goodbye properly. *(general enthusiasm from office)* What about Wednesday?

BROOKE *(pause)* Wednesday's not so good for me.

MARTY For me either.

KATE Thursday?

MARTY Actually, most of this week is bad.

BROOKE Does it have to be dinner? What about drinks?

There is more enthusiasm for this proposal. Emma emerges from Brian's office with a folder.

EMMA Marty, any word on Nicholas Martin?

MARTY Foreign Affairs say they still haven't found a body. I've hassled his family, hassled his mates, no-one's talking.

EMMA Well, keep . . .

MARTY Hassling.

Emma heads towards the whiteboard.

EMMA Righto, what have we got?

Mike realises a meeting is about to start. He cuts Emma off on the way to the board, clapping his hands.

MIKE We starting? OK, troops, listen up. You're probably wondering what went on in my meeting with Caville. *(general 'no' from staff)* Ha ha. Come on, I just said we were 100 per cent behind Brian and quite frankly we're disappointed, but anyway the show must go on. Now, we've got . . . um . . . *(he looks blankly at the board)* I'll let Emma handle the nuts and bolts.

EMMA Thanks, Mike. Now first up . . .

BROOKE Hang on, (let me get this right). You're executive producer now, are you?

EMMA *(stops to think)* Well, for the time being, Brooke, maybe I am.

BROOKE I see.

EMMA *(to Kate)* How are we going with our exorcist?

KATE Going well.

EMMA Have you spoken to her?

KATE Not to Mrs Loop de Loop personally, but I've got onto a sister. Could be a contact.

EMMA *(slightly bossy)* We need an interview with her. By tomorrow.

KATE *(taken aback)* All right . . .

EMMA Brooke, you got an interview lined up?

BROOKE You tell me – you're the executive producer.

EMMA (I see.) *(checking notes)* I've got Gareth Evans or Russell Crowe.

BROOKE I'll take Evans.

EMMA Now, our dodgy lawyer . . .

MARTY In court this afternoon. We'll be there.

STU Along with every other news crew in town.

EMMA I was looking through the legal notices this morning. Seems before Mr Scarletti hits court he's having a 'private' meeting with his creditors. *(passing paper)* Here's the address.

MARTY Very nice. Stu, Jase – let's go.

STU Let's get an apple pie on the way. Jase – you feel like an apple pie? *(the boys leave)*

EMMA OK, let's get going.

Emma heads back towards Brian's office. Mike realises the meeting is over.

MIKE OK, I think we've covered everything. Just a reminder, people: any problems you got, my door is always open.

Everyone is dispersing during this speech, going about their business.

MIKE So if you've got a query, or any problems that may . . .

Mike realises no-one is listening.

MIKE *(to Emma, quietly)* Brian made it look a lot more difficult than it is.

SCENE 4

THE CAR PARK

Marty, Stu and Jase walk through the car park on their way to do the lawyer story.

MARTY Come on, guys. Brian was contracted for three years; he would have walked away with half a mil. I'm tellin' ya, if you gotta go, that's the way to go. Golden handshake.

STU Golden kick up the arse.

MARTY Hey, they'll treat him well.

They see a workman removing the 'Brian Thompson' sign from a car space.

STU Yeah, real well.

SCENE 5

OUTSIDE BRIAN'S OFFICE

Mike looks mischievous as he prepares to play a joke on Emma.

MIKE *(to Domenica)* I'm going to do it now. If you want to see her reaction . . . Come on, Shell. Shell?

Shelley stares angrily at her computer screen.

SHELLEY Shit!

Mike walks into Brian's office. He hands over a coffee cup to Emma, who is meeting with Jan.

MIKE Cup of coffee, Em?

Emma is about to refuse but Mike presents her with a mug with 'Who's the boss?' on it. Emma gives a polite smile. Mike exits proudly.

MIKE *(to Domenica)* Got her a beauty, eh?

DOMENICA Yeah!

MIKE How did you think it went?

DOMENICA Great – pity no-one was here.

SCENE 6

BRIAN'S OFFICE

We cut back inside Brian's office. Emma and Jan meet.

EMMA Now, what about this network promo?

JAN 'One Big Family', darling. A somewhat dysfunctional one, but that's what we're running with. I've got Brooke scheduled for this afternoon and Mike tomorrow.

EMMA I thought the concept was all our celebrities . . .

JAN We prefer to call them 'on-air personalities', dear.

EMMA I thought we were going to have them shaking hands with each other. Don't they need to be in the same studio?

JAN *(looking suitably askance)* Darling, we're shooting in a way that no-one need be within a five-kilometre radius of each other.

EMMA Why?

JAN Emma, darling, this is television: everybody hates or mistrusts everybody else. That's why we spend so much time promoting how well we all get on. 'One Big Family'.

EMMA So . . . ?

JAN We're shooting the entire promo in bits, then patching it together later. That way everyone's happy.

Brooke bursts in without knocking. She holds a piece of paper.

BROOKE Jan, it says here I'm shaking hands with the weatherman.

JAN *(trying not to get angry)* Darling, nobody is shaking hands with anybody. It'll just *appear* that way.

BROOKE Good. 'Cause I don't want to touch him.

Brooke exits. Mike hovers outside.

MIKE *(to Brooke)* Did you see the mug I gave her? *(Brooke looks uninterested)* Go back in.

Brooke walks off.

SCENE 7

AN OFFICE BLOCK

Marty, Stu and Jase wait outside an office block. Marty smokes.

MARTY So who's gonna take over?

STU Who'd want the job? All that pressure.

MARTY All that money. Car. House payments. Travel.

STU And if the show doesn't rate? *(makes a throat-cutting gesture)*

Marty takes a drag on his cigarette.

STU Hey, I could sue you for passive smoking, you know.

MARTY Not if . . .

A lawyer emerges from the building.

STU Action.

As Stu and Jase grab their camera gear the lawyer spots them and bolts off up the street.

MARTY Let's go.

The three boys give chase but Marty quickly falls behind and becomes breathless. He tries shouting his questions.

MARTY Mr Scarletti! We just want to ask you a few questions about your client's trust fund. Mr Scarl . . .

Marty gets completely out of breath as Stu and Jase move on ahead of him. They stop and look back as Marty wheezes hopelessly. The lawyer escapes.

SCENE 8

GEOFF'S OFFICE

GEOFF So they sacked him?

MIKE Just like that. Whole office is pretty shook up. I'm doing my best to keep morale up.

GEOFF You're in charge?

MIKE No, well . . . I can tell you.

GEOFF You want me to keep this a secret?

MIKE Not really.

GEOFF I can.

MIKE No, I mean . . . Caville took me aside – upstairs – and, you know . . . asked me to help out. I'm doing the best I can. Emma's trying, but she's out of her depth. I feel the whole office is resting on me.

GEOFF You must be flat out.

MIKE You're telling me.

GEOFF Another coffee?

MIKE Sure.

GEOFF So the network promo's looking good.

MIKE Yeah, I got a memo from Jan about it. We're all shaking hands, apparently.

GEOFF Isn't that great? Sort of sums up the station's 'family' feel. Guess who I get to shake hands with?

MIKE Who?

GEOFF Brooke.

MIKE Phew! Good luck to you. Though . . . hang on, what are you doing here?

GEOFF What do you . . . ?

MIKE Brooke's down in the studio now. I just saw her. She's shooting her bit of the promo.

GEOFF But how can she if she's supposed to be shaking hands with me?

Mike gives a 'Who knows?' shrug.

SCENE 9

THE FRONTLINE STUDIO

Brooke is preparing to shoot the promo. Jan and the floor manager supervise. A make-up assistant is touching up Brooke's lips.

FLOOR MANAGER OK, I'll be the weatherman's hand.

JAN So Brooke, you turn from your right where the footy panel people will give you a high-five, turn and pass it on to . . .

BROOKE The weatherman! I thought we'd spoken about this.

JAN Darling, I'm running out of options. I've put you right up the front of the promo.

BROOKE So?

JAN So even when they screen the ten-second version you'll still be there . . .

BROOKE Shaking hands with a weatherman.

JAN *(losing patience)* Brooke, it's him or Wacko the Chook.

BROOKE I'll take the weatherman.

JAN All right, roll tape!

We hear audio roll-in of promo. Brooke sways to the music, receiving a handshake from her right and then reaching out to her left where she high-fives the floor manager.

JAN And cut. Darling, you'll have to smile.

BROOKE I was.

SCENE 10

BRIAN'S OFFICE

EMMA *(into the phone)* Right, just checking that the promos are at 3.15 and 3.45. Thanks, Gerry.

Emma hangs up. Kate enters with a piece of paper.

KATE Having a few problems getting in touch with our exorcist lady. She's disappeared all of a sudden. And now her sister's not talking.

EMMA Think someone else is sniffing around?

KATE Could be.

EMMA She still a registered nurse?

KATE Dunno. Think so.

EMMA Nurses' Federation will have a mailing address. Try them.

KATE Good one. *(she goes to walk out, then stops)* You're enjoying this.

EMMA What?

KATE You know. Being in charge.

EMMA *(defensive)* Kate! I . . .

KATE It's OK – it's good. You're doing well.

EMMA Do you think? I just feel bad about Brian and . . .

KATE Emma – relax.

EMMA Thanks, Kate.

As Kate exits, Shelley enters.

EMMA What's up, Shell?

SHELLEY I'm a little upset.

EMMA Shelley, this has come as a shock to us all. But Brian will be all right. He's . . .

SHELLEY *(sitting)* It's not about Brian. I was making a copy of that disk for him like you asked and . . . I get paid less than Kate.

EMMA What?

SHELLEY I'm her senior, Emma. I was Brian's personal secretary . . .

Domenica appears at the door.

DOMENICA Excuse me, Emma. Mr Caville wants to see you upstairs immediately.

Emma looks taken aback. She jumps up and starts hurrying out.

EMMA Look, we'll talk about this later, Shelley. In the meantime, I want that disk. That's going to cause trouble. Get it to me.

SCENE 11

CAVILLE'S OFFICE

Emma is seated awkwardly on a low comfy chair, balancing cup and saucer. Caville and Ed hover over her.

CAVILLE So how's it going downstairs?

EMMA Fine. Tonight's show is looking good, and we've got plenty for . . .

CAVILLE Of course, Emma, dear, no ship can carry on without a captain.

EMMA We're actually doing quite well . . .

CAVILLE Good that you are. And we've got some more good news. 'Sunday Forum' doesn't return for another week, so Ed here has kindly agreed to step in and keep an eye on things at Frontline until we find a permanent replacement.

EMMA As . . . ?

CAVILLE EP.

EMMA Executive producer?

CAVILLE Isn't that what it normally stands for, Ed?

ED I have heard it can also mean 'Enormous Penis'.

Ed and Caville share a blokey laugh. Emma tries to fake a smile.

EMMA Oh.

ED *(hand on Emma's knee)* Don't worry. I won't work you too hard.

SCENE 12

BRIAN'S OFFICE

Emma is packing up her stuff from Brian's desk. Mike watches her.

MIKE Come on Em, upstairs know what they're doing. *(Emma is silent)* Ed Forbes is a pretty smart operator; been EP of 'Sunday Forum' for years.

EMMA *(bitterly)* 'Sunday Forum' is a two-hour unwatched wank with a bit of classical music tacked on the end to make it look highbrow.

MIKE You know, you're sounding exactly like Brian.

EMMA Well, someone has to.

MIKE Hey. A little less sour grapes and you might just learn something from Ed. To me it represents opportunity.

EMMA Yes, Mike.

MIKE Hey! (This'll cheer you up.) Ed told me this. What does EP stand for?

EMMA I don't know, Mike.

MIKE Well, what does it usually stand for?

Emma refuses to give him the pleasure of an answer.

MIKE *(putting words into her mouth)* Not 'Executive Producer' – 'Extra-long Penis'. No, that's ELP. 'Extra Penis'.

Emma rolls her eyes and leaves Brian's office as Mike continues to fumble with his joke. Eventually he appears at the open door and calls, a little too exuberantly . . .

MIKE 'Enormous Penis'!

MARTY *(at his desk)* Yep, you are.

Day ❷

SCENE 13

THE PRODUCTION OFFICE

Ed emerges from Brian's office and sits at the table with Brooke, Kate, Emma and Mike, who are gathered for a production meeting. Shelley serves Ed a coffee.

ED Thanks, Shirley.

SHELLEY Shelley.

Ed ignores this correction. He holds a copy of the Age. His manner is a little slower than the Frontline team are used to: they almost lean forward as he speaks, willing him to speed up. Emma taps a pen impatiently.

ED All set? Welcome. Now I've looked at the rundowns; got a couple of story ideas.

Everyone looks interested.

ED There's this Russian conductor, Uri Isanisovich. He's in town; might make a good profile piece. That's on page fourteen.

Everyone nods politely.

ED And the . . . er . . . Government plans to privatise the electricity supply; lot of questions need to be asked there. I was thinking an investigative piece, perhaps over several nights. That's on page twenty.

More polite silence.

EMMA Um, there's a couple of things we're working on.

ED Shoot.

EMMA Kate's contacted a woman accused of being an exorcist.

ED Great. Great. Get her in.

EMMA And we're still waiting for word on Nicholas Martin.

ED Whoa, hold your horses. Nicholas Martin?

EMMA The kid missing in Cambodia. Page one.

ED Oh yes, strong story – see what you can get. Well, looks like we've got the ball rolling here. *(getting up)* Anything else?

There is no response. The meeting breaks up. Ed heads towards his office.

ED Shirley, could you get me some info on any good gyms round here? Price, terms – you can fill in the blanks.

Kate has screwed up a piece of paper and throws it in Shelley's bin. Shelley picks up the bin.

SHELLEY *(to Kate)* Would you mind putting that in your own bin?

KATE *(taken aback)* What?

DOMENICA *(answering the phone)* Hello, Frontline – One Big Family . . . *(calls to Emma)* It's Marty. He's got a problem in editing.

ED Oops, travelling. *(he leaves, obviously bound for the edit suite)*

DOMENICA *(to Emma)* I think Marty wanted you.

Ed reappears.

ED *(to Domenica)* Which floor is editing on?

DOMENICA Two.

ED Thanks, Dawn. *(he leaves)*

DOMENICA Dom.

EMMA *(under her breath, following Ed)* Dickhead.

DOMENICA *(picks up phone)* One Big Family . . .

SCENE 14

THE EDIT SUITE

Marty, Hugh, Ed, Stu and Jase view footage of the lawyer chase. Emma watches from the back. We see the lawyer running but barely hear Marty's questions.

STU It's unusable. You're miles away – can't even hear you.

MARTY Well, you guys moved like Carl Lewis.

STU Right, so we should have hung back with you, and got shots of a reporter with a fag in his mouth.

HUGH *(drawing on fag)* Gotta get fitter, mate. *(he breaks into an asthmatic wheeze)*

ED I don't think there's much we can do. Have to ditch it.

EMMA I've got an idea. We've got pictures; don't have audio. Let's go record some audio.

SCENE 15

THE PRODUCTION OFFICE

Marty runs around the desk as Jase records his questions.

MARTY *(slightly breathless)* Mr Scarletti! If we could just have a few words with you. It's no use trying to run, Mr Scarletti. Why won't you speak to us? *(he stops, panting)* How was that?

Stu checks with Jase.

STU Great. Now let's go for a take.

Marty fails to see the humour.

SCENE 16

THE KITCHEN

Brooke and Emma are making a coffee.

BROOKE Emma, I know he's a dead weight, but don't let it get you down.

EMMA I care about the show.

BROOKE Which is another thing – why are you busting your arse?

EMMA I told you. I care about the show.

BROOKE And?

EMMA And what?

BROOKE And in the back of your mind you think that when Ed leaves you're going to take over the job.

Emma offers a look of 'Don't be ridiculous' and goes to exit with her coffee.

BROOKE *(stopping her)* I'm telling you this for your own good. There is no way a woman, let alone a twenty-five-year-old one, is going to run a national current affairs program.

EMMA The people upstairs only care about ratings. If I can deliver then why shouldn't I run this show?

BROOKE *(smugly)* So you have been thinking about it.

Emma leaves. This time Brooke does not try to stop her. Ed enters.

ED Ah, women's talk. To be a fly on the wall . . . *(wink)* So, how's the promo coming along?

BROOKE Good.

ED You look great on camera.

BROOKE Thank you.

ED You really should be hosting this show.

BROOKE Thank you. I think Mike's pretty entrenched here. (Isn't he?)

ED Dunno. Ever feel like jumping this ship and coming across to 'Sunday Forum' – give me a ring.

BROOKE Sure.

ED In the meantime, I've got a few ideas I wouldn't mind running by you.

BROOKE OK.

ED How does tonight sound?

BROOKE Good.

ED Good.

BROOKE Great.

ED Great.

Ed lingers a little too long a little too close. Brooke doesn't fight it.

SCENE 17

THE FRONTLINE STUDIO

Mike is at the Frontline desk. We see Marty's story involving the chase going to air.

MARTY *(voice only)* Mr Scarletti! If we could just have a few words with you. It's no use trying to run, Mr Scarletti.

Marty delivers a final out-of-breath speech to camera.

MARTY *(on screen)* Well, he may have just given us the slip, but this slippery solicitor won't escape his creditors quite as easily. Martin di Stasio – Frontline.

Cut back to Mike.

MIKE Mmm, a lot of people with a lot of questions. Well, that's about it for tonight. But to take us out, Frontline funnyman Elliot Rhodes, with a rather cheeky look at the French Government.

Cut to Elliot in beret and striped shirt.

ELLIOT The French, they want to test a bomb
Why don't they do it at the Sorbonne?
Jacques Chirac wants Mururoa
Turn it in to Krakatoa . . .

Elliot's audio continues over the next scene.

ELLIOT *(audio only)* The French, they treat us all like dogs
That's what you get from eating frogs
But why must we put up with this?
'Oui oui' means they are full of piss

SCENE 18

THE CONTROL ROOM

Ed and Emma watch Elliot. The phone rings. Emma grabs it.

EMMA Hello? Mr Caville. It's Emma. Ward. Yeah, he's here – I can pass on a message . . .

Emma passes the phone over to Ed.

ED Bob. Thanks, mate. Yeah, I'll pass that on. Cheers. *(he hangs up)* Well, time to hit the road.

EMMA What did Mr Caville want?

ED Oh, he said he was very happy with the show, and well done . . . to everyone.

Emma looks pained.

SCENE 19

EMMA'S HOUSE

Emma is at home, listening to the radio. We hear a news theme.

NEWSREADER And heading our bulletin tonight, unconfirmed reports from the capital of Cambodia, Phnom Penh, suggest kidnapped Australian tourist Nicholas Martin has been found dead.

As the report continues, Emma reaches for the phone.

NEWSREADER The body of Mr Martin, twenty-seven, is believed to have been discovered in thick jungle . . . *(Emma turns down the volume)*

EMMA Marty? It's Em. The kid in Cambodia's been found dead. Yeah. You got his mother's address? I'll have Stu and Jase meet you there at dawn. OK, bye.

Emma hangs up and dials again. We hear an answering machine.

ED *(voice only)* Hi, I can't come to the phone right now (and the phone sure can't come to me), but if you want to you can leave a message after the beep.

Emma waits for the beep.

EMMA Hi Ed, it's Emma. Could you give me a call when you get in? I'm at home.

During Emma's message we cut to Ed's answering machine with her voice coming out. In the background we see Brooke and Ed making love.

Day ❸

SCENE 20

MRS MARTIN'S HOUSE

Marty, Stu and Jase arrive at the mother's suburban home. There is a huge media contingent camped on the front lawn. One journo is even on the roof.

JOURNO ON ROOF I think she's still inside.

MARTY Shit. This is hopeless.

STU She giving any interviews?

JOURNO #1 Not yet.

JOURNO #2 Hey, she's gotta come up for air eventually.

JOURNO ON ROOF *(calls)* Mrs Martin – if you really loved your son you'd talk to us!

STU *(admiring)* You hear that?

MARTY He's good.

There is no response from within the house. Marty and the boys try and find a spot to set up but all the good vantage points are taken. We see rose bushes etc. being trampled by crews jostling for position.

STU 'Scuse me, mate.

CAMERAMAN *(protesting)* Hey, mate!

STU You gotta take up the whole front lawn?

CAMERAMAN Shoulda got here earlier.

MARTY What about over there?

STU Oh yeah, great shot of the garage.

MARTY Shit.

SCENE 21

THE PRODUCTION OFFICE

Mike is walking around with tissues in his collar.

DOMENICA It must be exciting, Mike.

MIKE What?

DOMENICA Recording the promo.

MIKE *(feigns boredom)* Oh, bit of a drag really. Still, the network wants it. Apparently I'm the first person seen.

DOMENICA So what do you do, Mike?

MIKE Well, the whole thing starts with me.

DOMENICA Wow!

MIKE And I just sort of dance to a line . . . What's the line again, Em?

EMMA What? Oh . . . *(reads)* 'From the Frontline desk each evening'.

Mike acts this out for Domenica.

MIKE From the Frontline desk each evening . . .
I feel for the people who don't have rhythm.
Actually, Em – what key's it in?

EMMA *(slightly aggro)* Mike, you're not singing. It
doesn't matter what key it's in.

MIKE All right! Geez, Em, just because the show's
not falling apart like you expected it would.

EMMA I did not expect it would.

MIKE Well, whatever. I think Ed's doing a pretty
good job.

EMMA *(angrily)* He's not the only one!

MIKE Settle down. No wonder they pick blokes to
run things.

Emma can't believe this and turns away in disgust.

DOMENICA Hello, Frontline – One Big Family.
Kate – it's Mrs Rosen's sister on the phone.

*Kate is walking past Shelley's desk and goes to grab
her phone. Shelley takes the receiver from her.*

SHELLEY Use your own phone.

KATE *(taken aback)* What is wrong with you?

MIKE Hey, hey! Shell, can we have a word?

*Mike indicates his office. Shelley follows him in. Ed
arrives, in high spirits.*

ED Morning all!

Greetings from the staff.

ED *(to Emma)* Sorry I didn't get back to you last
night – I was in pretty late.

EMMA You heard about Nicholas Martin? *(Ed
looks blank)* Cambodia.

ED Oh yeah, I had some thoughts about that last
night. Doesn't his mother live here?

EMMA Yeah.

ED You might think about sending Marty out to
her house.

EMMA Consider it done.

Ed heads towards his office.

ED Dawn, could you get me one of those yoghurt
things from the canteen with the fruit in the corner?

DOMENICA OK.

Kate hangs up her phone.

KATE Shit! We lost her.

ED Who?

KATE Mrs Rosen. Our exorcist. She was going to
come in here for an interview but . . .

EMMA 'A Current Affair'?

Kate nods.

KATE Pre-record this afternoon.

ED Geez, you gotta hand it to them – they're slick
operators.

EMMA Money?

KATE Not interested. Wants to 'meet Ray'.

Emma looks disappointed.

ED Oh well, you win some, you lose some. Oh,
Dawn – a caffelatte as well.

Ed heads into his office.

EMMA *(under her breath)* Useless. *(to Kate)* You
know people at Nine; who would have booked her
for ACA?

KATE Sandra or Maureen, I guess.

EMMA Isn't Maureen having a baby?

KATE Yeah. Well, Sandra (then).

Emma grabs the phone.

EMMA Give us Mrs Rosen's number. *(Kate hands
Emma the number and she dials)* Hello, Mrs
Rosen? It's Sandra from 'A Current Affair' here.
Sandy, that's right. Yes, we just spoke. Look, slight
change of plans: would it be all right if we came
and picked you up right away? Well, it was Ray's
suggestion. Right, what was the address again? *(she
writes the address)* OK, be there in fifteen minutes.

*Emma hangs up. Kate looks at her in stunned
admiration.*

KATE Way to go, Em.

SCENE 22

MIKE'S OFFICE

Shelley and Mike meet.

MIKE I couldn't help notice you've been a bit narky
towards Kate lately. I know she's young, goes a bit
bull-at-a-gate sometimes . . .

SHELLEY It's not that, Mike.

MIKE Well, what is it? I'm here to help.

SHELLEY It's stupid really.

MIKE No, no – come on.

SHELLEY I've discovered that Kate gets paid more than me.

Mike smiles wisely and hitches up his pants.

MIKE Ah, Shelley . . .

SHELLEY I don't want to make a big deal of it.

MIKE They say 'Money is the root of all evil'. Listen, this is television: that's just the way it works. Everyone's on different deals.

SHELLEY I know.

MIKE I mean, you'd make more than Dom . . . *(Shelley nods)* Marty'd get more than Stu. *(she nods again)* I make more than Brooke.

SHELLEY No you don't.

Mike's jaw drops.

SCENE 23

THE STUDIO GREEN ROOM

Kate escorts Mrs Rosen in.

MRS ROSEN When do I meet Ray?

KATE Um . . . this is our producer, Emma Ward.

EMMA Hello, Mrs Rosen. Thanks for coming in so early. Have you been to make-up?

Kate mimes 'Don't ask', but it is too late.

MRS ROSEN *(creepily)* Make-up is the devil's work. Satan's face was painted white to hide the darkness of his soul.

EMMA Right, no make-up. What about tea or coffee?

MRS ROSEN When do I meet Ray?

EMMA Mrs Rosen, Ray's not here right now. Mike Moore will be doing the interview.

MRS ROSEN Oh, I like him too. Where is he?

EMMA Um . . . He's in a very important meeting.

SCENE 24

THE FRONTLINE STUDIO

Mike and Jan prepare to tape the promo. Mike is distracted. The music is rolled in. Mike moves in lacklustre fashion to the line 'From the Frontline desk each evening'.

JAN Cut! This is not the Mike Moore I know. What's wrong, poppet?

MIKE Oh, don't get me started, Jan.

JAN Mike, listen to me. You are the star of this promo. The first face we see. Face of the network. Even the ten-second version – you'll be in it.

MIKE *(starts to warm to the idea)* Yeah.

JAN And it's a great line. Far better than Brooke's lines.

MIKE Lines? Brooke has more than one line?

JAN *(realising her mistake)* No, well, it's one line – it's just longer. Er . . . quicker. Roll tape!

The music is rolled in again. Mike gives another lacklustre performance. Jan looks pained.

SCENE 25

THE PRODUCTION OFFICE

On the office monitor we see a tape of the media contingent, mainly backs to camera, on the front lawn of Mrs Martin's house. There is a brief glimpse of Mrs Martin as she braves the throng to get to her car. The tape is paused.

MARTY Jesus, this is crap. *(to Stu)* You managed to shoot the arse of every news crew in the country.

STU Least I didn't get the guy on the roof. Bloody hell – what's that?

MARTY Hello – it's the guy on the roof.

EMMA What about other members of the family?

MARTY The sister's out of town. No other kids. Christ, Stu even climbed the back fence with a camera.

Stu shows his torn jeans.

BROOKE You tried phoning?

MARTY *(sarcastic)* No, Brooke, that thought didn't cross our mind. We've been on the phone since seven a.m.! She's not talking.

BROOKE Well, maybe . . .

MARTY *(snaps)* Jesus, Brooke! We've been there since dawn. I didn't see you volunteering.

BROOKE I've been flat out, Marty.

MARTY Yeah, I've heard.

BROOKE What's that supposed to mean?

MARTY Oh, nothing. You're just doing your job. Working under Ed.

Brooke chokes on her rage.

SCENE 26

THE FRONTLINE STUDIO

Mike is just winding up his interview with Mrs Rosen.

MIKE And that's when you realised your daughter was possessed by the devil?

MRS ROSEN She had to be saved. I saved her.

MIKE Mrs Rosen, thanks for your time.

The interview is wound up. Emma and Kate approach.

MIKE That was fine, Mrs Rosen

MRS ROSEN Pity Ray couldn't make it.

MIKE *(confused)* Ray who?

EMMA Thanks, Mrs Rosen. We'll get you a cab. Actually, Kate, why don't you show Mrs Rosen around the station? Perhaps introduce her to a few of the stars.

KATE Sure.

MIKE Ray – who's Ray?

Emma pushes Kate towards Mrs Rosen. They head off.

MRS ROSEN I'd like to meet someone from 'Sale of the Century'.

Kate and Mrs Rosen leave.

MIKE What's the story?

EMMA 'A Current Affair' are after her for an interview.

MIKE Well, they can rack off – we got her first.

EMMA Yeah, but I think we should keep her here for a few hours, just to be sure.

MIKE Absolutely. Don't want her being poached.

ED *(entering)* Sorry, I got held up at lunch. How's it all going then?

EMMA Fine.

ED Great. *(he turns to leave then remembers something)* Did you get onto that conductor?

EMMA *(exhausted)* Um, no.

ED Come on Em, let's keep the pace up.

SCENE 27

THE PRODUCTION OFFICE

We see vision of a promo for 'A Current Affair', with shots of Mrs Martin's house.

VOICE-OVER Tonight on 'A Current Affair' we speak exclusively with the mother of murdered backpacker Nicholas Martin.

We see a shot of a distressed Mrs Martin inside her house.

MRS MARTIN I just want to . . . I can't believe this has happened . . . *(breaks into tears)*

VOICE-OVER That's tonight, on 'A Current Affair'.

The TV is switched off. We reveal everyone watching in the general office area.

ED They've got us.

MARTY Bastards must have talked their way inside.

MIKE Can we spoil?

ED What with? Marty's footage is just useless. Nah, we gotta cop it. Lie down.

MARTY (But) this is the biggest story in weeks. We can't ignore it just 'cause every journo in town beat us to the punch.

There is a pause as everyone thinks what to do.

EMMA Hang on – I've got an idea. That's the story.

MARTY What?

EMMA That. The media. The frenzy. The feeding frenzy.

MARTY (Oh I get it.) Sharks. Preying on a poor hapless grieving mother.

BROOKE Thank God we weren't part of it.

MARTY Thank God we were there to capture it, though.

Ed and Mike look on in slight confusion, then begin to catch on.

MIKE Ed, I think we're onto something.

SCENE 28

THE FRONTLINE STUDIO

Mike is on air.

MIKE Good evening, welcome to Frontline. I'm Mike Moore.

The opening titles run.

MIKE First up, the tragic story of Nicholas Martin, the Aussie backpacker whose body was found yesterday in a Cambodian jungle. Martin di Stasio reports on a sad chapter in television journalism.

We see a picture of a backpacker, then cut to Marty seated on a desk, casual Mike Munro-style.

MARTY For the last six weeks these sickening headlines have brought home the horror of missing backpacker Nicholas Martin.

Marty's voice continues as we see a montage of newspaper headlines: 'Backpacker Missing', 'Kidnap Fears', 'Martin Alive Say Captors', 'Hostage Fear', etc.

MARTY *(voice only)* His family and friends have been subjected to constant questioning and media harassment, as they waited for news of their son. This morning, the sickening feeding frenzy came to a head, as this headline was splashed across the daily newspapers. *(we see a headline reading 'Martin Found Dead')* But little could have prepared Nicholas Martin's family for the invasion that greeted them this morning.

Roll footage of journos at house, with Jaws theme music.

MARTY The media sharks were already sharpening their knives ready to feast on a banquet of grief, licking their lips as they devoured the anguish of a lost son. Stunned, horrified, I even heard one so-called journalist resort to the line: 'Mrs Martin, if you really loved your son you'd speak to us'. *(close-up of journo on roof)* What some call journalism, we call cannibalism . . .

Marty's voice drones on but we cut away from this story to the control room.

SCENE 29

THE CONTROL ROOM

Ed and Emma watch the show.

ED This is brilliant.

EMMA I thought so.

The phone rings. Emma reaches for it but Ed grabs it first.

ED Hello? Bob! Well, we had to pull something out of the fire. Yeah. Thanks, mate. *(he hangs up)* It was a very clever twist, Emma.

EMMA Thanks. Who was that?

ED Oh, Bob Caville – just saying well done . . . to everyone.

EMMA Great.

ED You certainly made me look good this week.

EMMA I know.

ED And I'd like to return the favour. Got a little surprise for you.

EMMA *(slightly interested)* Surprise?

ED *(smiling)* I know who the new executive producer is.

EMMA (My God, it's me.) Really?

ED Now I'm not really supposed to tell you, but since it's my last day, and he starts tomorrow . . .

EMMA He . . .

During Ed's speech we stay on Emma's despair.

Day ❹

SCENE 30

THE PRODUCTION OFFICE

Emma enters. Domenica looks excited.

DOMENICA Hi, Em!

EMMA Dom.

DOMENICA Guess what?

EMMA What?

DOMENICA Ed was down here before.

EMMA And?

Domenica indicates a bunch of flowers.

DOMENICA Surprise! From Ed . . . to you.

EMMA *(disgusted)* He really is an enormous penis.

BROOKE Don't bet on it.

Jan is holding a remote control and standing beside the video.

JAN All right, quieten down.

MIKE Come on, Jan!

JAN All right. Now this is just a first cut of . . .

Her explanation is howled down with cries of 'Get on with it', etc. She hits 'Play'. We see the network promo featuring various celebrities 'swaying' in time to the music. Each high-fives the next.

SONG From the Frontline desk each evening *(Mike smiles and dances)*

To the thrill of Jackpot *(a game-show host and hostess hold up cards)*

We'll take you to all the great places *(the Vacation hostess walks by with backpack and Akubra)*

For fun we've got the lot. *(the Comedy Bunch act wacky and zany)*

When the big name stars are talkin'
You know that you'll find them talkin' here . . .
(Brooke bops and smiles)

And if the weather is dreadful *(Geoff opens his umbrella)*

We've still got room to cheer and cheer. *(the sports show panel throw a football to each other)*

One Big Family *(a cooking show host in chef's hat tosses a pancake)*

I've got my whole family with me *(kids' show hosts with sock puppets)*

One Big Family *(a Vizard-style tonight show host)*

Come on everybody and sing . . . *(a Brian Naylor-style newsreader)*

The promo would continue but for our purposes this is all we need to see/hear. Jan pauses the tape and turns expectantly.

JAN Well?

General congratulations. Mike interrupts.

MIKE It is two lines.

BROOKE What?

MIKE You've got two lines.

BROOKE Well, I've got to shake hands with the fucking weatherman.

MIKE Excuse me, his name's Geoffrey Salter, you stuck-up shit!

Brooke and Mike go at each other. Jan tries to mediate. The following series of arguments erupt more or less simultaneously.

MARTY *(sarcastic)* Hey, you move well, Brooke.

BROOKE Oh, go get another exclusive, Marty.

SHELLEY *(to Kate)* Would you mind not sitting on my desk?

KATE Get off my back, Shelley.

EMMA Would you two just grow up?

SHELLEY I am grown up – I'm just not being paid like one.

DOMENICA Em, I've got 'A Current Affair' on the line . . .

EMMA Tell 'em to . . .

Sam enters the office carrying a briefcase. He stands and watches the entire place in conflict. Emma dumps her flowers in a bin before looking up and noticing him.

EMMA Sorry, can I help you?

SAM I'm Sam Murphy. *(raising his voice)* Your new executive producer.

Everyone falls silent.

EMMA Hi. Welcome to our family.

Episode 2

Workin' Class Man

Day ❶

SCENE 1

A MEETING ROOM

We open on an image of Mike at the Frontline desk, back-announcing a story.

MIKE And the cost for this high-tech home of the future? A cool 2.5 million dollars. Martin di Stasio reporting. And that's about it for Frontline tonight. Join us tomorrow when we take a look at the hidden dangers for first-time stock market investors. See you then.

The image is paused. Widen to reveal that Mike is on a monitor in a room where a focus group is being held. Barb (the convenor) holds a clipboard.

BARB Now, just like we did with the newsreader, I want to know what you think of him. How he comes across. Who of the people here watch Frontline?

A few mumble 'me', 'sometimes', 'a little'.

BARB What do you think of Mike Moore?

A pause.

WOMAN I like him. He's nicely dressed.

BARB Do you find him believable?

MAN #1 I don't like him.

BARB Why do you say that?

MAN #1 I dunno. Not the sort of guy you'd have a drink with.

MAN #2 He's a wanker.

MAN #1 See how smug he was when he was talkin' about the stock market?

MAN #2 Who gives a shit?

MAN #1 Wanker.

WOMAN *(having been swayed)* Yeah, wanker.

General agreement.

We reveal Sam is watching the last part of this on a TV screen in his office.

SAM *(calls)* Em! Could you come in here, please?

SCENE 2

A CITY STREET

Mike is speaking on his car phone while driving to work in his Saab. We hear Domenica's voice on the other end of the phone.

DOMENICA *(voice only)* No, Mike, Sam's out of the office. Anything wrong?

MIKE *(pissed off)* Yes. The flight back from Sydney this morning – I didn't get an upgrade. No, wasn't organised. Tell him it's not for me; it just reflects badly on the show. Yeah.

Mike pulls up at a red light during this conversation. We reveal a bloke in an old car next to him staring contemptuously at Mike and his car. Mike puts up his electric window.

SCENE 3

SAM'S OFFICE

Sam and Emma meet. Sam studies some papers.

SAM Let me read you a few random comments from the focus group. 'Wanker' came up quite a bit. 'Up himself'. 'Poncy'.

EMMA Were there any negatives?

SAM *(ignores joke)* They hated him. Emma, do you know what an AB audience is?

EMMA Isn't it, like, rich people?

SAM *(nods)* Upper end of the socioeconomic scale – brains and money. You know what DE's are?

EMMA The other end of the scale?

SAM Uh-huh. Plumbers. Blue collar. *(referring to figures)* We're starting to alienate our D's and E's.

EMMA Maybe that's a good thing. Means we're getting a better class of viewer.

SAM *(shakes his head)* Uh-uh, bad thing. D's and E's are our lifeblood. Why would anyone with brains or money be sitting round a telly at 6.30 each night?

EMMA So we've got to start appealing more to a blue-collar audience?

SAM *(nods)* 'A Current Affair' do it.

EMMA How?

SAM Two things. Right sort of stories: the Aussie battler, the pensioner who can't pay his gas bill. And they make sure it's hosted by a regular bloke.

EMMA Ray Martin's not a 'regular bloke'. He must be on a million a year. *(Sam gives a 'higher' signal)* Two million? *(Sam gives another 'higher' signal)* Whatever, he's hardly a regular bloke.

SAM As long as he says 'mate' and 'fair dinkum' a couple of times each night, he's a regular bloke.

EMMA So we've gotta take Mike and the show down-market?

SAM (No), just a bit of a tweak.

EMMA Not sure whether he'll like it.

SAM Ah, come on. Mike'd like to see himself as a man of the people.

SCENE 4

THE PRODUCTION OFFICE

Mike enters, talking to Domenica on his mobile. Halfway through his first sentence he hangs up and seamlessly continues the conversation 'live'.

MIKE No, it wasn't just the upgrade; it was the luggage too. No priority. I was waiting around an airport terminal for half an hour. That's why I'm late.

DOMENICA Late for what?

MIKE Well, just late.

DOMENICA For what?

Mike shrugs. Sam pokes his head out of his office.

SAM Mike – got a moment?

MIKE *(to Domenica)* See? For a meeting with Sam.

SCENE 5

SAM'S OFFICE

Mike meets with Sam. Emma is there.

SAM Been doing some thinking about the show. Looking at our audience breakdowns.

MIKE Uh-huh. Oh, when are we doing those focus groups?

SAM I'll let you know. Mike, who would you say is our typical audience?

MIKE *(thinks)* Twenty-five to forty, tertiary-educated, professionals . . .

SAM Take a look at these.

Sam hands Mike a page. He looks at it, obviously struggling to understand it.

MIKE Phew. Makes for some interesting reading.

SAM You understand the categories?

MIKE Just run them by me one more time.

SAM You know television audiences are divided into socioeconomic groups?

MIKE Uh-huh, of course.

SAM AB are the wealthy, educated viewers, C and D in the middle.

EMMA And the DE's . . .

MIKE Emma, I do understand this was just a refresher. So we've got a lot of these D's and E's?

SAM Huge amount.

MIKE Phew, that's a worry. Better get rid of them.

There is a fleeting look of fear from Sam.

SAM Yeah, we could. But what I'd really like to do is make the intelligent stories you're doing here on Frontline more 'accessible' to these viewers. I feel bad about excluding them.

MIKE Me too, but what can you do with these dodos?

SAM Look, I hear what you're saying. You're worried about compromising the intellectual integrity of the show.

MIKE Our AB's would never forgive us.

SAM Guess there's really not much we can do about it.

MIKE *(off-hand)* Short of tossing in a few stories that might appeal to the masses.

SAM *(feigns stunned amazement)* Emma, how many hours have we been in here trying to solve this problem?

EMMA Hours.

SAM And Mike Moore walks straight in off a plane . . .

MIKE Did Dom tell you? I was in economy.

SAM . . . and hits the nail on the head. 'Toss in a few stories' – write that exact phrase down, Em. *(to Mike)* You're saying we do a subtle repositioning. We skew the show towards the D's and E's.

MIKE Skew. Yeah. Write that down too, Em.

EMMA How do you spell it?

SCENE 6

THE CAR PARK

Marty is speaking on his mobile phone. He is pacing and obviously not happy. He holds a rolled-up magazine.

MARTY For Chrissakes, Dale, it's even in the *BRW*! We've got $250,000 tied up in this scheme and you're telling me the eggs aren't gonna hatch. What do we tell the investors? Of course I'm pissing myself – I could lose the house. Well, how long till we know? Shit. All right. I'm late, gotta go.

Marty hangs up and kicks Mike's car tyre in frustration. The alarm goes off.

MARTY Shit!

SCENE 7

THE PRODUCTION OFFICE

The staff are at a production meeting.

SAM So Mike's idea is we actively pursue the blue-collar demographic.

Mike looks chuffed.

BROOKE We're going down-market.

MIKE No! We're going to . . . What was the word I used, Sam?

SAM Skew.

MIKE Skew the show towards the E's and F's. Lower end of the alphabet.

SAM What Mike's suggested is a subtle repositioning.

MIKE *(nods)* Very subtle.

KATE How do we do that?

SAM You wanna DE audience? You appeal to their prejudices. Tell 'em things they want to hear. Aborigines are no-good drunks.

EMMA *(laughing)* Sam!

SAM *(unabashed)* Criminals are getting far too lenient sentences . . .

BROOKE *(getting into the swing of things)* And jails are nothing more than luxury hotels.

KATE Asian students are taking their kids' places at uni.

EMMA *(protesting)* Their kids don't go to uni!

Sam gives a 'doesn't matter' gesture.

MIKE She's missing the subtleties, Sam.

SAM *(looking at whiteboard)* We've got the budget out next week. That's a goldmine.

EMMA *(incredulous)* The budget?

SAM This time, no financial analysts, no-one with glasses from Canberra. We wanna find out how it's gonna affect the average punter.

EMMA Talk to people on the streets?

SAM Yeah, vox pops.

EMMA *(sarcastic)* Because let's face it – we need to hear the opinions of people wandering aimlessly around shopping malls during the middle of the day.

MIKE Hey, Em – D's and E's.

SAM All right, not the streets. How about we send Marty into a typical pub, find out what the average bloke is thinking.

MIKE I've got the perfect one. Blazers. Couple of old school mates have done it up . . . *(he sees that no-one is looking very encouraging)* What?

KATE It's a little . . . trendy.

MIKE No, they've deliberately gone down-market. Spent a fortune doing it. It's even got a billiard-table.

SAM Em, sort something out. Could be one for Marty.

Marty enters, in a rush. He carries a Business Review Weekly magazine open at a page.

MARTY Sorry I'm late. Car trouble.

MIKE Wouldn't happen in a Saab! *(he grabs the BRW magazine)* This yours, Marty? *(he takes the open magazine and begins reading)*

SAM Now, while we're still on the budget – Em, you had an idea for Brooke?

BROOKE What?

EMMA You visit a typical family out in the suburbs. Mum, dad, kids.

BROOKE Not one of these . . .

EMMA How they cope with the mortgage, cost of living, what the government's doing to help. A typical day.

BROOKE *(total disgust)* A day?

SAM Real grassroots stuff.

MIKE *(still reading)* Hey, here's a story.

MARTY *(reaching for magazine)* Mike, gimme that . . .

MIKE *(quoting article)* 'Hundreds of small investors stand to lose their life savings after putting money into an ostrich farming company teetering on the verge of bankruptcy.'

MARTY *(reaching for magazine)* Mike . . .

SAM *(grabbing magazine)* Hang on. *(he looks at the article)* Could be something in this.

EMMA Isn't it a bit 'up-market'?

MIKE Mmm, A's and B's.

SAM Nah, we go the small investor angle. Battlers getting their fingers burnt by rich bastards.

MIKE Battlers, now that's D and E. Probably a bit more D than E, but certainly in that part of the alphabet.

EMMA You right for that, Marty?

Marty looks shaken, but disguises his feelings.

MARTY Yeah.

DOMENICA *(with phone)* Mike, it's the gatehouse. Apparently your car alarm has gone off.

MIKE *(gets up)* Damn!

SCENE 8

GEOFF'S OFFICE

Mike and Geoff meet.

MIKE You want a piece of focaccia?

GEOFF No, I've got a sandwich. So what happened next?

MIKE Well, I said to him: we've gotta skew the show more towards the D and E demographic.

GEOFF You said that?

MIKE That's what I said. If we're being watched by D's and E's, that's who we've gotta appeal to.

GEOFF *(unconvinced)* Right.

MIKE What's wrong?

GEOFF Nothing.

MIKE No, Geoffrey Salter, I want to hear it.

GEOFF It just sounds a little cynical. Deliberately targeting the working-class viewer.

MIKE Deliberately targeting? No, subtly repositioning. Skewing . . . subtly skewing.

Geoff fails to be impressed by this distinction.

MIKE Do you really think it's cynical?

SCENE 9

SAM'S OFFICE

Mike and Sam meet.

SAM 'Cynical'! *(Mike nods)* Mike, that could not be further from the truth. We have enormous respect for all our viewers, right?

MIKE *(nods)* Uh-huh.

SAM A's, D's, whoever. What we've found though is that a certain section of our audience – the blue-collar viewer – is not being catered for.

MIKE *(starting to be convinced)* Right.

SAM Now we could say 'Stuff you – who cares?' Do you want to do that?

MIKE Of course not.

SAM Or we can 'broaden' the show a little. *(he pauses, waiting for Mike to acknowledge this, then a new thought arrives)* Because, Mike, you know what you are?

MIKE What?

SAM A communicator. You have this extraordinary ability to communicate stories and issues. That's why you're the host.

MIKE Right.

SAM You know, it doesn't stop with just the stories either. I think we 'reposition' you a little too.

MIKE What do you mean?

SAM A few language things. Toss in the words 'mate', 'bloke'. Instead of talking about children, they're . . .

MIKE Kids.

SAM *(nodding)* A communicator. Make yourself more accessible to our blue-collar viewers.

MIKE But I don't want to appear 'common'.

SAM Hey, everyone knows you're a smart guy – that came out in the focus groups.

MIKE I thought you hadn't done them yet.

SAM It will come out.

SCENE 10

THE PRODUCTION OFFICE

Kate is at Brooke's desk with a manila folder.

BROOKE A sewerage inspector?

KATE *(reads)* Daryl, Gwen and three kids. A model blue-collar family. *(Brooke gives a contemptuous look)* They're expecting you tomorrow.

BROOKE Where do they live?

KATE Gladstone Park.

BROOKE Where the hell is that?

KATE You know Caffè e Cucina?

BROOKE Uh-huh.

KATE It's about twenty-three kilometres north-west of there.

Brooke delivers a withering look as Kate hands her the folder.

SCENE 11

SAM'S OFFICE

Sam, Emma and Jan meet.

JAN It's not that easy, Sam.

SAM What, a slight change of image?

JAN Normally not a problem. But Mike is difficult. No matter what we do he comes across as sort of a private-school prefect.

EMMA He is.

SAM How do we get him to look more working class?

JAN Well, I guess we could take a leaf out of the Prime Minister's book and join Mike up with a football club.

SAM *(to Emma)* Does he follow the footy?

EMMA *(shakes her head)* Tennis.

SAM It's gotta be a blokey sport.

JAN What about his family? Does Mike by any chance come from a working-class background?

Sam looks to Emma. She shakes her head.

EMMA I think their nanny may have been working class.

JAN See what I mean? Think laterally – what do poor people do for entertainment?

They all think.

EMMA Um, sport?

SAM *(to Jan)* We'll get the footy team thing happening. What about something on air?

EMMA Interview a sportsman?

SAM Great.

Mike enters without knocking.

MIKE Oh, Jan – all set for the photo?

JAN Two o'clock, darling. I'll pick you up from make-up.

SAM What's this photo for?

JAN *Wheels* magazine.

SAM Good.

JAN 'Me and My Car'.

SAM *(looks worried)* Ah.

JAN *(looks worried)* Ah.

172

MIKE Ah what?

SAM Mate. It's the D's and E's. How are they going to react when they see you posing next to an $80,000 sports car?

MIKE Come on Sam, it's only a Saab. They're a dime a dozen.

SAM No wonder people think you're a wanker.

MIKE I beg your pardon?

SAM *(correcting himself)* People might think you're a wanker. I mean, if you're . . .

MIKE No, time out here. I think you could take any group of people, at random, ask 'em what they think of Mike Moore, and I very much doubt you'll hear the word 'wanker'.

Sam is lost for a reply, but he acknowledges Mike's comment as a 'point taken'.

MIKE *(to Jan)* So the photo shoot's off, is it?

SAM Mike, you can do it.

MIKE But I thought you said . . .

SAM No mate, it's good publicity. We'll just skew the idea slightly.

MIKE We're not over-skewing, are we?

EMMA What do you mean?

SAM *(to Emma)* Em, ask Marty if we can borrow his car keys.

SCENE 12

THE CAR PARK

Mike is posing for a photograph with Marty's Commodore. Jan supervises.

MIKE Yep, it's a Commodore. *(gesturing towards a Saab parked nearby)* You can keep your fancy foreign cars for the high-flyers. For me, it's the old Aussie Holden.

PHOTOGRAPHER Can we get a shot of maybe the door open and you sort of getting in?

MIKE Sure.

Mike pulls keys from his pocket and hits the auto button. We hear a beep and follow everyone's gaze over to Mike's Saab parked next to the photo shoot.

MIKE Whoops! Wrong keys.

SCENE 13

THE PRODUCTION OFFICE

Marty sits at his desk staring blankly. Kate comes over.

KATE OK Marty, I've got some background here . . . Marty?

MARTY *(on another planet)* What?

KATE *(handing over file)* The ostrich company.

MARTY The ostrich company . . . Didn't we drop that idea?

KATE No. It's run by some mob called AussieFarm Enterprises, based locally. Apparently they've stung investors for five grand each. There's some breeding problem with the eggs . . . the birds are carking it. Marty?

MARTY What?

KATE Walk-in?

MARTY Yeah, just leave it with me. I wanna . . .

Kate leaves and Marty picks up the phone.

MARTY Dale? It's me. You talked me into this. Now get me out of this mess.

SCENE 14

THE FRONTLINE STUDIO

Mike is at his desk as final checks are made. He practises reading the autocue to himself as Sam enters.

FLOOR MANAGER Thirty seconds to air.

MIKE Sam, I love it.

SAM What?

MIKE The new intro.

SAM Well, we just thought it might appeal to our . . .

MIKE D's and E's. I love speaking the language of the streets. Being a communicator. 'Gidday, I'm Mike Moore'.

SAM What did you say?

MIKE I said 'Gidday, I'm Mike Moore'.

SAM Did you say 'Gidday'?

MIKE No, I said 'Gidday'.

SAM Can you say 'G'day'?

MIKE That's what I'm saying.

SAM But . . .

FLOOR MANAGER In ten.

MIKE Hey, you want me to wink at the start?

SAM That might be a little too blue collar.

Sam backs out of shot as Mike composes himself. With a few seconds to go Sam darts back in, removing a gold pen from Mike's hand and replacing it with a biro. Mike has no time to react before saying:

MIKE *(winking)* Gidday, I'm Mike Moore. Thanks for joining us.

The opening theme is played. Mike speaks to Sam off air.

MIKE Sorry, Sam. Couldn't resist.

SAM That's OK, mate.

MIKE OK, mate.

Day 2

SCENE 15

A SUBURBAN STREET

Brooke, Stu and Jase pull up outside a suburban house.

STU And if you care to look out to your left you'll see Number 33, home to our typical struggling family. *(Brooke looks totally pissed off)* Ready, Brooke?

BROOKE I just know what it's gonna be. Screaming kids, stained carpet and instant coffee.

STU You're really not a DE kind of person, are you?

BROOKE Let's just say they weren't home.

SCENE 16

THE PRODUCTION OFFICE

Sam arrives. Marty looks as if he has been waiting for him.

MARTY Sam, can I have a word?

SAM Sure.

Sam heads to his office. Marty follows him in.

MARTY This ostrich story.

SAM Yeah?

MARTY I just don't think it's got legs.

Sam takes a folder from Marty and flicks through it.

SAM What?

MARTY *(trying new tack)* I spoke to someone, an accountant mate. Says the company might still bail itself out. (But) any adverse publicity could sink 'em.

SAM Great. Come on, Marty – stick it to 'em. *(calls)* Em! We found a sportsman for Mike yet?

Sam goes out into the production office. Marty follows forlornly.

EMMA Ric Charlesworth?

SAM Who?

EMMA Used to be captain of the hockey team.

SAM Hockey?

Sam gives a thumbs down and heads off to get a coffee.

EMMA Yeah, I know . . .

Emma keeps phoning people. Mike approaches Marty with some documents.

MIKE Marty, you're really thorough on your research for this story. *(Marty looks quizzical)* Found these in your Commodore yesterday. 'AussieFarm Enterprises – Articles of Association'. Don't know how you got your hands on these, but bloody good work. Nail 'em! Do it for our D's and E's.

Marty looks crushed. Mike walks off. We hear him speak to Domenica.

MIKE G'day Dom.

DOMENICA G'day Mike.

EMMA Fantastic! *(she hangs up and speaks to Sam, who is coming from the kitchen area)* Merv Hughes.

SAM *(pleased)* Oh, Em! He is blue-ribbon blue collar.

EMMA *(nods and then realises what he just said)* I don't think that makes sense.

SAM *(thinks)* When you write Mike's questions, make sure he looks like he's an old buddy of Merv's.

EMMA Got it. *(she goes over to Mike in the general office area)* Mike, we've got an interview with Merv Hughes.

MIKE Great. Who is he again?

SCENE 17

DARYL AND GWEN'S HOUSE

Stu and Jase set up in the kitchen of the house.

BROOKE OK Daryl, if you and Gwen want to have a seat at the kitchen table, then we'll put . . . *(she can't remember the kid's name)*

GWEN Kaila.

BROOKE Kaila here, and . . .

GWEN Briony.

BROOKE Over here, and . . . the curly-headed one there. I'll just check on . . . *(she goes over to check on Stu, then whispers)* Does anyone in the western suburbs have kids with a normal name?

STU Dunno. *(under his breath)* Brooke.

SCENE 18

THE FRONTLINE STUDIO

Mike winds up a pre-taped interview with Merv Hughes.

MIKE *(jovial)* Come on mate, you're a wacker. Always were, always will be.

MERV Oh, I like a bit of a laugh.

MIKE Well, don't forget – you still owe me that beer next time we play eighteen holes down Werribee way.

MERV No worries.

MIKE Mind you, you better swing a club better than you did last time we hit off together. Merv – thanks for your time.

MERV No worries, mate.

EMMA Cut. That was great.

MIKE Thanks, Mervyn.

MERV *(confused)* Sorry, I don't wanna be rude but . . . have we actually met before?

SCENE 19

DARYL AND GWEN'S HOUSE

Brooke is coaching Daryl and Gwen. The kids interrupt with 'I'm hungry' type comments throughout.

BROOKE OK Daryl, you're sitting here at the table with the bills, and Gwen – you bring the coffee across, sit down and say . . .

GWEN *(woodenly)* How are we going to afford to pay for all this?

BROOKE Great. OK, let's go for one. And – action.

Gwen turns and speaks almost over the top of the word 'action'.

GWEN How are we . . .

BROOKE Cut! Gwen, just leave a beat after I say 'action'.

GWEN A beat?

BROOKE Yeah. And – action.

Gwen stands immobile for several seconds. Thinking she has not heard, Brooke says 'action' again. Gwen speaks over the top of this. Brooke tries to hide her frustration. Stu cheekily indicates 'Take three' in front of camera.

BROOKE And one more time – action.

Gwen turns correctly and comes over to Daryl but looks at camera as she delivers her line.

BROOKE Cut!

GWEN I left a beat!

BROOKE You looked at the camera.

GWEN No I didn't.

DARYL Yes you did.

GWEN Well it's all right for you – you've just gotta sit there . . .

A full-on domestic starts as the kids demand food and Brooke sinks her head into her hands.

SCENE 20

THE FRONTLINE STUDIO

We catch the tail end of Mike's interview with Merv Hughes, then cut back to Mike at the Frontline desk.

MIKE Merv Hughes – great bowler and a great bloke, a good mate. Well, the budget's due out next week, and for his larrikin look it's over to Friday night funnyman Elliot Rhodes . . .

Cut to Elliot, dressed in workman's blue singlet, shorts and hard hat.

ELLIOT The rich are gettin' richer
And the poor can only bitch about
The way this country's goin' down the drain.
While the yuppies all send faxes
We're just gettin' taxes
And I tell you it's the government to blame.
Budget blues
Workers lose
And it's a struggle just to keep the family home.
You can tax the wife
Might even get me out of strife
But you better leave me beer and smokes alone.

Elliot gives a cheesy thumbs up.

MIKE Elliot Rhodes with 'The Budget Blues'. It's an anthem for us all – I'm already feeling it in the hip-pocket nerve. Well, that's about it for this week. Have a good weekend, or should I say: 'Avagoodweekend'. *(slight look of surprise)* Go Swans!

Over Mike's shoulder we see the words 'Go Swans' written on the autocue.

Cut to the control room, where Emma and Sam watch as the final credits run.

EMMA 'Go Swans'? Since when has Mike been a footy fan?

SAM Since about 4.30. Jan's signed him up with some team.

Day

SCENE 21

SAM'S OFFICE

Marty enters, looking like he hasn't slept. He goes to the door of Sam's office.

SAM Good weekend?

MARTY Not really. I'm worried about this ostrich story.

SAM Yeah?

MARTY I really don't think it's worth putting our time into. Small company, not many . . .

SAM Marty. Close the door and sit down. *(Marty does so)* Why don't you want to do this story?

MARTY I'm in big trouble, mate.

SCENE 22

THE PRODUCTION OFFICE

Mike enters.

DOMENICA Hi, Mike.

MIKE G'day, Dom.

DOMENICA Guess what? *(she holds open a TV Week to show a photo of Mike)* 'Fair Dinkum Footy Fan' . . .

MIKE *(grabbing mag)* Wow, that's a beauty. *(disappointed)* Oh, page four.

DOMENICA And guess what? Jan just phoned; they want you to be Celebrity Angler on the 'Rex Hunt Fishing Show'!

MIKE Wow! I love fishing.

DOMENICA So tell us about the match.

MIKE *(conspiratorial)* TV Week'd kill me if this got out, but I wasn't actually there.

DOMENICA Really?

MIKE No, no. The spectators are models – we hired them.

DOMENICA Why didn't you just go?

MIKE Oh, too crowded. And the sort of people who go to the footy – they would have been recognising me, wanting my autograph . . . Yobbos.

A motorcycle courier enters.

COURIER *(to Domenica)* Delivery for Mike Moore. Can you sign for it?

MIKE *(indicating himself)* I think I can sign for it.

COURIER Oh, sure mate. *(he hands clipboard to Mike, obviously failing to recognise him)*

MIKE *(as he writes his name)* Mike – Moore.

The courier leaves. Mike calls after him.

MIKE It's me!

SCENE 23

SAM'S OFFICE

Marty and Sam continue their meeting.

SAM So you and a couple of old school mates decided to set up this ostrich scheme. *(Marty nods)* Marty, you do stories on these shonky investment set-ups every week. How could you have been sucked in?

MARTY The accountant said it was no risk. Just a standard tax-minimisation scheme. All we had to do was talk enough people into investing.

SAM How many suckers so far?

MARTY Not 'suckers'. As long as we get enough money we'll probably, generally, be OK.

SAM How many more do you need?

MARTY Five hundred. But the eggs haven't hatched and the bank's . . .

SAM All right, all right. So you don't exactly want an exposé on the operation.

MARTY It'd kill us for sure.

SAM But we gotta do something.

MARTY Why?

SAM You and your mates go down the drain, you don't think that'll get out? 'The scourge of the shonky businessman gets a taste of his own medicine'. Besides, it's still a good story.

MARTY What?

SAM Small company, small investors – it's got blue collar stamped all over it.

MARTY Sam, it's got 'bankruptcy' stamped all over it. We can't do an exposé.

SAM Who said it had to be an exposé?

SCENE 24

THE FRONTLINE STUDIO

Mike is at the Frontline desk watching the end of Marty's ostrich story. We hear Marty's voice over vision of ostriches.

MARTY *(voice only)* For a nation that's always ridden on the sheep's back it may well come as a surprise that so many of our farmers are going to the birds.

We cut to a farmer.

FARMER It's amazing. One chick can provide eggs,

leather, even meat. It could be our biggest export by the turn of the century.

Cut to Marty squatting in rural vista, picking up dirt and doing a final speech to camera. He is wearing moleskins.

MARTY But best of all, this all-Aussie enterprise is about honest investors – not the Mr Bigs, but people like you and me – having a share in this country's future. And that's gotta be good for Australia.

Cut back to Mike at his desk.

MIKE Mmm, good luck to them. Seems like a good bloke. Martin di Stasio with that report.

Cut to the control room, where Emma and Sam watch Marty's story.

EMMA Martin di Stasio with that ad.

SAM Silly bugger. I had to save his arse. Made it clear I wanted him out of the scheme by tomorrow.

EMMA He still in debt?

SAM *(checking watch)* Give it about half an hour.

Cut back to Mike at his desk.

MIKE Coming up after the break, Brooke Vandenberg spends a day on Struggle Street with some suburban battlers.

Cut to vision of Gwen and Daryl at their kitchen table. Gwen walks over to Daryl.

GWEN How are we going to afford all these bills?

SCENE 25

A RESTAURANT

It is later that evening. Sam, Jan, Mike, Marty and Brooke are seated at a table.

SAM Well, it's been a great week all. I just wanna say thanks for going with us on this blue-collar thing, subtle as it was.

MIKE We skewed.

SAM I'm sure our efforts will be reflected in the ratings.

JAN Hear, hear.

MIKE Must say it's nice to be back in an AB kind of place. I was starting to forget what they're like. *(to waiter)* No, I'll stay on the red, thanks.

A patron approaches the table.

MIKE *(pulling out pen)* Uh-oh. Autograph time.

The patron goes straight to Brooke, gets her autograph, and leaves.

MARTY I'd like to propose a toast. To our EP, for backing an all-Aussie company during a slightly shaky period. *(everyone toasts Sam)*

BROOKE *(to Marty)* I take it we're out of the financial woods?

MARTY Two hundred calls from potential investors . . .

SAM Potential suckers.

MARTY . . . since the show went to air. Dinner's on me.

MIKE *(referring to patron)* I think that's very rude interrupting dinner like that – probably a DE. Marty, I'm quite interested in this ostrich thing. You said you knew someone in the company?

Sam glares at Marty.

MARTY Er . . . Not any more, Mike.

MIKE That's a pity, 'cause I put ten grand in after we ran that story. Very impressive piece.

SAM *(almost choking on his drink)* Christ.

JAN *(changing the topic)* I'd like to propose a toast to Mike, our celebrity angler.

MIKE *(chuffed)* Oh, come on Jan . . .

JAN No, as we speak Michael is appearing on the 'Rex Hunt Fishing Show', probably sitting on the end of a pier – a normal Aussie bloke reeling in flatheads . . .

SAM Reeling in viewers.

JAN *(toasting)* I give you our new working-class hero.

SCENE 26

A RIVER

We see vision of Rex Hunt's fishing show. Rex stands next to a river.

REX So how's it going, Mike?

Widen to reveal Mike in full fly-fishing gear, casting.

MIKE Not bad, Rex.

REX I see you got all the gear there, one of these high-flying fly-fishermen. What's this rod worth?

MIKE Well, it's handmade, Rex – Loomis, about two and a half grand. I honestly couldn't fish with anything else.

REX Still, a fella like you would be on a couple of mil a year, eh?

MIKE *(not actually denying)* Well . . .

REX So when did you first turn your back on us commoners and take up fly-fishing?

MIKE I was staying, believe it or not, in a castle in Scotland with friends who got me 'hooked', as it were. Since then it's a hobby that's taken me all over the world.

REX Where's your favourite hot spot?

MIKE Ooh, there's a couple. Off the coast of Florida; Argentina, of course; New Zealand – I remember once we took a chopper . . .

As Mike continues his poncing on, we cut to Gwen and Daryl's house where the family is watching TV. The husband and wife look at each other.

DARYL Wanker.

He flicks the remote over to Ray Martin.

RAY *(on screen)* G'day. Thanks for joining us.

Episode 3
Heroes and Villains

SCENE 1

A PUBLISHER'S OFFICE

There is a meeting between a professor and a book publisher.

PUBLISHER I realise that it's been released through University Press; I just feel that with a re-jig of the cover and publicity push, it could be a mainstream release.

PROF Why can't you release it as is? *(he holds up a relatively boring university-type book)*

PUBLISHER Well, people will think that it's just facts and figures.

PROF It is.

PUBLISHER But you're saying things as well.

PROF Not really. I deliberately avoided any interpretations; people just pick up on the wrong things.

PUBLISHER I think people would find it interesting.

PROF Really?

PUBLISHER Really. And one chapter in particular – that one on race.

Day

SCENE 2

THE PRODUCTION OFFICE

A production meeting is starting. Sam pokes his head into the kitchen to find Marty.

SAM *(holding up newspaper)* Marty, what do you know about this professor bloke?

MARTY 'Professor bloke'?

SAM The racist guy.

MARTY Oh, right. Only what I've read.

SAM You read his book?

MARTY I read the weekend papers.

SAM *(walking back to office area)* Sounds like he's got some way-out views.

MARTY That race stuff, (dynamite).

We follow Sam and Marty out into the production office. There is general turmoil as everyone fights for coffee and a seat.

SAM Come on, let's get into it.

EMMA Where's Mike?

DOMENICA His plane landed an hour ago.

BROOKE *(holding up* TV Week*)* Good to see he's kept a low profile on this holiday.

We see a TV Week *article of Mike in scuba gear with a dolphin.*

STU His *TV Week* articles make it back before he does.

MARTY Beautiful creature. Can be trained to do all sorts of things.

DOMENICA Yeah.

MARTY Like he hosts this show, he drives a car . . .

DOMENICA *(protesting)* Marty, he was there trying to help dolphins.

MARTY Yeah, he gave them a superiority complex.

SAM *(irritated)* Shut up, everyone.

A few register shock at Sam's mood.

SAM Got a show to do. *(he tosses the newspaper on the table)* Tell me more about this racist professor.

MARTY Came out of nowhere.

KATE Sounds like a Nazi. *(others join in:* It's terrible, *etc)*

SAM Em, what's his story? A racist?

EMMA Well, it's 800 pages long. I've only read the first couple of chapters, and he does touch on race, but then it's a lot of statistics: health, education . . .

SAM Yeah yeah yeah, but he does talk about race?

EMMA Well, in one of the chapters there's a breakdown on the basis of race, like what is the average wage and occupation and . . .

MARTY IQ.

EMMA Yeah . . .

Everyone goes 'Oooh'.

SAM Get him in.

EMMA *(shrugs)* You sure it's not a big stir over nothing?

SAM Dunno. But it's about to get bigger. Let's get him on the show.

EMMA When?

SAM Um, in a couple of weeks. Tonight, you dope – what else?

BROOKE I got a call yesterday from this doctor.

MARTY Still got that rash?

BROOKE *(ignoring joke)* You may have seen him in the *Woman's Day*. Did a heart transplant on the weekend. *(she holds up the magazine article; we see a shot of an Asian-looking kid)*

KATE Yeah, I saw that.

BROOKE This kid was flown in from Asia for it.

EMMA Don't think it was a transplant, was it? The kid had a hole in the heart.

BROOKE (Are) you a cardiologist now?

SAM Not a bad story. Pity the kid's Asian-looking.

KATE *(grabbing magazine)* Speaking of looks, check out the doctor.

Kate shows a photo of Ben Caffey. Emma, Kate and Brooke give a little 'va va voom'.

SAM Are we talking potential miracle worker?

KATE I'm talking potential husband.

EMMA I'll call him.

KATE Hey, hey – you've got the racist.

SAM I want both stories for tonight.

EMMA That's it?

SAM Yeah, that's it. Let's move . . . and let's congratulate Brooke on a great job hosting last week. *(they clap)* Marty (can I see you for a sec)?

Mike walks in.

MIKE Hi, everyone.

SAM Hi, Mike. *(Sam walks into his office)*

MARTY Hi, Mike. *(Marty does the same)*

MIKE Hm, welcome back! *(to Domenica)* Was there a meeting?

DOMENICA Yeah, just a little one. How was Bali?

MIKE Great.

DOMENICA Scuba diving? *(Mike pulls out a scuba licence)* Wow.

MIKE You're looking at a fully qualified diver.

Domenica's 'wow' is still going.

MIKE *(softly)* How'd Brooke go last week?

DOMENICA Fantastic.

MIKE Really?

DOMENICA *(realising what she's just said)* Sort of. She wasn't that good.

SCENE 3

SAM'S OFFICE

SAM We have to make this week a winner, mate. *(he hands over the ratings from Friday)* We stayed a couple of points off the whole week.

MARTY Brooke?

SAM Nothing to do with her. Whole show's looking tired. We need to fire up.

MARTY A little controversy?

SAM Which is why I want this racist bloke. You think we can nail him?

MARTY He's a sitting duck. Any time you touch race . . .

SAM If we do interview him I don't want it to degenerate into a boring scientific discussion.

MARTY That's up to Mike. He's gotta run over the top of him, stick to the race stuff.

SAM You're right. I might just fire Mike up a bit . . .

Marty smiles.

SCENE 4

MIKE'S OFFICE

Mike lazes back in his chair, feet on desk. Domenica sits on a chair holding a TV Week.

MIKE I am so relaxed. Bali is just the best place to unwind.

DOMENICA You want to hear this letter?

MIKE Sure.

DOMENICA *(reading from* TV Week*)* 'Dear Editor, As a big fan of Frontline and in particular Mike Moore, I am glad he is back hosting the show. Brooke Vandenberg did a good job but let's face it, she is no match for Mike.'

MIKE Great.

DOM0ENICA *(revealing her notepad inside the* TV Week*)* And you want me to mail it today?

MIKE Yeah.

Domenica gets up. Mike stops her just as she leaves.

MIKE Oh, and Dom . . .

DOMENICA Use a false name.

Mike indicates 'correct'. Domenica exits as Sam enters.

SAM Mike. How are you, mate? How was Bali?

MIKE Great. The Balinese were a bit annoying, but if you know how to deal with them . . . Like with all Asians, you lay down the ground rules.

SAM Go back there?

MIKE Oh yeah. Well, what a difference from France, my last holiday. You know what the French are like.

SAM Yeah.

MIKE So Brooke did all right last week?

SAM Yeah. Ratings were a little down.

MIKE *(excited)* Were they?

SAM Mike . . .

MIKE I agree, Sam. Let's not say a thing. She did her best; the week's over; the matter's closed.

SAM Thanks, Mike.

Mike gives a magnanimous gesture. Sam holds up the newspaper.

SAM Now this university bloke. Know about it?

MIKE Outrageous book, absolutely outrageous.

SAM Looks like we're interviewing him tonight. You can really hit him hard.

MIKE I reckon we can be cleverer than that, Sam. Focus on the book – turn it into a scientific discussion.

SAM Let's not be too clever.

MIKE But he must have some evidence to back up what's he's saying. I mean, 800 pages . . .

SAM You don't agree with him?

MIKE Hey, I'm not racist. But I just think I should read . . .

SAM Scientific mumbo jumbo. The guy wants you to talk about science to hide the fact he's racist.

MIKE *(understanding dawns)* I see his game.

SAM Get stuck into him. Land some punches tonight. This is like something from . . . *(pretends to think)* oh . . .

MIKE Nazi Germany.

SAM *(pretends to be amazed)* Mike, nailed it in one. It's Third Reich, Hitler . . .

MIKE Actually, is this guy German? 'Cause the Germans are shockers like that.

Sam goes to exit.

MIKE Don't worry, Sam. *(feigns punching)*

SCENE 5

THE PRODUCTION OFFICE

Brooke is in the office on the phone.

BROOKE Great. *(hangs up)* Our heart surgeon's happy to do the story. Stu, Jase – in five?

Sam walks out of Mike's office and comes over to Brooke.

SAM Hey, Brooke. With the doc, up a couple of notches – you know . . .

BROOKE 'Hero, miracle worker . . . '

SAM *(nodding)* Give it a bit of szhoozh.

BROOKE And if he's not a miracle worker?

SAM *(smiles)* Make him one. *(he heads for his office)* Em, what's happening with Professor Goebbels?

EMMA (He's) more than happy to come on. Live interview tonight.

SAM Good stuff.

EMMA He's actually in a bit of shock.

SAM (not hearing) Can you find out whether he's got any right-wing affiliations – political, social . . . Does he like Wagner . . . Are his parents German . . .

EMMA Is that a joke?

SAM Yeah, but find out anyway.

SCENE 6

THE PRODUCTION OFFICE

Mike leaves his office and comes over to Brooke's desk.

MIKE Just wanted to say 'Well done' for last week.

BROOKE (busy at desk) Thanks, Mike.

There is a pause.

MIKE I wouldn't worry about the figures.

Brooke fails to bite.

MIKE Sam was just telling me they were down a little. Frankly, I don't think there are enough people meters out there to accurately record a drop-off of viewers. As far as I'm concerned, you did your best, the week's over, the matter's closed. I'm not gonna say another word.

SCENE 7

GEOFF'S OFFICE

GEOFF Really? Ratings were down, were they?

MIKE Ooh yeah. Everyone reckons it's because Brooke was hosting the show while I was away. (But) I don't think so.

GEOFF (agreeing) No, it's probably not her fault.

MIKE It might be.

GEOFF (shaking his head) No . . .

MIKE It is. I'm just playing it down.

GEOFF Do you want me to play it down too?

MIKE Yeah . . . Not too down. You can tell your friends.

GEOFF People in the newsroom?

MIKE Yeah. Anyway, I'm back now. Trend's about to change. I've got a very big interview tonight.

GEOFF Really?

MIKE Yeah – that racist professor.

GEOFF Who's that?

MIKE The one that wrote the book, *Above Average*.

GEOFF Oh, he's a racist, is he?

MIKE Yeah. Haven't you read it?

GEOFF No. Have you?

MIKE No. I've read the papers though. He's definitely a racist.

GEOFF Oh well, if it's in the papers . . .

MIKE Everyone agrees.

SCENE 8

SAM'S OFFICE

EMMA You got a minute?

SAM (holding the phone) Not really.

EMMA Sam, I don't think this guy is what everyone's making him out to be.

SAM He probably isn't.

EMMA It's not really a racist book – that stuff has been taken out of context. For a start it's only twenty pages out of 800, it's a statistical study, there's more graphs than words . . .

SAM Em, Em, Em – I don't care.

EMMA Sam, I don't want to sound naive . . .

SAM You're doing a bloody good job.

EMMA He's just a lab coat who's going to be destroyed.

SAM He can defend himself. He's a smart guy. Wrote an 800-page book.

EMMA I suppose.

SAM Em, this is current affairs. We're observers in this; we don't take sides.

SCENE 9

GEOFF'S OFFICE

MIKE It's us against him. We're gonna nail that professor tonight, Geoffrey Salter.

GEOFF Are we?

MIKE Crucify him.

GEOFF Hey Mike, you can turn this into a comprehensive scientific discussion. You can focus on all the facts, and then you can prove him wrong on statistics . . .

MIKE No, no, Geoff. You're falling into exactly the same trap that Sam did.

GEOFF Really?

MIKE I said to him: 'Sam, no. We can be cleverer than that.'

GEOFF Really? How?

MIKE 'Let's ignore the evidence.'

GEOFF Oh, ignore the evidence!

MIKE Yeah. Ignore that scientific mumbo jumbo. Let's just expose him for what he really is.

GEOFF Yeah! A statistician!

MIKE No, a racist.

GEOFF (not entirely convinced) Oh yeah, a racist.

MIKE (changing topic) Did you see *TV Week*?

GEOFF Sure did. So tell us about Bali.

MIKE Best holiday I've had.

GEOFF Better than the Greek Islands?

MIKE Well, you don't have the Greeks trying to rip you off all the time.

GEOFF Balinese good?

MIKE Yeah. Not too smart, but what they lack in intelligence they make up for in hearts of gold.

SCENE 10

THE KITCHEN

Marty is making a coffee as Sam enters.

SAM Help me out here, will ya? What's the deal with Emma?

MARTY Deal?

SAM I'm trying to nail this racist guy; she's become counsel for the defence.

MARTY (smiles knowingly) She's a bloody good producer. Half the things that happen round this place wouldn't without her. But she comes at a price. Every now and then she's inclined to go for the moral high ground.

SAM Bit like Mike.

MARTY Yeah, only (worse) she's got brains.

Sam nods, grateful for the advice.

MARTY (calls) Where are the biscuits?

EMMA (off screen) Top shelf, behind the coffee.

Marty checks. The biscuits are in fact there.

SCENE 11

A HOSPITAL

Brooke is walking along a hospital corridor with Stu and Jase.

BROOKE Are you guys ready to go?

STU (slightly testy) Yes, Brooke.

BROOKE 'Cause he won't have a lot of time.

Dr Ben Caffey comes in, all smiles.

BEN Hi.

BROOKE Brooke Vandenberg.

BEN Ben Caffey.

BROOKE Thanks for agreeing to the story.

BEN My pleasure – no problem at all. (to Stu) Ben Caffey.

STU Stu, doctor.

BEN Please – Ben.

STU And this is Jase.

BEN G'day Jase. Now what would you like to see? Where would you like to go?

BROOKE Well, I guess we should spend some time in the operating theatre, maybe your office, with a couple of patients, and if you have time, you relaxing at home.

BEN No problem. The operating theatres are through here. I thought you'd want to speak to some patients so I've got that covered.

BROOKE Terrific. Sorry, Ben – have you got time right now?

BEN Sure.

BROOKE I thought . . . (referring to his surgical garb)

BEN Oh no, I cancelled theatre today after you rang. I just thought it'd look better in the uniform.

SCENE 12

THE PRODUCTION OFFICE

Mike is going towards his office with the professor's book. Domenica is walking back to her desk.

MIKE *(to Domenica)* No calls for the next few hours.

DOMENICA Are you going to read the book?

MIKE Already started. Preface. Acknowledgements. It's dedicated to his mother.

Mike opens his office door. Khor is in there, vacuuming.

MIKE No, not now, Khor! I've got research to do. Choppee choppee.

SCENE 13

MIKE'S OFFICE

Mike is sitting at his desk. He opens the book and turns to the first page, ready for a long haul. He starts reading. (we dissolve to the future) Mike is a little tired this time and we see him turning another page. (dissolve again) Mike is really tired and he's struggling. (dissolve again) This time Mike has his nose in a copy of Magic Eye. *There is a knock on the door. Mike quickly swaps the book for* Above Average.

MIKE Come.

DOMENICA How'd you go?

MIKE *(his eyes are still crossed)* A racist!

SCENE 14

THE EDIT SUITE

Marty walks in, eating.

MARTY Brooke, what's up?

BROOKE I'm having a little trouble making our heart surgeon a hero of the people.

MARTY Was he a prick?

BROOKE No, no, on the contrary – Dr Smoothie. But it doesn't seem like he does many transplants; it's mostly bypasses.

MARTY Of . . . ? The heart?

BROOKE Yeah, but that operation's done every day.

MARTY Let's go back to 30,000 feet. It's the heart – that means life to most people. The man spends his day saving lives, whether it's transplants or . . . In fact that's what you say: 'It's not just transplants for the doctor – he does lifesaving heart surgery every day.'

BROOKE Actually that's good. *(she starts writing it down)* I'm also having a bit of trouble with him relaxing at his multimillion-dollar home.

MARTY *(unperturbed)* Even more impressive. 'And Dr Miracle Worker doesn't even need to do this.'

BROOKE 'He could easily retire now . . . '

MARTY ' . . . but blah, blah, blah.' Exactly.

BROOKE This is brilliant. Don't move – let's keep going.

MARTY *(while she writes)* So what was he like?

BROOKE Bit up himself. Very comfortable with the spotlight.

MARTY So you two had a fair bit in common.

Brooke nods, before realising this may not have been a compliment.

SCENE 15

THE MAKE-UP ROOM

Mike is in the chair being made up for camera. Sam walks in.

SAM Ready, Mike?

MIKE Yeah.

SAM *(slightly worried)* Dom was saying you read the book.

MIKE *(proudly)* Yep.

SAM Not sucked in by that scientific mumbo jumbo, were you?

MIKE Hey, I could tell after the first ten pages what he was up to.

SAM *(relieved)* Good man. You right with the questions and the intro?

MIKE *(holds up papers)* Emma's prepared them.

SAM *(taking papers and reading)* What happened to all the Nazi stuff we were talking about this morning?

MIKE She said it was a little 'predictable'.

SAM *(feigning shock)* Hang on, let me get this right. Emma is telling you – the host of a national current affairs show – what you should and shouldn't say?

MIKE *(realising the absurdity)* Crazy. *(pause)* So what should I say?

SCENE 16

THE FRONTLINE STUDIO

We see vision of Brooke's doctor story.

BROOKE *(voice only)* Dr Caffey doesn't need to carry on his lifesaving work – he could easily retire to a life of Porsches, palatial mansions and polo. But this miracle worker limits that part of life to the weekend. Monday to Friday he gives hope to people from as far away as Singapore and Hong Kong and to little boys like Jin. *(we hear the song 'Dreams')*

Cut back to Mike in the studio.

MIKE Mmm. Dreams *can* come true. Brooke Vandenberg there, with a modern-day miracle worker. Back after the break.

Mike gets up and meets the professor, who is quite pleasant.

MIKE Professor, welcome.

PROF How do you do, Mr Moore.

FLOOR MANAGER Thirty seconds, Mike.

MIKE Oh yeah, sure. Professor, you sit there.

As he's getting his microphone on the professor chats with Mike.

PROF Thank you for having me on – I hope this will clear it up. It's been a horrid three days.

MIKE Uh-huh.

PROF You see, my book doesn't make judgements. It's a statistical regression of completely independent variables. It's for other people to interpret.

Mike mouths the words 'mumbo jumbo' to Sam.

FLOOR MANAGER Five to go, Mike.

Cut to control room. Marty is there with Emma and Sam.

SAM Fire it up, Mike.

Cut back to studio.

MIKE Welcome back. Our nation has been rocked over recent days by the release of a book that some are calling a Third Reich-type document. Entitled *Above Average*, it threatens to tear this country's social fabric apart. It was written by controversial professor Desmond Lowe, and he joins me now. Thanks for coming on.

PROF Thank you. I certainly didn't set out to be controversial.

MIKE Professor, you wrote a book that says some races are better than others.

PROF No, no. Er, this is . . . (where people misunderstand the whole thing). My point was to identify prevalence and frequency on a wide range of criteria. It's not a static commentary of predetermination or causal relationships.

MIKE *(not grasping this)* Sure. I mean, that's obvious. But you mention race.

PROF Yes . . .

MIKE You attribute characteristics on the basis of race.

PROF Statistical characteristics.

MIKE *(interrupting)* That's racism.

PROF No.

MIKE You said it.

PROF But I . . . It was . . .

MIKE *(aggressively)* You said it, professor. That's racism.

Cut back to control room.

SAM *(impressed)* Wow, Mike.

Emma isn't comfortable. Cut back to studio.

PROF I was pointing to elements that can be altered.

MIKE Social engineering – isn't that what Hitler did?

PROF No, no. That's not social engineering.

MIKE (You're) an apologist for Hitler.

PROF I'm referring to my book.

MIKE So I guess you would deny the holocaust, yes?

Cut to control room.

SAM Yes.

MARTY Yes.

EMMA *(protesting)* No.

Cut back to studio.

PROF No, no, it's mathematics. *(he's pretty much broken now)*

MIKE *(stops and thinks briefly as if he's changing direction)* What do you say to immigrants – the immigrant friends of mine who for the past week have been asking me one question: 'Is he saying some races are better than others?'

The professor hardly answers; he's nearly broken. Cut back to control room, where everyone almost whoops at Mike's manoeuvre.

SAM This guy's dead.

MARTY He's flatlining.

Emma is not happy about it.

SCENE 17

A PUB

Emma, Kate, Shelley and Domenica meet at the pub.

SHELLEY Why?

EMMA I don't know. I don't think he likes me.

DOMENICA He called you a dope.

SHELLEY Maybe he's just shy.

KATE Sam Murphy is not shy.

SHELLEY He's just settling in.

EMMA He's just so patronising and dismissive. He's really short with me.

SHELLEY He's my eleventh executive producer – they're all the same.

KATE So what are you going to do?

EMMA I know exactly what I'm going to do. I am going to get really, really drunk.

DOMENICA I don't think he's short. He's quite tall.

Day ❷

SCENE 18

THE PRODUCTION OFFICE

Sam and Jan greet Mike as he walks in the door.

SAM It's fantastic, Mike. Half the calls are saying they hate the racist and the other half how much they love the heart guy. Who said current affairs isn't balanced? *(he goes into his office)*

JAN Mike, you were wonderful last night. Gave that nasty racist a real drubbing.

MIKE Well, I tried to present a balanced view. He was getting a little irrational.

Emma enters, wearing dark glasses. She does not look well.

JAN My God, darling. What happened to you?

MARTY I believe all the girls went out for a bit of a drink last night.

BROOKE No we didn't. Did you?

None of the girls respond.

JAN *(to Brooke)* Darling, your story last night on the heart surgeon – wonderful television. That little Asian boy, plucked from some Third World hovel and saved by gorgeous Dr Caffey. I had goose bumps.

SAM *(calls)* Jan!

JAN Coming! *(she goes into Sam's office)*

MIKE Oh Dom, I'm expecting someone from Southern Divers today.

DOMENICA *(writes)* Southern Divers . . . Oh Mike – I got your postcard.

MIKE Today! Oh, that's typical of Indonesians – slow, bureaucratic . . .

DOMENICA Are they?

MIKE Oh, almost as slow as Indians. Remember that holiday?

DOMENICA Oh yeah. You hated them.

SCENE 19

SAM'S OFFICE

Sam, Jan and Marty meet.

SAM There's more in these stories. Both of 'em.

JAN Absolutely.

SAM We've gotta make 'em run, side by side, like we've got a hero and a villain.

MARTY The racist'll run – he's money for old rope. But the heart guy's kind of a one-off.

SAM AND JAN No, no.

JAN We can make him last.

MARTY How?

Jan and Sam smile.

JAN Are you thinking what I'm thinking?

SAM Does it have something to do with Dr Caffey becoming Frontline's new medical expert?

JAN By the time we've finished he'll be a national celebrity.

SAM But still a humble, publicity-shy surgeon.

JAN Absolutely. I'll take care of my hero.

MARTY Leave the villain to me.

SAM OK. Let's do it. *(calls)* Shelley, can you tell Mike to come in here for a moment?

Jan and Marty exit. Emma enters with papers.

EMMA *(drops the papers on Sam's desk)* I think Mike went a bit overboard last night.

SAM Yeah, (I) don't know what got into him.

EMMA That Hitler stuff. *(Sam nods)* He had no defence to that.

SAM Agreed. *(looks down to get on with his work)*

EMMA Now can we leave this man in peace?

SAM No.

EMMA We destroyed him last night. What more is there to be done?

SAM He can handle a bit of controversy, until it dies down.

Mike enters in a full wetsuit.

EMMA How can it 'die down' if we keep feeding it?

MIKE Did you call me, Sam? I'm just getting measured up. Feeding what?

SAM Oh, this racist professor. Emma reckons we're just feeding the controversy.

MIKE Feeding it! Let me take over here, Sam. There's a bit of history to all this bleeding heart stuff.

Emma scoffs.

MIKE Have you read the book?

EMMA Yes.

MIKE Well I haven't, so I'm still objective. Do you honestly think we caused this controversy? Like, we sat down at a whiteboard and mapped it out?

SCENE 20

THE PRODUCTION OFFICE

Marty is at the whiteboard with Kate.

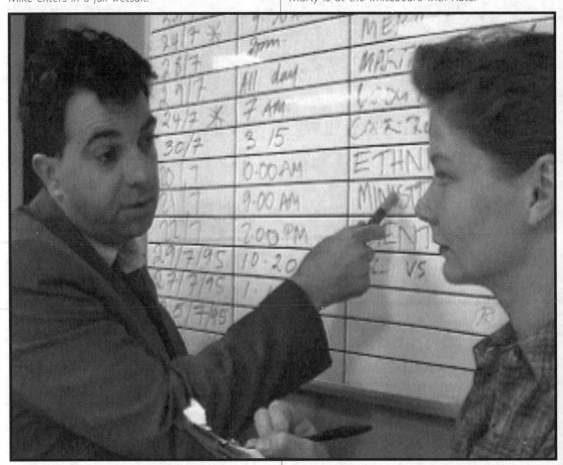

MARTY We'll have the ethnic groups attack him today. Tomorrow, the government's response – they'll spot a populist cause miles off. Thursday, other scientists' anger, his own peers kinda thing. Friday . . .

STU His funeral?

MARTY That was last night. Now we're just dancing on his grave.

SCENE 21

SAM'S OFFICE

MIKE We don't take issues and artificially pump them up. We just report what's happening. The fact is, and I know Sam will back me on this, we're just observers. Complex scientific argument like this – we nurture the facts to the surface and let the public make up their own mind. We don't take sides.

EMMA (leaving) Thanks, Mike.

MIKE (to Sam) She needs guidance every now and then.

Day 5

SCENE 22

THE FRONTLINE STUDIO

Mike is sitting at the desk watching a story going to air.

MARTY (voice only) And so as the week comes to a close, Professor Lowe's book is still walking off the shelves, and the government is talking about using its racial vilification legislation to ban it from sale. This comes on top of a letter in this morning's paper signed by seventeen scientists who have distanced themselves from the professor.

Cut to the control room where Sam is a little concerned about Mike. He gets up and walks into the studio.

SAM Mike.

MIKE Yeah?

SAM Don't telegraph your opinion. We're not taking sides – we're observers.

MIKE You're right . . . I've got a good 'look'. (he does a look)

SAM Good. Earnest ambivalence.

MIKE Yeah. (not knowing what that is) I'm sure there's a bit of that in there.

FLOOR MANAGER In two.

MIKE (playing it out perfectly) Mmm, Martin di Stasio there with a story that just won't go away. Well, it wouldn't be Friday without Frontline funnyman Elliot Rhodes. And I wonder what he has to say about this current trade dispute? Sock it to us, Elliot.

Cut to Elliot dressed as a clichéd Japanese warrior: headband, samurai sword, glasses, hat and a Fu Manchu moustache.

ELLIOT I am Japanese
I come from far across the seas
I think your land is very nice
But there's no way that we will buy your rice.

Your country here is very grand
So I keep on buying up your land
Half of Queensland I've now got
But me, I want the bloody lot.

You maybe beat us in the war
But I tell you now this thing for sure
Mitsubishi will always beat Ford
'Cause the yen is mightier than the sword.

(bows) Ah-so.

Cut back to Mike.

MIKE Ha ha. (bows) Ah-so, Elliot – or 'Erriot'. Very clever. All good fun. That's it for us – have a good weekend.

The closing music is heard. Mike loosens his tie.

MIKE Better get moving.

ELLIOT Going out, Mike?

MIKE Got a fundraising dinner for Dr Caffey.

ELLIOT The heart surgeon?

MIKE (nods) Marty, Brooke and I have been invited. Although only one of us has been asked to give a speech.

ELLIOT Yeah, who?

MIKE Me! It's a beauty.

SCENE 23

A DINING ROOM

Mike is giving his speech. Behind him is a banner: 'The Caffey Foundation'.

MIKE We're here to hail one man, and to help him. The cynics told us medical stories don't rate: 'People don't like disease and sickness and hospitals.' Well, Frontline took a punt. Not only did it rate, but we helped raise over 100,000 dollars for the foundation.

Polite applause. Brooke and Marty are sitting at a table near the front. Brooke gets up to leave, and Marty watches her go with a look of helpless desperation.

MIKE Now I know how important a heart is when you're fifty feet underwater, but that's a healthy heart. So something like scuba diving, which I had the privilege to learn only last week in Bali, is fine for me. I can don a scuba outfit . . .

SCENE 24

A CORRIDOR OUTSIDE THE DINNER

Brooke walks out into the corridor and sees Mike's doctor there.

BROOKE Hi.

JONATHAN Hello. Brooke, isn't it?

BROOKE Yes. You're Mike's doctor.

JONATHAN That's right – Jonathan.

BROOKE I didn't know you were connected with all this.

JONATHAN Only partially – we've got ties to the same research council.

BROOKE Mike a little too much for you?

JONATHAN Oh no, no, no. I'm just having a cigarette . . . and you?

BROOKE Mike's too much for me.

JONATHAN Mind you, it is a bit rich.

Brooke cocks her head.

JONATHAN Heart transplants sound all glamorous, but they're basically advanced plumbing done just about anywhere these days.

BROOKE Then it's not a world first?

JONATHAN *(laughs)* No. I mean he's good but he's basically a bypass surgeon. Now that *is* plumbing and almost as lucrative . . .

BROOKE And glamorous?

JONATHAN Oh yeah, all that. Heart means life.

BROOKE What about the little Asian boy?

JONATHAN 'Plucked from the ghetto and saved'?

BROOKE Uh-huh.

JONATHAN I don't want to put your reports down.

BROOKE Go ahead.

JONATHAN He was the Sultan of Brunei's nephew. Most of Caffey's Asian patients are rich businessmen who pay a fortune to have a 'top' surgeon. It's like a status symbol for them.

BROOKE (Then) why are we raising money for him?

JONATHAN *(laughs)* The question had crossed my mind.

The door opens and Mike's voice floats out.

MIKE *(voice only)* When I think of Asia I think of great diving locations, but he thinks of great lifesaving locations. *(applause)*

JONATHAN You see, I'm trying to get some money for my little research program.

BROOKE On?

JONATHAN Chlamydia and fertility. *(Brooke reacts with distaste)* Yes, not glamorous but effective. It'd get more people pregnant than IVF but I'm fighting . . .

BROOKE Us.

JONATHAN In a way, it's funny. It was one of the things raised in that professor's book – how research dollars go to popular causes – but it's not like we can quote him now, is it?

Mike's voice floats out again.

MIKE *(voice only)* Just as the aqualung gives life, so too does the transplant.

Jonathan and Brooke look at each other and smile. The door opens and Marty staggers out with a drink.

MARTY I think I've got the bends.

Day 8

SCENE 25

THE PRODUCTION OFFICE

EMMA Production meeting in ten minutes.

Marty comes out of the kitchen with a bowl of cereal and holding the cereal packet.

MARTY Recognise this face?

He shows a photo of Dr Caffey on the side of the packet.

EMMA My God. How'd he have time to organise that?

BROOKE I think it was in the wind already.

MARTY Shy petal.

MIKE You know Ben Caffey also scuba dives? We were chatting about it after my speech.

MARTY He was the only one still awake.

MIKE We happen to be going diving together this weekend.

Sam approaches.

SAM Marty.

MARTY Yo?

SAM Just heard our resident racist is giving some talk at the university today. Could be fireworks – get out there and cover it.

MARTY Can I have my breakfast first? *(reading box)* 'A healthy heart is a . . . '

SAM Move it!

MARTY Travelling. Come on, guys.

Stu, Marty and Jase fall back on their chairs à la scuba diving.

MIKE Very funny. And that's not the way you do it.

SCENE 26

THE FRONTLINE STUDIO

We see vision of the professor arriving at the university and being pelted with eggs and paint, with people chanting with placards.

MARTY *(voice only)* And it didn't change once he was inside. Every time the man dubbed 'Professor Hate' tried to speak, angry students would shout him down.

Cut to Mike watching, practising his earnest ambivalence.

Cut to Sam and Emma watching in control room. Emma is not happy.

Day 9

SCENE 27

THE EDIT SUITE

Emma enters with a tape.

EMMA This is our interview for tonight. Can we make a dub?

HUGH OK if I dump it onto this tape – the professor guy and the uni demo?

EMMA Yeah. Poor guy couldn't even get a word out.

HUGH Sorry?

EMMA Marty said he got shouted down; he didn't get to speak.

HUGH Oh, he got to speak.

EMMA When?

HUGH Take a look.

Hugh hits the 'Play' button. We hear the professor's voice.

PROF *(voice only)* . . . and so we see that at no time did I express an opinion. It was mathematics pure and simple.

EMMA Sorry?

HUGH He got to speak. Sam just thought it was boring, so we concentrated on the protest and all the shouting.

Emma looks distinctly unimpressed.

SCENE 28

SAM'S OFFICE

Cut to Emma standing firmly in Sam's office. Sam looks up, knowing in some way what is to come.

EMMA The professor may be naive, but I'm not.

SAM Sorry?

EMMA I understand exactly what you did. You destroyed a man's reputation. You knew his book wasn't racist, but saying he's a decent bloke who's caught in the middle of a media frenzy is boring.

SAM So . . .

EMMA So you fire up Mike to make this old bloke look like the devil himself, 'cause no-one understands science but everyone hates racism.

SAM This was always going to be controversial.

EMMA For a day, not three weeks. But resolve this thing – that's the last thing we could let happen because what would we do the next night?

SAM And?

EMMA And I know it's our job to fudge stories slightly to make them work for television and you decided to go all the way. You're executive producer – that's fine. But show me a bit of respect here.

SAM Em . . .

EMMA Sam, I don't know you well enough yet to say this, but don't bullshit me. And it's the irony that kills me. You and Marty and Mike are 100 times more racist than our professor could ever be.

SAM *(tacitly admitting that she's right)* So what do you want me to do about it?

EMMA *(pause, knowing there is nothing he can do about it)* Nothing. I just want you to know that I know . . . so don't treat me like Mike.

She turns and leaves. Mike walks in with the top of a scuba wetsuit indicating that the seam has split under his arm.

MIKE Look at this. The Koreans really don't know how to make a wetsuit.

Episode 4
Office Mole

Day ❶

SCENE 1

THE PRODUCTION OFFICE

A morose Mike is wandering around aimlessly. No-one is taking too much notice of him. He strolls over to Marty's desk.

MIKE Marty.

Marty gives him a wave without even looking up from something he is punching into his laptop.

MIKE Good story on the marathon runner last night. Determined young man. If you want to follow it up, I'd love to give you a hand . . .

MARTY *(eating a banana)* I don't think we're going to follow it up.

EMMA *(on phone, calls to Marty)* Marty – the woman with all the cats you interviewed last week . . .

MARTY Yeah?

EMMA You guys tread on her rose garden?

MARTY *(uninterested)* Maybe.

EMMA *(holding up phone)* You want to handle it?

Marty gives the thumbs down. Emma resumes her phone conversation.

EMMA *(into phone)* Mrs Cranitch, we're very sorry if any damage was . . .

Mike spots Stu and Jase at the whiteboard and approaches.

MIKE Guys.

They keep sorting out something on the board.

MIKE I was just saying to Marty that the marathon story was dynamite. Good photography, Stu – especially that shot at the end when the guy runs off and you pan around to the setting sun.

STU Tilt. *(doing actions)* This is a tilt. That's a pan. Brooke, are we finished with this High Court thing? 'Cause we're having trouble fitting in all this other stuff.

BROOKE *(eating cereal)* Yep. All done.

Stu and Jase walk off to Emma leaving Mike stranded.

MIKE See ya, guys. You sound busy . . .

His voice trails off pathetically, then he saunters over to Brooke. She is on the phone, obviously waiting for someone.

MIKE How's it going, Brooke?

BROOKE *(into phone)* Great.

MIKE *(thinking she is speaking to him)* Great. I was just saying to Marty . . .

Brooke continues speaking. Mike realises she is on the phone.

BROOKE *(not looking up)* Uh-huh. And you've got the prescription with you now? OK. *(checking watch)* We'll be there in about an hour. *(she hangs up and goes over to Stu and Jase)* OK boys, it's on.

Mike is left standing alone pathetically in the middle of the office.

SCENE 2

MIKE'S OFFICE

Mike, eating a Kit Kat, is sitting at his desk looking very bored. Suddenly Domenica enters excitedly.

DOMENICA Mike! Guess what?!

MIKE *(suddenly excited)* He's called!

DOMENICA Who?

MIKE Glenn Ridge.

DOMENICA No. Ratings! Twenty-eight!

MIKE *(unable to hide his disappointment)* Oh, great. So he hasn't answered any of my calls?

Domenica shakes her head 'no'. Suddenly Mike gets upset.

MIKE Just SO RUDE!

DOMENICA Doesn't matter. He'll call. What about the ratings, huh? Emma says this is the tenth straight night we beat the others!

MIKE I'm sick of chasing him down! That's it!

DOMENICA Oh! And you're in the paper today.

MIKE *(in his own world)* He's let me down.

DOMENICA Do you want me to cut it out for your *(mimes 'clip clip')* book?

MIKE What's it about?

DOMENICA *(holds up article)* You doing the 40 Hour Famine.

MIKE *(not realising he is eating)* Don't worry about it.

DOMENICA Are you all right?

MIKE I don't get it, Dom. Why isn't he calling back? I'm starting to think he's not getting my messages . . .

DOMENICA We're about to have a production meeting. You coming?

MIKE Well, I'm sick of chasing him up.

Mike picks up the phone and dials. Domenica exits.

VOICE #1 *(on speaker-phone)* Hello, Channel Nine.

SCENE 3

THE PRODUCTION OFFICE

Domenica exits Mike's office and goes discreetly over to Shelley's desk.

DOMENICA How's it going?

SHELLEY Good.

DOMENICA Does anyone know?

Shelley shakes her head 'no'.

SCENE 4

MIKE'S OFFICE

Mike speaks into the speaker-phone.

MIKE Glenn Ridge, please.

VOICE #1 Hold the line.

VOICE #2 'Sale of the Century'.

MIKE Glenn Ridge, please.

VOICE #2 Who's speaking?

MIKE Mike Moore.

VOICE #2 He's not in. Can I leave a message?

MIKE *(jokingly)* He's not in all that often, is he?

VOICE #2 *(no reaction to joke – pause)* Can I leave a message for him?

MIKE Er, no . . . He knows my number. He can call me at work, or at home, any time . . . but it's not urgent.

VOICE #2 I'll pass that on.

MIKE Yeah, sure you will. *(he hangs up)* Arseholes.

VOICE #2 Thank you for calling.

Mike realises he didn't hang up properly.

SCENE 5

THE KITCHEN

Sam and Emma are making coffee. Marty is eating Twisties and drinking a Coke.

EMMA *(with ratings)* You want the good news or the good news?

SAM Twenty-five?

EMMA Twenty-eight! *(Sam looks pleased)* We've had some great stories.

SAM It's more than just stories, Em. It's the mix.

Emma looks quizzical.

SAM *(explaining)* Current affairs is like a well-balanced diet.

Emma notices Marty eating and drinking.

EMMA *(to Marty)* I thought you were on the 40 Hour Famine.

MARTY No, I said I was 'supporting' it, not on it.

SAM You've got to have the right mix. Last night – lead story?

EMMA The Ebola virus down under.

SAM We scared people. Then we made them feel good.

EMMA The boy who cared for his grandmother with Alzheimer's.

SAM Then Mike interviewed the Foreign Minister . . .

MARTY Comedy.

SAM You get the point. Good stories, good balance.

EMMA There's a good vibe out there.

SAM I wanna keep it that way.

SCENE 6

THE PRODUCTION OFFICE

There is a production meeting. Everyone is cheering at the news of the ratings figures.

SAM Everyone! As of tomorrow, there'll be Tim Tams for all – except of course our on-air fasters.

Brooke and Marty look at each other. They are both still eating. The others cheer Sam.

SAM *(grabbing ratings)* Well done, all of you! We're on a roll. You've worked real hard – but believe me, now's the time to work even harder. Let's kick these clowns while they're down.

MARTY Absolutely.

SAM OK, what have we got?

EMMA *(reading from list)* Brooke's chasing a dodgy doctor.

SAM Great. Haven't had one of those for a while.

EMMA *(to Brooke)* What's he do?

BROOKE Hands out methadone to just about anyone.

SAM We got footage of him?

BROOKE How would you feel about a hidden camera?

SAM Great. Next?

EMMA In a doctor's surgery? Should we run it past legal?

SAM (Nah.) Next.

EMMA But . . .

SAM Next!

MARTY Colin Manteri. Name mean anything to you?

SAM Nuh.

MARTY It will. Teenage kid; attacked his parents last night with a carving knife. Topped 'em both.

SAM Where is he now?

MARTY Helping police with their inquiries.

SAM Follow it. Anything you can get. Cops, neighbours, court . . . Anything else?

BROOKE My High Court story's ready. Been sitting on the shelf for three days now.

SAM Good. What is it again?

BROOKE Sexism in the High Court. All the judges who say it's OK to rape prostitutes, or your wife . . . (etc.)

SAM They said that?

BROOKE Some judge said it last week. And we've got a few other examples . . .

EMMA *(under her breath)* From the late nineteenth century.

BROOKE It's a good story.

EMMA It's a great story.

SAM *(looking at rundown)* (Actually,) when have we got the Penthouse Pet piece?

EMMA AND KATE Tomorrow.

SAM *(gives a 'Yeah, all right girls' look)* Let's save the High Court for then. It'll take the mozz off – nudity and a femmo story.

MARTY *(aside, to Emma)* The perfect mix.

BROOKE You don't think someone might beat us to it?

SAM *(dismissive)* Relax. *(getting up)* Good meeting.

MARTY And we managed to get through it before Mike rolled up.

DOMENICA He's here.

SAM *(concerned)* Eh?

DOMENICA He's in his office. Didn't want to come.

SAM *(concerned)* Is he all right?

DOMENICA I dunno.

Jan enters.

JAN Morning all. How are my three fasting sweeties?

Jan is intercepted by Mike, who steps out of his office.

MIKE Jan, can I have a word?

JAN Darling, I just have to speak with . . . (Sam).

SAM It's OK, Jan. We can do it later.

Jan follows Mike into his office.

SCENE 7

MIKE'S OFFICE

MIKE *(eating)* Nine?

JAN *(confused)* Twenty-eight.

MIKE Twenty-eight?

JAN Nine?

MIKE Channel Nine.

JAN Oh, Channel Nine. I thought you were talking about the ratings. What a funny little mix-up. What about them?

MIKE 'Celebrity Sale of the Century' – my 'Battle of the Current Affairs Hosts' idea . . .

JAN I'm having a little trouble getting through.

MIKE So am I. Glenn isn't answering my calls. That's not like him. Bet they're not passing on my messages . . . I know! You've got Glenn Ridge's personal fax number.

JAN I may have misplaced it.

MIKE *(pause)* Jan, you don't want me to do this either, do you?

JAN It's a wonderful idea – it's just the logistics . . .

MIKE I've solved the logistics. It's out of your hands, Jan. Give me the number! It's in your diary.

Emma knocks and enters.

EMMA Jan, you right for . . . (that meeting with Sam)?

JAN Coming, dear.

Jan reluctantly writes the number on a strip of paper. Mike takes it and starts to leave.

MIKE This'll make him sit up and take notice. *(leaving his office)* I'm faxing him right now!

EMMA Do you know how to do it, Mike?

MIKE *(patronisingly)* I think I'll be right, Emma.

Mike exits with the number. As Emma passes Shelley's desk she notices a piece of paper on the ground. She picks it up. It is covered in a strange scrawl.

EMMA *(to Shelley)* This yours?

Shelley takes it, a little too quickly. Emma continues into Sam's office. Shelley gives a worried look to Domenica. Domenica looks reassuring. Sam stands at his door.

SAM Brooke – you got a minute?

SCENE 8

SAM'S OFFICE

Jan, Brooke and Emma enter. Sam shuts the door.

BROOKE I've got an interview in twenty minutes.

SAM This won't take long. Folks, I'm worried about Mike. He's distracted.

JAN Perhaps I might be able to shed some light. He's persisting with his 'Sale of the Century' idea.

SAM *(disbelieving)* Not that 'Battle of the Current Affairs Hosts'?

JAN *(nods)* (He) won't be talked out of it.

SAM You know the problem here? Mike's bored. Where is he now?

JAN Faxing Glenn Ridge with the idea.

SAM Jesus.

Shelley buzzes through on the speaker-phone.

SHELLEY *(voice only)* Em? It's urgent.

Emma quickly picks up the phone.

EMMA Hello . . . Yeah, Mike? No, the document goes face down . . . then dial the number . . . then hit 'Fax'. *(hangs up)*

SAM We're on a roll at the moment, and I don't want it jeopardised by a host whose mind's not on the job.

Marty enters carrying a videotape.

MARTY Sam . . . *(realises who's in the office)* Who got sacked?

SAM What do you want?

MARTY Our teen murderer's been refused bail.

EMMA There's a surprise.

Marty puts the tape in the VCR and hits 'Play'.

SAM You get any footage?

MARTY This is all News had.

We see a fairly distant shot of our murderer being led from court and into a police van. He is partly obscured and glimpsed only fleetingly.

SAM That's it? Three seconds worth?

MARTY We could slo-mo it.

SAM Great, six seconds of nothing. We need an interview. What about his parents?

EMMA Sam!

SAM What?

EMMA He killed them.

SAM Oh yeah. Relatives? Friends?

MARTY It's your standard 'We're so shocked; he was such a quiet guy.'

EMMA This is a long shot, but contact his local video shop. May have been one of those psychos who watched a lot of violent videos.

SAM *(excited)* Great! It'll pad out the story and give us a chance to play some grabs from the real nasty ones. Talk about how terrible they are. Then play more grabs. Think you can get the list?

MARTY They may not give it to me, but they're about to get a phone call from Senior Detective M. di Stasio. *(he starts to leave)*

SAM Marty, we've got a problem with Mike.

MARTY So someone is about to be sacked.

SAM He's bored. We need to occupy him with something – make him feel like he's part of a team, working hard.

JAN Easy. I could organise an article. 'Captain of the Team', 'Mike's Manic Day' . . .

SAM Yeah. But it's more than just perception. I actually want him to be part of the team and working hard.

EMMA Suits me. There's a few things he could do round the office, lighten my load.

SAM Great. What?

EMMA He could keep a tab on the editing schedule.

SAM Nah.

EMMA Oversee the staffing roster.

MARTY Write questions for his own interviews.

SAM Shut up, Marty.

EMMA *(to Marty)* Apologise on behalf of reporters.

SAM *(shaking his head 'no')* Any more?

EMMA About twenty.

SAM Are they all as pissy?

EMMA Pretty much so.

SAM We're after something that sounds important but means nothing.

EMMA There's the London Weekend Television thing.

SAM Tell me more.

EMMA Told you about it last week.

SAM Wasn't listening.

EMMA Standard reciprocal deal, straight swap – our crap for theirs. They give us a tacky royal story, we give them a wacky outback piece.

SAM Getting warmer. Much work?

EMMA We send them a copy of our story rundowns every morning – they pick something off the satellite if it sounds interesting. Takes me five minutes.

SAM It'll take him an hour – and he even knows how to use the fax machine now. Tell Mike he's our new . . . *(thinks)* International Story Coordinator.

Everybody laughs.

EMMA Come on, Sam. Mike's not going to buy this.

SCENE 9

GEOFF'S OFFICE

MIKE . . . International Story Coordinator!

GEOFF Wow!

MIKE Big job. Start tomorrow.

GEOFF You do it yourself?

MIKE Mmm, there's a fair bit of responsibility. I have to supply our London bureau with a complete rundown of all the stories that go to air that night.

GEOFF Uh-huh. Then what?

MIKE Then what?

GEOFF After you've sent the rundown, then what?

MIKE Oh, er . . . then it's a waiting game.

GEOFF That's the hardest part.

MIKE Still, it's a real buzz knowing your stories will be seen halfway round the globe.

GEOFF I'll say. But they're not actually *your* stories.

MIKE Yeah, but I present them.

GEOFF Not all of them.

MIKE I oversee them all.

GEOFF I didn't know that.

MIKE Most of them.

SCENE 10

A CITY STREET

Brooke is talking with Robyn. They are standing next to the crew's car.

BROOKE So you've made another appointment with him for this afternoon? *(Robyn nods)* And you know what to say?

ROBYN *(reciting)* I lost the prescription and can I have another one.

BROOKE *(studying prescription)* And this is for methadone, right? *(Robyn nods again)* Guys, are we going?

Stu brings a large handbag over.

STU Set to go. *(pointing)* Camera and mike's in here. We'll start it for you. All you gotta do is sit down, hold it on your lap like this and point it at him. Understand?

Robyn nods.

ROBYN When do I get paid?

SCENE 11

GEOFF'S OFFICE

GEOFF So tell me, has Glenn Ridge called? He would have got your fax by now.

MIKE *(shaking head)* I am so pissed off! What happens to some people, Geoffrey Salter? A thimbleful of fame and bang – goes straight to their heads. Promise me, Geoff – if ever I start becoming one of these showbiz arseholes, please stop me.

GEOFF I will, Mike. Know exactly what you mean. I see them every night – two-bit weathermen. Weathermen, mind you, not meteorologists. Monte from 'Today' . . .

MIKE You're friends with Monte?!

GEOFF We talk – but not as much as we used to, not since he went 'national'. Thinks he's the cat's pyjamas. And just quietly, who introduced him to Steve Liebmann? (Me.)

MIKE I know that story by heart – but back to what I was talking about. What was I talking about?

GEOFF Er . . . the London job?

MIKE No, after that. Hang on – Steve Liebmann . . .

GEOFF Monte?

MIKE Before Monte . . . Oh yeah, Glenn Ridge! I swear, I've written him off.

GEOFF Good on you.

MIKE I'm all done chasing him. *(getting up)* I might just give him one more call.

SCENE 12

A DOCTOR'S SURGERY

Robyn is seated in a doctor's surgery. The doctor is writing out a prescription. As he hands it to her, we cut to the point of view of a hidden camera.

SCENE 13

THE FRONTLINE STUDIO

Mike is at the desk watching Brooke's hidden camera story go to air. We see vision of Robyn in the surgery and hear Brooke as voice-over.

BROOKE *(voice only)* Three hours later she was back, asking for another prescription. And our free-dealing doctor? Once again he's doling out drugs like candy.

Cut to Mike on air.

MIKE Mmm, Brooke Vandenberg there with the man they've dubbed 'Doctor Yes'. Back after the break.

Day ②

SCENE 14

THE PRODUCTION OFFICE

Emma is spooling through video footage on the office monitor. We see file footage of Aboriginal children living in squalor. Sam walks past.

SAM 'Current Affair' promo been on yet? *(Kate shakes her head 'no')* That's cheery.

EMMA *(holding up newspaper)* UN Report came out today. Aboriginal living standards come in for a bucketing.

Sam gives a sigh of concern.

EMMA What?

SAM Do we have to?

EMMA It's a huge story. Can't ignore it.

SAM I want up – you're giving me down. I've got my down story for tonight. Damn. *(thinks)* We hit the positives.

EMMA There *are* no positives.

SAM There's always positives. Gimme . . .

EMMA Infant mortality, alcoholism, illiteracy, leprosy . . .

SAM OK, let's create some positives. Got it! Who's that Aboriginal girl? Sport . . .

EMMA Evonne Cawley?

SAM Let's move forward a few centuries from the dreamtime. The runner.

EMMA Cathy Freeman?

SAM *(nods)* Easy. Profile piece. 'Koori kid triumphs over adversity'. Mention the report in passing but just show shots of her winning medals. Good one for tomorrow.

EMMA You're the only person I know who can turn a national disgrace into a feel-good piece.

SAM Thank you, Emma.

Emma hits 'Stop' on the video. As she and Sam are about to turn away from the monitor Kate calls to them.

KATE *(looking up at TV)* 'Current Affair' promo!

We cut back to the office monitor just in time to see the end of an 'ACA' promo for a story about sexism in the High Court.

VOICE-OVER *(over stock footage of the High Court)* . . . out of touch and behind the times. Is it high time the High Court put women first? Find out tonight, on 'A Current Affair'.

The TV is muted. Brooke gives a filthy look to Sam.

BROOKE I told you we should have run it last night!

EMMA We dump the story?

BROOKE Yes.

SAM No.

BROOKE What?

SAM We still run your piece tonight. I wanna take 'em on.

BROOKE It was going to be an exclusive!

SAM Big deal. We take 'em on head to head. We come out on top, (and) it's an even bigger victory for you.

BROOKE We're not gonna win, Sam. I can feel it.

Day ③

SCENE 15

BROOKE IS ON AIR AT 3LO WITH PETER COUCHMAN.

BROOKE Yes, it was a good win, Peter. We were very confident with the story.

PETER Sexism in the High Court – obviously a big problem, as both you and 'A Current Affair' ran with it. *(looking at figures)* With a narrow ratings victory to Frontline. Congratulations.

BROOKE Thanks, Peter.

PETER Just finally, Mike Moore – he's not well?

BROOKE Touch of the flu, Peter, but he'll be back at the desk tonight.

SCENE 16

THE PRODUCTION OFFICE

BROOKE That's the last time I cover your arse, Mike.

MIKE I forgot about the radio interview. Dom didn't put it in my book.

SAM Em, phone LO and apologise again.

BROOKE I practically killed myself getting there.

MIKE Listen Brooke, I've got a lot on my shoulders. Hosting, recording interviews . . . International Story Coordination doesn't just take care of itself. *(he exits)*

SAM I told you – he's distracted. I thought this overseas bullshit might have helped. *(he walks over to Marty)* Marty, how we going with our teen killer?

MARTY *(getting papers from desk)* Not so good. I got the list of videos he's taken out. (He's got) fairly tame tastes. *(reading)* Turner and Hooch, Betsy's Wedding, Home Alone 2, Naked Gun . . .

SAM That sounds psycho.

MARTY It's a comedy, Sam. *(continues reading)* Hudson Hawk, Reality Bites, Terminator 2 . . .

SAM *(clicking fingers)* That'll do – Terminator 2. It's violent, lot of killings . . .

MARTY It's one out of thirty. The rest are musical comedies.

SAM *(on a roll)* Forget the rest. We grab some bits from *Terminator 2*, get a psychologist to talk about the possible effects, show some more bits. It's our lead tonight.

SHELLEY *(holding phone)* Sam, the general manager wants to see you and Brooke.

SCENE 17

CAVILLE'S OFFICE

SAM We had the footage.

CAVILLE You had nothing! The word of some spaced-out drug addict.

BROOKE Ex drug addict.

Caville gives a 'Don't split hairs with me' look.

SAM She was in that consulting room for just sixty seconds. That's not long enough to start handing out methadone.

CAVILLE To someone you haven't met before, maybe. But that girl was a regular patient. Been seeing the doctor for years.

Sam and Brooke look almost chastened.

SAM He gonna sue?

CAVILLE *(nodding)* His lawyer did make it clear, however, that the amount could be lessened via a personal apology.

SAM *(worried)* On air?

CAVILLE He said 'personal', not 'public'. The man's obviously not into grandstanding. But he does want an apology from us.

Sam and Brooke look at each other.

BROOKE OK.

SAM He'll get one.

SCENE 18

THE DOCTOR'S SURGERY

The doctor is seated behind his desk.

DOCTOR You came in here, abused my trust, wasted my time and then held me up to public contempt without once checking your facts.

We reveal Emma is sitting opposite.

EMMA And on behalf of Frontline I apologise for the story.

SCENE 19

THE PRODUCTION OFFICE

Marty is reading from a newspaper.

MARTY *(reading)* ' . . . but Mike's gruelling workload doesn't end there. No sooner does he oversee the daily production schedule . . . '

Marty puts the paper down and pretends to look for Mike, then continues reading.

MARTY ' . . . than he is out on location, putting together stories for the top-rating show.'

General mirth.

DOMENICA Come on, he works really hard.

MARTY Let's just go through a typical Mike Moore day, shall we? *(writing)* Eleven o'clock – arrives. Complains about car park. Eleven-thirty – gruelling session in canteen. Complains about coffee. One o'clock – gruelling lunch. Eventually spends time in the office, which is gruelling – for us.

STU Don't forget his gruelling load as International Story Coordinator.

MARTY Gruelling.

Sam comes out of his office. He accidentally bumps into Emma.

SAM Sorry, love.

EMMA No, allow me to apologise.

Sam ignores the sarcasm.

SAM Marty – teen killer looking good for tonight?

MARTY All systems go. Found some gory scenes from *Terminator 2.*

Emma comes over.

EMMA How's this for a promo? *(reads)* 'What sort of movies would make a man want to kill? Video violence taking over the home.'

SAM Sounds good.

EMMA 'That's tonight on "A Current Affair".'

All register shock.

SAM Is this a joke?

EMMA I'm not finished. They're also covering the UN report. Exclusive interview with Cathy Freeman.

SAM All right. Meeting. Now. Shelley?

SHELLEY *(nervous)* What?

SAM You OK?

SHELLEY *(flustered)* I'm fine . . .

SAM You sure? *(Shelley nods)* I need some memos sent out.

SCENE 20

THE PRODUCTION OFFICE

Sam is addressing the staff.

SAM When they did our High Court story yesterday, I thought, 'Damn, they beat us to it.' Then the Cathy Freeman thing – 'Strange, but could be a coincidence.' But the violent video thing? Nah. Has anyone been talking to anyone at Channel Nine about our stories?

There is no response.

EMMA We running with Marty's video story?

SAM Yep. Worked for us yesterday – it'll work tonight. We take 'em on head to head again. These guys wanna keep playin' dirty – we'll teach 'em a lesson.

General 'All right!/Let's get 'em!' from everyone. The meeting starts to break up.

SCENE 21

THE FRONTLINE STUDIO

Mike is at his desk, listening to the end of Marty's story. We see vision of the teen murderer being led from court in slo-mo.

MARTY *(voice only)* No one can guess what went through the mind of Colin Manteri, but there is little doubt that films like this played a part on the night he said 'Hasta la vista' to his parents . . . *(we hear a grab from* Terminator 2*)*

MIKE *(off air)* I didn't think *Terminator 2* was as good as the first.

Mike is cued.

MIKE Mmm, Martin di Stasio with that disturbing report on videos that could turn your child into a killer. Coming up after the break, our Aboriginal anguish. Evonne Cawley speaks about the UN report and her life at the top.

Day 4

SCENE 22

SAM'S OFFICE

Sam is on the phone in his office. Marty watches on.

SAM Right, understood. Yes sir. *(hangs up)* This is not my week.

MARTY What?

SAM That was upstairs, about the violent videos.

MARTY *(picking up ratings)* We won! Beat 'A Current Affair' by three points. *(Sam looks unhappy)* What?

SAM The film we suggested could 'turn your child into a teen murderer'.

MARTY Yeah?

SAM It's our Sunday night movie.

Marty doesn't know whether to laugh. Sam does. Mike enters, eating. He shuts the door behind him.

MARTY Uh-oh. This looks ominous.

MIKE Been doing a little thinking about our mole.

SAM Our . . . ?

MIKE Person who's leaking the stories. Guys, I think Shelley's been acting strange, don't you?

MARTY Eh?

SAM She has, actually.

MIKE And have you noticed how many things she's been writing down in shorthand?

SAM *(concerned)* I didn't even know she *knew* shorthand.

MIKE *(nodding)* Fellas, I think this calls for a bit of investigating.

SCENE 23

THE PRODUCTION OFFICE

Mike is snooping around Shelley's desk. He finds a pad full of shorthand notes. Domenica looks across nervously.

DOMENICA What are you looking for, Mike?

MIKE Didn't know Shelley knew shorthand.

DOMENICA Um . . . she doesn't.

MIKE *(holding pad)* What's this then? Shorthand. I think she's hiding something.

DOMENICA *(pause)* Please, Mike. Don't tell anyone I told you, please. Shelley made me promise to tell nobody about this.

MIKE Bang! Got her! Channel Nine, yeah?

DOMENICA You know everything?

MIKE I've put the pieces together.

DOMENICA She really wants to go for that new job, and she thought she had to learn shorthand. Please don't tell Sam. She's really scared he'll find out and get mad.

MIKE New job?

DOMENICA In sales at Channel Nine. I thought you said you knew everything.

MIKE I do . . .

DOMENICA Please don't tell Sam. She'll get into real trouble and so will Kerry.

MIKE Who?

DOMENICA Marty's girlfriend. She's the one who told Shelley about the job.

MIKE Marty's girlfriend works at Channel Nine? I'm picking up another scent.

SCENE 24

THE PRODUCTION OFFICE

It is later. Mike is standing at Marty's desk. Stu and Jase are at the whiteboard behind Mike and Marty.

MIKE Martin.

MARTY How'd you go with Shelley?

MIKE Fine.

MARTY Find out anything?

MIKE Few things. How's Kerry?

MARTY Sorry?

MIKE Marty, you really should be careful who you talk about work to. *(Marty is confused)* Did you talk to your girlfriend about the violent videos story?

MARTY What are you (talking about)?

MIKE That *Terminator 2* stuff.

MARTY *(realising what Mike is on about)* Mike, we said 'Hasta la vista' to each other weeks ago.

STU Got your clothes back yet, mate?

MIKE I wouldn't laugh about this, Stu. It's very important who you talk to about work. *(pause)*

STU What?

MIKE Those cameraman mates of yours.

STU Yeah.

MIKE The ones you have a drink with.

STU Yeah?

MIKE Any from Channel Nine?

STU Some, yeah.

MIKE Do you swap any 'information'?

STU They tell me stories about Ray, I tell them stories about . . . *(he is about to say 'Mike', but stops himself)* Brooke and Marty.

MARTY Mike, I think you're getting a little carried away here.

MIKE Someone's leaking our stories, Marty. *(thinking aloud)* If it's not you, or Stu or Shelley, it's gotta be someone who wants to get in their good books, maybe score a job . . .

Brooke pokes her head out of the kitchen.

BROOKE Would people please put the milk back in the fridge when they've finished with it?

MIKE Fellas, I got a feeling I know who the mole is.

Mike walks off into the kitchen.

STU Not the first time she's been called that.

SCENE 25

THE KITCHEN

MIKE Remember when we were talking about how it would be if we worked at a different network?

BROOKE Mmm, no.

MIKE You said Channel Nine is the place to be.

BROOKE Did I? Sounds like me.

MIKE You said you've had the occasional informal chat with them.

BROOKE What are you on about, Mike?

MIKE Had one recently?

BROOKE Hang on, (let me read between the lines). You think I'm passing on our stories to Channel Nine in return for a job.

MIKE You're saying it.

BROOKE Mike, the only person who blabs on about our stories is you.

MIKE Me?! Yeah, sure – I'm the mole. Who do I go and blab to? *(he makes a horrifying realisation)*

SCENE 26

GEOFF'S OFFICE

MIKE Geoff, you said you know that weatherman from Channel Nine – Monte.

GEOFF Uh-huh. Not that well, but we have spoken. He's a bit up himself . . .

MIKE Ever talk to him about Frontline stories that go to air that night?

GEOFF No. Why?

MIKE I told you about Brooke's High Court story, didn't I?

GEOFF Yeah.

MIKE And Marty's violent videos?

GEOFF *(shocked)* You think I'm the mole!

MIKE Don't be ridiculous, Geoff.

GEOFF I can't believe it! You think I'm leaking your stories to Nine!

MIKE Geoff! Stop! *(uncomfortable pause)* But you *are* friends with Monte?

GEOFF Mike, am I the *only* person you talk to about stories?

SCENE 27

VARIOUS LOCATIONS

We see a montage featuring the following shots, separated by dissolves (no audio).

Domenica's desk – Domenica shaking her head.

Emma's desk – Emma and Kate shaking their heads.

The edit suite – Hugh mouthing the words 'Fuck off'.

The production office at night – Khor shaking his head.

The Frontline studio – Elliot shaking his head.

The production office the next day – Colin Konica shaking his head while Mike holds up originals of show rundowns sitting under the photocopier flap.

Day ❺

SCENE 28

SAM'S OFFICE

Emma and Sam meet.

SAM What?

EMMA Nine have beaten us.

SAM I could kick myself, Em. Nine haven't beaten us. We've beaten ourselves. Too busy looking over our shoulder. The vibe was good. The mix was right. We were kicking arse. Five days later, the vibe is dead. The mix is out the window. And *our* arses are getting kicked.

EMMA Yeah, thanks to someone feeding them half our stories.

SAM Yeah, and that's not the only problem.

EMMA Mike?

SAM He's running round playing Inspector Clouseau, instead of concentrating on the show.

EMMA While we're on the subject of concentration, I just got a call from London Weekend Television. They're ropeable. Apparently our International Story Coordinator's been a bit slack in his correspondence.

SAM *(quietly)* Right. Where's Mike?

EMMA Fax room.

SCENE 29

THE FAX ROOM

SAM Mike, this Sherlock Holmes thing has to stop. I want your mind back on the job. Em's just been given a serve from England.

MIKE Why?

EMMA They haven't even received one show rundown yet!

MIKE What? I've been faxing them every day. Just finished doing this morning's.

EMMA *(taking a piece of paper from Mike)* That's not their number.

MIKE You gave it to me.

EMMA That's not my handwriting.

SAM It's Jan's.

SCENE 30

GLENN RIDGE'S OFFICE

Glenn pulls a fax of a rundown out of his fax machine, picks up the phone and dials.

GLENN Ray, it's Glenn. Sorry – came a little late this morning. Got a pen? Great. 'Lead story. Electricity bills too expensive . . . '

Episode 5
Basic Instincts

Day

SCENE I

THE LOCAL PUB

On the pub television Geoff is finishing off the weather report. Marty, Stu and Jase are talking over a beer.

GEOFF *(on screen)* So, Tim, I'm afraid it's more of the same the next few days.

NEWSREADER *(on screen)* Let's just keep our fingers crossed for the weekend then.

GEOFF My word, let's keep our fingers crossed. Although I think we'll need to cross more than just our fingers.

NEWSREADER Indeed. Thanks, Geoff. And that's all the news for tonight. Join us again tomorrow at six o'clock for the latest. But right now, stay tuned for Frontline with Mike Mo . . .

The TV channel is changed. Jase and Stu have a good laugh.

BARMAN Sorry, boys. Nothin' personal.

STU That's a vote of confidence.

MARTY Guys, don't turn round now . . . *(Stu and Jase both turn around to look)* I don't know why I bother.

STU Hello . . .

We see where the boys are looking. A woman sits with her back to them on the other side of the room.

MARTY Hey, I spotted her first.

The woman turns slightly to reveal it is in fact Emma. The boys react with distaste.

STU It's Emma!

MARTY My God, we were actually . . . perving.

STU What's she doing here? Normally doesn't leave the office till eight o'clock.

MARTY Fellas, don't look now . . .

Stu and Jase both turn. We see them see a guy bring two drinks over and sit with Emma. They are obviously friends.

STU Well, bugger me.

MARTY No wonder she nicked off early.

STU You wanna go over and hang shit on her?

MARTY I'm keeping out of this, fellas. I'm off.

STU Wanna lift?

MARTY You're pissed.

STU No, I always look like this when I've spent an afternoon with Brooke.

MARTY You'll stack your car.

STU I got the unit van.

MARTY Fair enough then. See ya tomorrow.

Marty walks off. Stu turns to take another look at Emma.

SCENE 2

STU'S VAN

Stu is driving home via the back streets, listening to music on the radio. Suddenly he sees something. He switches the radio off and pulls over to the side of the road. He is looking intently off to the other side of the road. His van stops, and without taking his gaze off some action he reaches back, pulls out his camera and films what he is looking at.

SCENE 3

MARTY'S FRONT DOOR

A hand knocks on Marty's door. Marty opens to find Stu, looking strange.

MARTY You've stacked the car. *(Stu shakes his head)* You got picked up by the cops.

Stu breaks out into a smile and holds up a videotape.

STU Mate, I just shot two and a half minutes of the best footage you'll ever get.

SCENE 4

MARTY'S HOUSE

On Marty's TV, we see the footage that Stu has shot. It is of a bashing. Marty cannot believe his eyes.

MARTY What a gift!

STU Can you believe it? I was just driving by.

MARTY You are the luckiest arsehole around!

STU You dream about this kinda stuff.

MARTY It just goes on and on and on.

STU (I know.) I couldn't believe my luck.

MARTY (winces at a particularly bad blow) Was the kid all right?

STU (pause) I dunno.

There is another pause. Marty hasn't stopped looking at the screen.

STU They started coming after me.

MARTY Shit. I hope that kid's all right.

STU I called the cops. Should I have done something? I should have done something. I just kept filming.

MARTY Hey, you called the cops.

STU Yeah.

MARTY (refers to the screen) Mate, you're a legend.

STU Yeah . . .

MARTY A bloody legend.

Day ❷

SCENE 5

THE PRODUCTION OFFICE

Emma enters.

DOMENICA Morning, Em!

Mike emerges from his office, intercepting Emma.

MIKE Oh, you're in at last.

Emma lets this pointed remark go.

EMMA Hi, Mike.

MIKE What's happening with my debate?

EMMA Your . . . ?

MIKE The euthanasia debate. This has been going on for a week. We said we were going to nail it down this morning.

EMMA I'm on the case, Mike.

Emma continues walking to her desk, leaving Mike looking pissed off. He goes over to Domenica.

MIKE (Look at that!) We're trying to get up a debate on one of the most contentious, divisive issues and did you see what time she got in?

DOMENICA Yeah, it was about five minutes after you.

SCENE 6

SAM'S OFFICE

Sam, Marty and Stu are watching the bashing footage.

SAM You're a legend.

STU Thanks, Sam.

MARTY This is one of the most brutal bashings I've ever seen captured on film.

STU It's not bad.

SAM Not bad! They'll be showing this on news reports overseas.

MARTY Either that or 'Funniest Home Videos'.

SAM (calls) Em, get in here!

MARTY Actually, it's not quite brutal enough for 'Funniest Home Videos'.

EMMA (enters with clipboard, smiling) Yeah?

SAM You spoken with police media liaison today?

EMMA Yes.

SAM Any assaults?

EMMA (checking) Just one. Fifteen-year-old kid; two attackers arrested.

SAM This one.

Sam smiles, indicating the footage on screen to Emma.

EMMA You're kidding?! Where did that come from?

STU I shot it.

MARTY This man is a legend.

STU I was lucky.

SAM Hey, you make your own luck in this game. You've got the right instincts.

MARTY Em, he got two and a half minutes worth. Look at it. It goes on and on.

They admire the footage.

EMMA Is this a joke?

STU What?

EMMA Are you setting me up?

STU No.

EMMA You stood by and filmed that for two and a half minutes.

MARTY Hey, he called the cops.

SAM If Stu wasn't there they wouldn't have been caught.

There is an uncomfortable silence.

STU The kid. He's not dead?

Emma shakes her head.

STU Is he OK?

Emma shakes her head again.

STU How not OK?

EMMA Critically not OK.

SCENE 7

THE PRODUCTION OFFICE

Domenica is signing for a huge bunch of flowers.

BROOKE *(pretending she doesn't know they're for her)* Oh-oh. Who are they for?

DOMENICA *(walking past her)* Emma.

Emma emerges from Sam's office. Her eyes light up.

DOMENICA (They're) from David! He sounds really nice.

EMMA They're gorgeous!

KATE Bring him in here. We want to meet him.

General girlie chatter.

BROOKE *(wanting to spoil the party)* Emma, is that Hutchence interview confirmed? *(the laughter suddenly stops)*

EMMA Sorry?

BROOKE My interview with Michael Hutchence. Has it been confirmed?

EMMA Yes.

BROOKE *(surprised)* When did we get the OK?

EMMA Yesterday.

BROOKE Thanks for telling me.

Mike enters.

MIKE So who's the flowers for?

KATE Em.

MIKE You're kidding.

EMMA What's that supposed to mean?

MIKE *(stumbling)* Well, I mean . . . you know . . . You're not normally . . .

EMMA Sorry?

MIKE Hang on, let me choose my words carefully . . . Oh, they know what I mean. *(cutaway of the other girls, stony-faced)* Oh, you do. So do you. You've got me all wrong . . . I have to see Sam.

SCENE 8

SAM'S OFFICE

Sam, Marty and Stu continue to view the tape of the bashing.

STU Did I stuff up?

SAM What? You're a legend.

STU You saw Emma's reaction.

MARTY Emma's reac . . . This is award-winning stuff.

STU What if the kid carks it?

SAM It's not the point. Mate, this issue's been around since cameras were invented. Do you intervene or do you do your job? In the end it's more important that the cameraman does his job.

STU Yeah, but I still feel bad. People are gonna know I stood by while a kid got his head kicked in.

SAM Stu, they won't have to know. Because this tape was handed in to us . . . anonymously.

Stu thinks this over for a second.

STU It doesn't look like amateur footage, mate.

MARTY Don't flatter yourself.

Mike enters.

MIKE What's amateur footage?

SAM This, Mike. *(he hits 'Play' and the footage runs again)*

MIKE Wow!

SAM It was handed in to us anonymously.

MIKE That is incredible. I mean, those handicams – the quality . . . It must have had one of those stabilisers. Geez, it goes on.

SAM It's in tonight's show.

MIKE Great. I'll write some links.

MARTY It's OK, Mike. I'll do that.

MIKE I'll handle it.

MARTY Actually, if you don't mind . . .

MIKE I do mind. Big story. I'm the show's host.

STU Guys, if you ask me, I reckon . . .

MIKE Sorry, Stu? I don't even know what you've got to do with any of this.

STU I'll just leave you guys to decide, then. *(he exits)*

MARTY Sam, tell him it's *my* story!

MIKE It's mine!

MARTY Mike!

SCENE 9

THE PRODUCTION OFFICE

STU Em, don't tell anyone I shot that stuff.

Emma nods while she looks at the bunch of flowers.

STU And if you hear any news about the kid, let me know.

Emma nods and takes the flowers to the kitchen. Marty comes out of Sam's office in a huff.

MARTY *(to Stu)* This place is stuffed! That was *my* piece. Shit.

Meanwhile, the girls gather round and chat.

DOMENICA He's really nice, apparently.

KATE Do we know what he looks like?

DOMENICA Nuh.

SHELLEY What does he do?

The phones are ringing. No-one answers.

BROOKE Is someone going to get the phone?

DOMENICA *(answering phone)* Hello, Frontline . . . Sure, I'll just get her. Em! *(Emma emerges from the kitchen with her flowers in a vase)* Michael Hutchence's manager.

Mike and Sam emerge from Sam's office.

MIKE Oh Sam, can I grab a copy of that when you're finished with it? Got an idea for the introduction.

SAM Great. You need a hand?

MIKE I'm fine.

Sam goes back into his office while Mike heads off to his own office. Brooke enters Sam's office.

BROOKE Did you know that Emma has a boyfriend?

SAM Nope.

BROOKE Well she does.

SAM Good on her.

Pause.

BROOKE Don't you think . . . I mean, isn't it . . .

SAM What?

BROOKE You know, it could um . . .

SAM Brooke, where are you coming from here?

BROOKE Doesn't matter. *(changing topic)* What's that?

SAM Handed into us anonymously. Amateur footage.

BROOKE Amateur? That's SP Betacam.

SAM OK. Stu shot it. But he doesn't want anyone to know.

BROOKE Why?

SAM He didn't help. Kid's in really bad shape.

BROOKE Oh. It's good footage.

Brooke and Sam exit Sam's office.

SAM *(to Emma)* Em, we need promos. I want this hammered for the rest of the afternoon. Hit the exclusive angle.

EMMA *(on phone)* Righto.

SAM And Em . . . *(referring to Mike)* He's writing an intro – he'll need a hand. Otherwise it'll get too 'flowery'. And Hugh's waiting for you in editing. I want you two to weave some magic with this footage.

EMMA OK. One at a time, Sam. *(into phone)* Sorry, Lydia. Ten-thirty tomorrow's fine for Michael? Bit early for him . . . OK, let's make it 11.30. Sure, one o'clock it is. No, we won't ask him anything 'delicate'. Promise. What? OK, what doesn't he want to talk about? Uh-huh, yeah, uh-huh . . . Yes, Lydia, I am writing it down . . . *(she's not)*

DOMENICA Emma, Hugh's waiting for you.

EMMA Travelling.

DOMENICA And David's on hold.

EMMA *(into phone)* Yeah, Lydia, got all that. Positive. Bye. *(hangs up)* Kate, write this down quickly: 'Paula Yates. Kylie Minogue. Last album flop.'

KATE What's it for?

EMMA *(rushing out)* Tell David I'll call him back and they're gorgeous.

Kate shrugs and writes down the words.

SCENE 10

GEOFF'S OFFICE

Stu's footage is playing on Geoff's monitor. Mike is trying to write his story.

MIKE How about this? 'Like a bloodcurdling cloud of terror, the horror of street violence spreads insidiously over the horizon of . . . ' and that's where I need an 'h' word – preferably something rhyming with 'horizon'.

GEOFF That's hard. Homogenising?

MIKE Yeah, that's more about milk . . .

GEOFF I can't believe you've been left to write this on your own.

MIKE Can't rely on Emma. That euthanasia debate – hasn't done a thing for it yet.

GEOFF Why not?

MIKE Apparently she's got a boyfriend.

GEOFF Really?

MIKE Yeah. I'm surprised too.

GEOFF *(distracted, half to himself)* You're kidding.

MIKE *(not noticing Geoff's face)* My reaction exactly.

GEOFF *(miserably, to himself)* A boyfriend . . .

MIKE *(looks up)* Geoff . . . Geoff – are you all right? *(Geoff is still silent)* What's the matter?

GEOFF Nothing.

MIKE *(indicating TV screen)* Pretty amazing stuff, huh? *(Geoff looks)* Amateur footage.

GEOFF Looks like broadcast-quality SP Betacam to me.

MIKE Sorry?

GEOFF I reckon that's been filmed by a professional.

MIKE *(uncertain)* It hasn't.

GEOFF It has.

SCENE 11

SAM'S OFFICE

SAM It hasn't.

MIKE *(strongly)* It has! This has been filmed by a professional!

SAM All right, Mike – close the door. *(Mike does)* I knew I was never going to fool you. It's not amateur footage.

MIKE I knew it!

SAM Stu shot it.

MIKE Stu!

SAM Keep it down.

MIKE Stu was there? Aaah . . . now it's all starting to make sense.

SAM Yeah, so there's a slight problem.

MIKE Right. (pause) What is it?

SAM Mike . . .

MIKE He's not happy with the way he filmed it.

SAM No, Mike.

MIKE It was a bit shaky.

SAM He filmed for two and a half minutes while the kid got his head kicked in.

MIKE Disgraceful. People are gonna pick that up like . . . (clicks fingers)

SAM It's not disgraceful.

MIKE It is. There's a guy who put self-interest ahead of personal principle, and that's the way the people will view it.

SAM That's why we've said it was handed in anonymously. Hugh's gonna make it look like home video.

MIKE So I go to air and lie. Then I'm doing what Stu did. That's even more disgraceful.

SAM All right, then. I'll give it to Marty.

SCENE 12

THE FRONTLINE STUDIO

Mike is at the Frontline desk, on air.

MIKE . . . earlier today a tape was handed to me anonymously. What it shows is first-hand evidence of the growing sickness that is street violence. We warn viewers the following scenes may cause distress.

Cut to control room, where Sam and Emma watch.

SAM That'll get 'em in.

The footage is screened. It has been de-graded and a date has been superimposed in one corner.

SAM That looks great. You and Hughie are champions. Well done, Em.

EMMA Thanks. God knows how I fitted everything in today.

SAM Let me shout you a drink after the show.

EMMA Can't tonight. But thanks.

SCENE 13

THE PRODUCTION OFFICE

It is after the show. General celebrations.

SAM Good story, Mike.

MIKE (modestly) Thanks, Sam. I really didn't do much.

MARTY (under breath) I'll drink to that.

SAM (proposing toast) Hey, what about a toast to our 'amateur cameraman'?

All toast. Stu looks decidedly uncomfortable.

SAM I was just saying to Em . . . Where is she?

KATE Gone home.

SAM (remembering) That's right.

MARTY She sick?

Domenica, Kate and Shelley shrug. Sam doesn't understand.

BROOKE In love. Sam – it's a worry. The Michael Hutchence interview's tomorrow, and she hasn't done a scrap of research yet.

MARTY My God, you might even have to think of your own questions!

BROOKE At least I can hold onto my own stories.

MIKE Actually I'm concerned too. This euthanasia debate just hasn't got off the ground.

SAM What?

MIKE Hasn't booked a guest. Might as well do it myself.

SAM I'll speak to her.

STU (slightly down) I'm outta here.

MARTY Don't forget your camera.

STU (quietly and seriously) Not funny.

SAM (indicating for Stu to follow him into his office) Mate . . . (they go into his office)

KATE What's wrong with Stu?

MARTY Don't worry about it.

MIKE He shot the footage.

ALL THE OTHERS What?!

MARTY Mike!

MIKE Well, he did. You were all going to find out eventually!

Marty just shakes his head in a 'You dickhead' gesture. Mike looks feeble.

SCENE 14

SAM'S OFFICE

SAM Great stuff tonight, mate.

STU Thanks.

SAM You OK?

STU Em says the kid's not getting any better.

SAM Mate, what were you supposed to do?

STU Help him?

SAM Stu, we've gone through this before. Do you do your job or do you help out? (What about) the guy that filmed the My Lai massacre? You don't think he could have tried to help the villagers who were getting shot? But then the world would never have seen what the Americans were really doing in Vietnam. You've got a duty to film, not intervene.

STU Sam – this wasn't My Lai. It was one kid being belted by two kids. I could have helped. What I filmed didn't help anyone.

SAM All right, so it wasn't a My Lai massacre. It was more like the Rodney King footage. People are now aware of what goes on on their streets.

STU And they didn't know before? Come on – we can spend all night justifying it but when it all boils down, I did what I did out of instinct and you're playing it 'cause it's good television.

SAM Mate, you're being too hard on yourself. I've seen some dynamite footage in my time, but what you shot last night was up with the best of it. You are a legend.

Day ③

SCENE 15

THE KITCHEN

Emma is cutting the stems off her flowers. She is in a perky mood and is singing. Brooke enters.

BROOKE Good morning, Emma.

EMMA What's wrong?

BROOKE Nothing. I just said 'Good morning'.

EMMA Good morning, Brooke.

BROOKE Nice flowers.

EMMA Uh-huh.

BROOKE This fellow of yours sounds lovely.

EMMA He is.

BROOKE Do you spend much time together?

EMMA Brooke, your Michael Hutchence questions will be ready before your interview, as usual.

BROOKE Hey, hey . . .

EMMA The reason you don't have them on your desk this morning has nothing to do with David. I'm very busy at the moment.

BROOKE Emma . . . I just want to say one thing. We work in current affairs. We're extremely lucky girls. We're good at our jobs because we've always been focused.

EMMA That's funny – I thought *we* were good at *our* jobs because *we've* always had someone to write our questions for us.

BROOKE I'm just trying to help out.

SCENE 16

SAM'S OFFICE

Sam and Mike meet.

MIKE Brooke took me aside last night. I tell you what – we think that Emma's lacking . . . focus. *(he gets distracted)*

SAM Mike?

MIKE Sam?

SAM Emma's lacking focus.

MIKE She is, but I don't mind . . . Could be a blessing in disguise. Euthanasia debate . . . I'm happy to organise it myself.

SAM Mike, I don't think . . .

MIKE Sam, don't worry. I know what you want – fireworks. And this issue will deliver.

SAM OK – but talk to Emma too.

MIKE Any fallout from last night?

SAM Are you kidding? *(points upstairs)* They're rapt.

MIKE I really think Stu should've helped that kid.

SAM I know, Mike. But I mean, journalists have been arguing this dilemma for decades.

MIKE *(agreeing)* We have.

SAM *(I mean)* what's the difference between a cameraman who films a war and a cameraman who films a local bashing?

MIKE It's an old chestnut.

SAM We've got a duty to the public, to let them know what's happening.

MIKE It's a burden.

SAM It's the My Lai massacre principle.

MIKE Of course. My Lai massacre. That puts it in perspective. My Lai.

SCENE 17

MIKE IS ON AIR AT 3LO WITH PETER COUCHMAN.

PETER Congratulations, Mike – powerful story last night. No doubt it rated through the roof?

MIKE Yep. Twenty-eights in Melbourne, twenty-seven Sydney. The same elsewhere, but you know I've never taken much notice of ratings.

PETER Right.

MIKE And that's just a HUT figure. The audience averages would be higher.

PETER Hmm. But last night's story . . .

Cut to the production office, where everybody is listening to Mike on the radio.

MIKE *(voice only)* Well, I guess it reflects genuine community concern over the issue of street violence.

PETER *(voice only)* Do you know whether the person who filmed it helped the boy?

Cut to Stu looking uncomfortable.

MIKE No, no, maybe, but not that it matters . . .

PETER Why doesn't it matter?

MIKE Well, it's that whole My Lai massacre theory, isn't it?

PETER How is it?

Sam looks worried. Cut back to the 3LO studio.

MIKE Well, it just is.

PETER Which particular facets of My Lai?

MIKE None in particular, just generally . . .

PETER Mike, we've got the woman on the line who took the kid to hospital. Andrea, hello.

Mike looks worried.

ANDREA *(voice only)* Yes, hello Mr Couchman. I want to ask Mr Moore a question.

PETER Go ahead.

ANDREA If he says that they got the footage anonymously, how can he explain the Frontline van opposite the park?

Mike is somewhat like a rabbit in a spotlight.

SCENE 18

SAM'S OFFICE

The shit has hit the fan.

MIKE I can't believe it! I cop the flak when Stu's the culprit!

SAM You're not copping flak.

MIKE *(What!)* I've been called a liar on radio! I didn't want to lie! I came in here yesterday and said 'Sam, I'm not going to lie.' And you made me go on air and lie!

SAM Hey, I offered the story to Marty. You practically begged me to give it to you!

EMMA *(popping head in)* Sam, the *Australian.*

SAM Right.

MIKE Sam . . .

SAM Mike, (leave me alone will ya?) If I don't put out some major bushfires, every paper will be calling us a bunch of opportunistic scumbags.

MIKE What about the My Lai massacre theory?

SAM It's got nothing to do with that. We lied.

MIKE I'm not taking the blame, Sam. Is that clear? Stu stuffed up. I think I deserve some protection!

SCENE 19

THE PRODUCTION OFFICE

Mike exits Sam's office in a huff.

MARTY Tell me, Mike – when was the My Lai massacre?

MIKE Shut up, Marty. You're just as responsible as Stu for this mess.

MARTY Hey, you're the one who went on air and bullshitted.

MIKE If anyone bullshitted it was you two. *(he indicates Marty and Stu)* You told me it was amateur footage.

MARTY You didn't complain when you found out it wasn't.

MIKE You know who should take the rap? Sam! He's the EP. He should take the fall.

DOMENICA *(calls)* Ronald Marks of the Euthanasia Council on the line.

MIKE Oh, I've forgotten! That's this afternoon. My whole life is fireworks.

BROOKE Come on, Stu. We're gonna be late for Mr Hutchence. *(she sifts through the stuff on her desk)*

EMMA Interview's been changed to one o'clock.

BROOKE When did that happen?

EMMA Yesterday.

BROOKE Why didn't you tell me? *(she sidles over to Emma)* Haven't we spoken about things like this? This guy *(pointing to flowers)* is affecting your work.

EMMA Brooke, it's up there. *(points at whiteboard)* Has been for the last twenty-four hours. I know you expect me to write your questions, but I think you can manage an occasional glance at the whiteboard on your own.

BROOKE Hey Emma – guess what? I do not expect you to write my questions. Never have, never will.

EMMA Suits me.

BROOKE Fine.

SCENE 20

GEOFF'S OFFICE

Mike and Geoff are looking through an encyclopaedia.

GEOFF Mei Lei . . . Meilei . . .

MIKE Maybe it's a hyphenated word. Try under Hawaii – it sounds Hawaiian.

GEOFF Here we go.

MIKE No, that's Maui.

GEOFF Maui, Meilei – could just be different pronunciation.

MIKE Right. Was there a massacre there?

GEOFF There's a volcano . . .

MIKE Well, that would've killed people.

GEOFF This sounds like it.

SCENE 21

THE CREW'S CAR

Stu, Jase and Brooke are driving to the Hutchence interview.

STU You know what, Jase? I reckon I stuffed up. I wish I'd never shot that bloody attack. The thing that shits me is that everybody in the office is trying to cover their own arse and no-one is stopping to . . .

BROOKE Sshh, Stu – I'm trying to concentrate. Did Michael Hutchence do a song for the new *Die Hard* film or the latest *Batman* film?

STU I dunno.

BROOKE Well, come on – we've got to come up with some questions.

STU Haven't you got any questions?

BROOKE Of course I've got questions. Give me the phone.

SCENE 22

THE PRODUCTION OFFICE

DOMENICA Afternoon – Frontline.

BROOKE *(voice only)* It's me.

DOMENICA Who?

BROOKE Me, Brooke. I want to talk to Emma.

DOMENICA She's gone to lunch.

BROOKE Lunch!

DOMENICA David's taken her to that new cafe in . . .

BROOKE Get me Kate.

DOMENICA Hang on.

KATE Hello.

BROOKE Did Emma leave any info for this Hutchence piece?

KATE No.

BROOKE Nothing?

KATE I remember she asked me to write out a list of things while she was speaking to his manager.

BROOKE That's something. Read them to me.

KATE Got a pen? 'Paula Yates. Kylie Minogue. Last album flop.'

SCENE 23

THE PRODUCTION OFFICE

It is later. Emma enters in a rush. She has been crying.

EMMA Sorry.

KATE How was lunch? *(Emma doesn't answer)* Are you all right?

EMMA *(obviously not wanting to talk about it)* Where is everyone?

KATE Mike's pre-recording his euthanasia interview.

EMMA What? With who?

KATE He's organised the guests himself.

EMMA Oh, Jesus. *(exits)*

SCENE 24

THE FRONTLINE STUDIO

Mike is at the Frontline desk talking to his guests.

MIKE All right, let's just all . . . We can express our opinions but let's keep our shirts on. *(Emma walks in)* Oh Em – good of you to join us.

The floor manager counts down from five to go.

MIKE Welcome back. Well, the vexed issue of euthanasia continues to divide the community. Few debates have been as emotionally charged and never have two sides been further apart. Tonight we look at both sides of this controversial issue. Ronald Marks, head of the Euthanasia Council of Australia . . .

RONALD Good evening.

MIKE . . . and Vanessa Gibbs, acting chairperson of the Civil Liberties Council.

Vanessa nods.

MIKE To you first, Ronald – you believe euthanasia should be legalised?

RONALD Absolutely. It's a fundamental right, currently denied us all.

MIKE Well Vanessa, what do you have to say to that?

VANESSA I agree.

MIKE Sorry?

VANESSA The Civil Liberties Council fully supports euthanasia. We always have.

MIKE *(thrown)* Right. Well, we seem to have found consensus.

SCENE 25

SAM'S OFFICE

Mike and Brooke are both competing for Sam's attention.

MIKE How was I to know they're on the same side? Emma should have been there.

BROOKE At least your guest hung around.

MIKE What happened?

BROOKE I got halfway through her first question and Michael Hutchence is out the door. This is a joke, Sam.

MIKE It's a joke.

SAM *(after a dramatic pause)* Are you both finished?

Mike and Brooke nod.

SAM I'll speak to Emma.

SHELLEY *(entering)* Sam, Caville wants you upstairs.

SCENE 26

CAVILLE'S OFFICE

Sam is on the couch.

CAVILLE What did you tell the press?

SAM Exactly what you said. (Told them that) we acted responsibly by showing people what goes on rather than trying to stop a one-off act. Said we'd done nothing illegal and actually helped the police by giving them the footage.

CAVILLE Good.

There is an uncomfortable pause.

SAM It's not enough though, is it?

CAVILLE No. We did lie unfortunately and someone needs to take the blame.

SAM It's slightly complicated. The decision was taken by a few people. I mean, technically Mike made the announcement but I should . . .

CAVILLE Sam, Sam. *(stopping him)* I don't care who's to blame. I just want someone to *take* the blame.

SCENE 27

THE FRONTLINE STUDIO

The show is going to air.

MIKE Well, that's about it for tonight. Just before we go, last night I stated I had personally received an anonymous videotape. It's with a great deal of sadness that I admit that I, Mike Moore, was misled, lied to. The tape was actually shot by a senior Frontline cameraman who will be disciplined accordingly. *(changes tone of voice)* But on a lighter note, Friday night funnyman Elliot Rhodes is set to shine his satirical light on the weekly news.

Cut to Elliot at his keyboard.

ELLIOT Petrol prices keep going up
Like a nightie on a bride
Canberra's taking more and more
And taking us for a ride.

Super, diesel, unleaded, gas
Everything's taking a hike
While drivers stuck at the petrol pump
Say 'Keating – get on ya bike.'

We can't afford these prices
But the government's all talk
If they keep on taking their slices
I'm gonna get out and walk. *(honks bike horn)*

During this song Mike speaks to the crew.

MIKE You don't think we should actually name him? I mean, we know it's Stu, but maybe we should, you know, say his name?

There is no response from the crew.

SCENE 28

THE LADIES' BATHROOM

BROOKE Em, I know it hurts, but you did the right thing.

EMMA What?

BROOKE It's for the best.

EMMA *(astonished)* You think I broke up with David on your advice? You – telling me about relationships!

BROOKE Just keep it down a bit, Em.

EMMA I am not your de facto personal assistant. Technically, I don't have to do half the crap I do for you.

BROOKE Emma. *(she gestures to be quiet)* You may not have seen it, but having a boyfriend was affecting your focus.

EMMA God, Brooke! You are so hypocritical. I'm glad all your boyfriends never affect *your* focus. You weren't worried David was going to damage my career – you were worried he was going to damage yours.

BROOKE *(lost for words)* Time heals the pain, Em.

Emma exits, annoyed. The toilet flushes and Domenica emerges spraying a can of air freshener.

DOMENICA Excuse me.

SCENE 29

THE PRODUCTION OFFICE

The staff are having a drink after the show.

MIKE Honestly, I think it's for the best. There's a code of ethics. Stu transgressed the code; now he's paying the price.

KATE So he's been sacked?

MARTY 'Disciplined', Kate. Six weeks' holiday on full pay.

KATE Oh! *(she goes towards the kitchen)*

MARTY That's the beauty of this form of discipline. Everybody's happy, including the fall guy. You do the crime, you do the time – but in style.

MIKE I think he should have been sacked for causing this whole thing. He risked my reputation. He should have been hung out to dry.

MARTY Mike, they sack Stu and he can go out and say anything about us. Even say *we* were responsible for the whole thing.

MIKE Wouldn't put it past him. He's got a spiteful streak.

MARTY Sam disciplined him just enough so that justice is seen to be done, but not so much that he turns against us. Get it?

MIKE Right.

Kate comes back from the kitchen with a coffee. She speaks discreetly.

KATE Uh-oh.

SHELLEY Emma?

KATE *(nods)* Still a little teary.

MIKE Still? I'll have a word with her.

The girls react in horror.

GIRLS No, Mike!

Mike cannot be stopped. He walks over to the kitchen and out of sight. After a brief pause Emma runs out of the kitchen crying. Mike re-emerges.

MIKE She's fine.

SIX WEEKS LATER

SCENE 30

THE SUPREME COURT

Several news crews wait around on the Supreme Court steps, their gear on the ground. Marty, Stu and Jase are amongst them.

MARTY So after that?

STU I spent the last two weeks with my sister in Noosa.

MARTY Christ, I'd kill for some sun.

STU Hey, it wasn't a holiday, Marty. Took the rap for all you bastards.

MARTY The thing that gets me . . .

Marty is cut off by the sound of screeching brakes and a crash. The camera pans to see a car accident, then pans back to the crowd of cameramen. They grab their cameras and leave frame. Stu is left in frame. He pauses, then grabs his camera and leaves frame. The frame is left empty.

Episode 6
Let the Children Play

Day ❶

SCENE 1

THE KITCHEN

Mike, Rebecca and Domenica are making a coffee. Marty enters.

DOMENICA So how long are you here for, Rebecca?

REBECCA A week. Mike's showing me round.

DOMENICA *Uncle* Mike.

MIKE No, come on Dom. I let her call me Mike. She's a grown-up after all. Doing media studies.

MARTY Wasn't that the one you failed, Mike?

MIKE *(pretending to laugh)* Come on, Marty. Actually, I'd like you to meet my niece Rebecca.

MARTY G'day. So you here on work experience?

REBECCA Uh-huh.

MARTY I was talking to Mike.

Rebecca laughs. Domenica and Marty leave.

MIKE Told you he was funny.

MARTY *(calling as he leaves)* Em, tell Sam we could have a walk-in.

MIKE *(explaining)* Sam's our EP. You know what EP stands for?

REBECCA Enormous penis.

MIKE Where'd you hear that? He's executive producer.

REBECCA He's the boss.

MIKE Sort of. More a partnership. He and I work hand in hand to shape the show.

REBECCA But isn't it just a formula?

MIKE Not with Frontline. We're trying to throw out the old formulas. That's the great thing about Sam. He doesn't care what the opposition are doing. He's not looking over his shoulder.

SCENE 2

SAM'S OFFICE

Sam, Emma and Kate are watching the end of a story from 'A Current Affair'. The girls are a little teary. We see slo-mo footage of young children opening presents, accompanied by Whitney Houston singing 'The Greatest Love of All'. We hear a voice-over.

VOICE-OVER Thanks to Angry and his team of volunteers, Christmas has finally arrived for these very special kids.

Just as the story ends and an image of Ray Martin appears, Sam hits the 'Pause' button.

SAM I reckon we do what Nine is doing.

EMMA Sam!

SAM It was brilliant telly last night. You two are both bawling.

EMMA We can't just pinch the idea.

SAM Why not?

EMMA It's got 'A Current Affair' stamped all over it.

SAM Well, let's stamp the name 'Frontline' over the top.

KATE I don't know why these things suck me in. But you see sick kids, the music . . .

SAM It's a formula! You know they didn't really find all those presents in a week.

KATE I know, Sam. I'm not an idiot. But they did it, and it helped the kids, and I know it's set up, but it's a good thing.

SAM (This whole thing is) just a cynical attempt to tug at the heartstrings.

EMMA Cynical! You're the one who wants to pinch it!

SAM Hey, let's clear one thing up right now. Channel Nine pinched the entire concept from England.

EMMA Are you sure?

SAM I was at Nine when we did it. Listen, we do one of these specials – in the end, who benefits?

EMMA AND KATE (reluctantly) The kids.

SAM Exactly. And us, in ratings terms maybe, so it's a win-win situation. All we gotta do is make our version look different.

KATE How?

SAM (unsure) Oh, he does kids with life-threatening diseases, we'll do kids with . . .

EMMA Coughs and colds?

KATE Tinea?

SAM We'll do kids with something. Sort it out.

EMMA And who do you want hosting this entirely new concept?

SAM Well, seeing as we're pinching the concept, we might as well pinch the host.

Emma and Kate look horrified.

SCENE 3

A BISTRO

Sam is having lunch with a bald man wearing an earring. We do not see his face.

SAM I mean, Angry, ACA are burying you - the odd special once every three months. Come across to Frontline and you'll be weekly. What do you think?

SCENE 4

MIKE'S OFFICE

Mike is showing Rebecca some ratings figures.

MIKE This column here is the number of people watching us, and these are the other networks.

REBECCA Do you mean the number of people watching or the percentage of sets actually in use?

Mike pauses.

MIKE Look, if I had a bit more time I'd explain it to you. Ooh, ouch – look at that. 'Current Affair' gave us a hiding last night.

REBECCA Wow.

MIKE Mind you, they had one of those Angry Anderson 'challenges' on. Did you see it?

REBECCA No.

MIKE Gotta hand it to him. (He) found all these presents in a week. Must have moved like lightning.

Domenica enters holding a fax.

DOMENICA Mike, you heard of Astral Lodge?

MIKE Falls Creek? Uh-huh.

DOMENICA They're offering free accommodation to celebrities this weekend as part of the ski season opening.

MIKE Dom . . . (gives thumbs up)

DOMENICA (leaving) You really deserve this, Mike.

MIKE (pretending to be modest) Well . . .

REBECCA What's this column here? 'HUTS'?

MIKE Oh, 'HUTS'. Um, well, that's an acronym.

REBECCA What's it stand for?

MIKE I think it's Latin. 'Humanus . . . under . . . ' I mean, there's some English in there as well. 'Humanus under . . . '

REBECCA 'Homes Using Television'.

MIKE You know?

REBECCA Uh-huh.

MIKE Well, why'd you ask me if you knew?

REBECCA Marty told me to ask you.

MIKE Look, that's just wasting my time.

Mike looks out of his office and sees Marty. He indicates for Rebecca to follow him into the general office area.

MIKE Might just go and speak to him.

Mike leads Rebecca out of his office. Marty is waiting next to Kate as she hangs up the phone.

KATE Not talking.

MARTY Bitch.

KATE Marty! Her husband's just been shot.

MARTY Got an address?

KATE But . . .

Marty indicates for Kate to give it to him. She writes the address out. He speaks to Stu and Jase.

MARTY *(impatient)* Come on, fellas.

STU *(grabbing camera)* Travelling.

MIKE Marty.

MARTY Hey Mike. *(to Rebecca)* You ask him? *(Rebecca nods)*

MIKE I was wondering if Rebecca could tag along with you guys. She'd love to see a story being put together.

MARTY We're leaving now.

STU *(leaving)* Come on.

STU AND MARTY Hut, hut, hut, hut . . .

Sam enters the office as the boys and Rebecca prepare to leave.

EMMA How was lunch?

SAM Not great.

EMMA Keep looking?

Sam nods. He spots Mike.

SAM How's it going, Mike?

MIKE Fine. Oh, Sam – have you met my niece Rebecca?

SAM G'day, sweetheart. Mike, can we have a word?

MIKE Sure. *(to Rebecca, making 'hand in hand' gesture)* Gotta 'shape the show'. You run along with Marty. I'll just be in with . . . *(indicates Sam's office)* Dom – hold all calls. And can you organise some . . . *(skiing motion)*

SCENE 5

SAM'S OFFICE

SAM You see the ratings last night?

Mike indicates he has with a nod and a frown.

SAM Every time one of these Angry Anderson Challenge specials is screened we get thrashed. So I think to myself: what would any normal EP do in this situation?

MIKE They'd do the predictable, Sam. Copy the concept and milk it for all it's worth.

SAM That's right.

MIKE But you're different. You're your own man. You wouldn't be party to such a cynical, knee-jerk response.

Sam turns away from Mike and mouths the word 'Fuck'.

SAM *(turning back)* Right again. But what if we were to come up with something completely different?

MIKE Completely different. Yep, sure.

SAM Yet harnessing the same concept.

Mike looks a little unsure.

SAM I mean, Channel Nine don't have a monopoly on charity, do they?

MIKE No.

SAM And the bottom line is, these specials help the needy . . .

MIKE Absolutely.

SAM Sick kids, poor people . . .

MIKE Sure.

SAM So the more of them, when you think about it, the more people helped. John Stuart Mill, utilitarianism, the greatest good to the greatest number . . .

MIKE *(nods knowingly)* He summed it up.

SAM *(winding himself up)* I mean, God damn it, there's a need there. We want to help and all of a sudden we can't do anything because they 'own' charity!

MIKE Oh, it makes your blood boil.

SAM You know what? Let's do it.

MIKE Absolutely! *(pause)* Do what?

SAM A charity special.

MIKE Great!

SAM Let's whack a host in the centre . . .

MIKE Yep.

SAM Maybe a muso, a challenge to meet, a deadline . . .

MIKE Um . . .

SAM What?

MIKE Aren't we getting a bit close to what Nine are doing?

SAM Bugger them, Mike. We thought it up totally independently. Right then. You were there.

MIKE Yeah, we fleshed it out.

SAM Now we should get started.

MIKE Let's get the ball rolling.

Emma enters without knocking.

EMMA Sam, found some really good charity causes.

MIKE For what?

Emma sees Sam's 'Don't tell him' expression.

EMMA Um, for you to donate to . . . that whole tax thing.

SAM Later, Em.

MIKE Sam and I *are* having a meeting. We've just come up with an idea.

SCENE 6

SAM'S OFFICE

Emma, Kate and Sam meet. They are looking at a whiteboard with two columns of writing. We see:

Cancer Kids	Farnham
Aids Babies	Neil Finn
Abos	Tim Finn
Spas. Kids	Glenn Shorrock
Homeless Youths	Daddo(s)
Schizos	Stevie Wright
Chernobyl Kids	Shirl *(crossed out)*

EMMA So it's a toss-up between the Chernobyl kids and the inner-city homeless.

SAM I like the inner-city kids. Don't want anyone dying on us.

EMMA *(facetiously)* Heaven forbid.

SAM OK, inner-city kids. What do we provide for them?

EMMA Drugs.

KATE A rifle range?

SAM Can we just limit our suggestions to the category 'useful'?

EMMA A playground?

SAM Now we're talking! Swings, grass, skateboard ramp. How we going with a host?

EMMA *(consults list)* Not good.

SAM Hmm. *(calls)* Brooke!

Brooke comes to the door.

SAM We're chasing a host for this charity special. Ex-muso, bit of TV experience . . .

EMMA Drug-free.

BROOKE That narrows the field. What about Jon English?

SAM Not bad. Where'd you pull that name out of, Brooke?

Brooke catches Emma smiling.

BROOKE Excuse me. We met on the 40 Hour Famine launch.

EMMA Which was about as long as the relationship lasted.

BROOKE You asked for suggestions.

SAM *(to Emma)* Suss him out.

EMMA Sure. *(to Brooke)* You got a number?

BROOKE It's in my book.

SCENE 7

SAM'S OFFICE

Sam, Emma and Jon English meet.

SAM So what's Em told you?

JON You're putting together a charity special. Building a playground for some kids.

SAM Yeah. And we want you to host it.

JON Sort of like those Angry Anderson things?

SAM Oh, I guess in a way the lines intersect somewhere. Whatever – you're doing stuff for kids.

JON Great. How long have we got?

SAM Long as we need – weeks – but we gotta make it *look* like it's all been done in twenty-four hours.

JON Why?

SAM You know – just a bit of showbiz. A race against time.

JON *(understanding)* Right . . .

SAM Here's how it works. We'll get you to roll up, ask the kids what they really want. They'll say 'a playground' . . .

EMMA They actually want a basketball court.

SAM *(to Emma)* Too late. We're going with the playground. *(to Jon)* Then you've got 'twenty-four hours' to meet the challenge.

EMMA Though, according to legal, we can't use the word 'challenge'.

SCENE 8

THE FRONTLINE STUDIO

Mike is showing Rebecca around the studio.

MIKE So – you have a good time with Marty?

REBECCA Uh-huh.

MIKE He's a good operator.

REBECCA Real good. He tricked this woman into giving him a photo of her dead husband.

MIKE How'd he do that?

REBECCA Said if she gave it to him, he'd make sure it was distributed to all media outlets.

MIKE Oh, that's kind of him.

REBECCA I don't think he's going to.

MIKE Ah well, you're new to this game. Anyway, this is the 'engine room' of the show. You've got your desk, cameras, autocue . . .

REBECCA Everything's written out for you?

MIKE It's not for *me*. They *(points to control room)* need it.

REBECCA *(reading autocue screen)* Even your reactions are written.

MIKE For them. And I often improvise. I mean, sure it says 'smile', but there's a lot of room for interpretation there. The whole smile spectrum is pretty broad . . .

REBECCA What's the story about?

Mike consults rundown on desk.

MIKE Well, it's all here, on the rundown. I get a copy. *(reads)* 'Used cars'. One of Brooke's.

REBECCA But what's it about?

MIKE Oh well, cars. Used ones.

REBECCA So you won't really know until it's gone to air?

MIKE No. They like me to see the story as it goes to air, so my reactions stay fresh. Now, we can stay here and I can show you round the rest of the studio, or we can go to the edit suite.

SCENE 9

THE EDIT SUITE

Brooke and Hugh are working on a story. Mike and Rebecca watch from behind. We see a bit of the story. Brooke stands in a used-car yard.

BROOKE *(on screen)* Well, we've done our homework, compared prices and selected a model. Now it's just a matter of choosing the car.

The image goes to fast motion as Brooke 'runs' around the car yard, to the tune of 'She Drives Me Crazy' by Fine Young Cannibals. Hugh hits 'Stop' as he and Brooke look at each other with a satisfied 'Job's done' expression.

MIKE Now that story's edited it can go into the show.

REBECCA So when a story's a little boring you add music, and when it's really boring you put it in fast motion?

Brooke gives an 'I'll kill the little bitch' expression. Hugh has an asthma attack. Mike escorts Rebecca out. Their last few lines are heard as they depart.

MIKE Why don't we pop down to the canteen?

REBECCA Then can we go to the production meeting?

MIKE There's no production meeting today. I checked with Dom.

REBECCA Yes there is. Four o'clock. I heard them talking about it.

MIKE When?

REBECCA After you left.

SCENE 10

THE PRODUCTION OFFICE

Everyone is at the production meeting. Rebecca is helping to hand out rundowns.

MIKE *(to Domenica)* This meeting wasn't in my diary. *(coming over to the table)* Oh, just before we start – I presume everyone here has met my niece Rebecca?

There are general 'hello/hi's from the room.

SAM OK, how we doing? Marty, the murdered guy's wife?

MARTY Saying 'no' to all interviews. But we did manage to find this little exclusive.

Marty casually produces the photo. Congratulations from all present.

EMMA How'd you get that?

REBECCA He tricked . . .

MARTY *(cutting her off)* Could have an interview with the cops as well.

SAM OK, what else?

EMMA *(reads)* Brooke's got a gay teacher.

BROOKE (Been) contacted by a guy who claims he's been dismissed from the Education Department because he's homosexual.

MARTY Is he a poof?

MIKE Hey! Marty! (Watch your language in front of Rebecca.)

Brooke shrugs her shoulders. She couldn't care less.

SAM Story set to go?

BROOKE Just waiting for the ABC to give us permission for some overlay.

MIKE *(explains to Rebecca)* 'Overlay' is extra footage we use to help illustrate a story.

REBECCA Oh, like in this one you'd be using stuff from the Gay Mardi Gras.

The look on Brooke's face tells us Rebecca is right. The others laugh.

MIKE How'd you know that?

REBECCA Whenever you do a story on homosexuals you usually show stuff from the Gay Mardi Gras.

EMMA (Moving right along.) The charity challenge.

MIKE Oh yeah. Listen up. This is an idea Sam and I have been tossing around. We need a host and a cause.

EMMA We're getting Jon English to build a playground for underprivileged kids in the inner city.

MIKE *(surprised)* Great.

REBECCA Sounds like a rip-off of those Angry Anderson challenge spec . . .

KATE Why don't I take you to meet Mike's friend the weatherman?

MIKE *(irritated)* His name's Geoff. *(to Rebecca)* I'll be right up.

Everybody (with the possible exception of Rebecca) agrees this is a great idea. Kate gently guides Rebecca away.

MIKE Phew! Out of her depth. Still, we're going to face a bit of that. People not realising that we're harnessing the same concept, thinking it's a copy.

SAM *(to Emma)* So – all looking good?

EMMA *(nods)* Suzuki are keen to supply a car. Mitre 10 have agreed to kick in for the hardware but they want more than a credit.

SAM Meaning?

EMMA On-camera visit to the store.

SAM Jesus.

EMMA And first ad out of the break.

MARTY Well, that's really entering into the spirit of things.

SAM All right, but they've got to look 'surprised' when we walk in.

EMMA I've explained that.

SAM What else?

EMMA We're still chasing a builder who's available and we need some playground gear.

SAM Phone a few toyshops. Lean on 'em.

EMMA How?

SAM '(If) you don't donate, your competition's gonna get the glory.'

EMMA Got it.

MIKE If there's anything I can do to help, Em . . .

EMMA It's fine, Mike.

MIKE No, this is my idea. Only fair I do a bit of the legwork.

SAM Are we done?

EMMA Oh, just one other thing. Slight hitch with phones. Ericsson have said they'll supply them but Optus are a main network sponsor.

SAM Mmm, dodgy.

MARTY Perhaps we should run it past . . . *(points upstairs)*

EMMA The managing director?

MARTY No, Mike's niece.

General mirth.

MIKE Come on, she's a good kid.

SCENE 11

GEOFF'S OFFICE

Mike, Geoff and Rebecca meet. Mike rubs his neck.

MIKE Man, what a day.

GEOFF You've got to pace yourself, Mike.

MIKE If only I could! Been flat out since we got in.

REBECCA At eleven o'clock.

MIKE *(ignoring her)* Walk into the office – Sam wants an ideas session. Then we had a production meeting – Em's asking for help. You weren't there for that bit, Rebecca.

REBECCA You told us before.

MIKE Did I? Geoff, did I?

GEOFF Oh, maybe you did. I forget. I'm a little distracted . . .

MIKE I've noticed that.

GEOFF I'm helping to organise a charity auction this Friday . . .

MIKE You just give that Spastic Society so much of your time.

GEOFF *(genuinely modest)* Well . . .

MIKE I mean, if you weren't a friend of mine I wouldn't have a clue. You really ought to get Jan to organise something.

GEOFF But I don't want . . .

MIKE Geoff, if you're going to do charity you've got to let people know about it.

GEOFF Sure.

MIKE So how's the auction looking?

GEOFF Problem. John was going to be celebrity auctioneer. . .

MIKE John?

GEOFF John – you know, the host of 'Jackpot'.

MIKE Oh – John Phelps.

GEOFF Yeah. Anyway apparently he's double-booked and had to pull out.

MIKE I don't accept that.

GEOFF Oh, he's done it for the past two years.

MIKE I don't care. You make a commitment – you keep it.

GEOFF He's really disappointed. Anyway, I was wondering – please say 'no' if it's a hassle – is there any chance of you stepping in?

MIKE Geoffrey Salter, I'd be honoured.

GEOFF Mike!

MIKE No, (don't say another word). Being in a position to help other people is one of the few fringe benefits of this job. Speaking of which, you hear what we're doing with Jon English?

GEOFF No.

MIKE My idea. We're getting him to build a playground for underprivileged kids.

GEOFF *(excited, with no hint of accusation)* Oh, like one of those Angry Anderson . . .

MIKE Ah! I know what you're going to say. This is what happens when you harness a concept. First of all, it's very different from Angry Anderson. Secondly, what if it is? The greatest good for the greatest amount. Utilitarianism. Sir John Mills.

GEOFF The actor?

MIKE *(unsure)* Uh-huh.

SCENE 12

A SUZUKI VEHICLE

Emma, Jon, Stu and Jase are in a Suzuki. Stu films Jon, who is driving.

EMMA How we looking?

STU Set.

EMMA *(to Jon)* Jon, we'll just put down the opening bit. Don't forget to wave at everybody.

JON There's no-one around.

EMMA We'll pick up some shots of people waving back later. And – action.

JON Well, as you can see, it's a pretty run-down neighbourhood; not much for kids to do. But we're gonna try and fix that. We're gonna need a lot of help from a lot of people. But the funny thing about us Aussies – we always dig deep without asking for anything in return.

STU Cut. One more time.

EMMA What's wrong?

STU Couldn't see the Suzuki sign.

Jon removes his hands from the steering wheel to reveal the Suzuki logo.

SCENE 13

THE PRODUCTION OFFICE

KATE *(holding phone)* Sam, someone from Toyworld. Can give us swings and stuff but they want 'Tonight's Frontline proudly brought to you by . . .'

SAM These people are pariahs. Get Em to . . .

SHELLEY She's out taping.

SAM *(flustered)* Um, put 'em through to . . . (my office). Hate it when she leaves the office.

Mike approaches, Rebecca in tow.

MIKE Anything I can do?

SAM We're fine, Mike.

MIKE Sam, don't freeze me out on this one. What are we short?

SAM Oh, we still need a builder. There's . . .

MIKE Leave it with me.

SAM *(going into his office)* Emma may have started . . .

Mike cuts him off with his hand and gives a smug 'Here I go again, saving the office' look to Rebecca as he begins sifting through the contents of Emma's desk.

MIKE Let's see what's here. Geez, what a mess. Thank God my desk doesn't end up like this.

REBECCA There's nothing on your desk.

MIKE *(searching)* Because I value order, Rebecca. Now, what's this? *(holds up paper)* A builder. *(calls)* Sam – got one! *(to Rebecca)* What they'd do without me round here . . .

SCENE 14

COUNCIL OFFICES

Emma is on her mobile phone.

EMMA Yep, OK. *(she hangs up and checks the back of her phone)* We'll need an Ericsson sticker on this. *(to Jon)* You set?

JON Yeah.

EMMA Now remember – try and keep a sense that you've just arrived.

JON We've been here two hours.

EMMA I know. Ready, Stu?

Stu starts to film as Jon walks into the building talking to camera.

JON Well, before we build our playground we're gonna need a place to build it. And who better to find us a piece of local real estate than the local mayor. We're taking a bit of a punt dropping in unannounced – let's just hope he's in. *(he approaches the receptionist)* G'day.

CHERYL Hi, Jon.

JON Is the Lord Mayor in?

CHERYL Yes, he's expecting you.

Jon looks flummoxed. Emma steps in.

EMMA Cheryl, this whole thing's a surprise to you.

CHERYL Oh yeah.

EMMA Let's try it again.

The mayor, in full robes, pokes his head out from his office.

MAYOR Is this my bit?

EMMA We're going again.

MAYOR *(rolling his eyes)* Phew.

SCENE 15

THE FRONTLINE STUDIO

A story is going to air. We hear Marty's voice-over. Mike speaks to Rebecca during the story. She stands just off set.

MARTY *(voice only)* But with the police ducking for cover and his wife too distressed to speak, there's still many questions to be answered about the tragic death of Liam Naughton. Martin di Stasio, Frontline.

MIKE So I, as anchor, back-announce the story and reflect what the audience are thinking. I crystallise their reaction.

REBECCA Even when you haven't watched it.

MIKE Oh well, that's part of the skill.

FLOOR MANAGER In five.

Cut to Mike at desk.

MIKE Mmm, some disturbing elements there. Coming up after the break, the teacher sacked for simply being gay.

Cut to footage of Gay Mardi Gras: men in cheekless leather pants etc.

Day

SCENE 16

A HARDWARE STORE

Jon is speaking to the shop-owner. Stu's shot starts off on the Mitre 10 sign and pans down to the interview.

JON You see, we're building a playground for underprivileged kids and we're going to need some hardware. For free.

SHOP-OWNER Well Jon, here at Mitre 10 we'd be glad to help. I think you'll find we've got everything you need. *(starts physically showing)* Hammers, saws, nails, a wide range of poly . . .

JON *(cutting him off)* That's great.

SHOP-OWNER . . . fillers, paints and paintbrushes . . .

JON Plenty there.

There is a pause as the shop-owner looks towards Emma.

JON What?

SHOP-OWNER The deal was I could mention everything in the winter catalogue.

SCENE 17

THE EDIT SUITE

Rebecca watches as Hugh cues up a tape. They both smoke.

HUGH Better hope your uncle don't walk in and catch you.

REBECCA He's at home doing some research.

Hugh has an asthma-inducing laughter fit. We see Brooke through the glass standing at a mike, with headphones on. She holds a script. She knocks on the window and gives Hugh an impatient 'Get on with it' gesture.

HUGH Christ, she's a bitch. *(into mike)* Stand by for a listen.

Brooke listens as Hugh plays footage from a Bosnian-type story. We hear a distinctly BBC voice-over.

VOICE-OVER Here in the Muslim enclave of Bihac, shelling has continued non-stop since the last UN-brokered ceasefire collapsed on the weekend. For the residents, time is running out.

The tape is stopped and rewound by Hugh. Brooke consults her script.

HUGH *(into mike)* Just got this last bit to re-voice.

Brooke gives the thumbs up. Hugh starts the vision again, this time minus the BBC voice-over. Brooke reads.

BROOKE Here in the Muslim enclave of Bihac, shelling has continued non-stop since the last UN-brokered ceasefire collapsed on the weekend. For the residents, time is running out.

Hugh gives the thumbs up.

REBECCA So she just reads what he said, but in her own voice?

HUGH Uh-huh.

REBECCA Does she add anything?

HUGH Oh yeah.

REBECCA What?

BROOKE *(heard from next door)* Brooke Vandenberg reporting.

SCENE 18

AN ABANDONED INNER-CITY LOT

A bunch of hoonish-looking kids stand around watching as Emma tries to organise things. She has a megaphone.

EMMA OK, if we can have the kids over here. Perhaps those with tattoos can stay up the back. And anyone with McDonald's – make sure we can see the wrappers. Hold the burgers up nice and high. You set, Jon?

JON Ready.

Stu indicates he is ready to film and Jon takes his own cue.

JON Right. Now this is just an abandoned lot. But thanks to the generosity of the people we've spoken to today . . .

Stu pans slightly across to reveal a pile of treated pine with a strategically placed sign reading 'Ozchip Timber Supplies'. He pans back to Jon as Jon continues.

JON . . . we plan on turning it into a playground. A playground for needy kids like Josh.

Jon steps across and crouches next to Josh. He has obviously been chosen as the most presentable face of the kids.

JON What do you reckon, Josh?

JOSH It's great.

JON Where do you normally play?

JOSH We don't have nowhere.

JON So if we . . . *(he stops and stands up)* Who took my wallet?

The mass of kids stands with no response.

STU *(to kids)* For Christ's sake – we're trying to help you little shits.

EMMA Stu!

STU They're old enough.

KID #1 This playground sucks.

KID #2 We wanted a basketball court.

SCENE 19

SAM'S OFFICE

Jan, Mike and Sam meet.

JAN Now I've written out a few of your reactions for the press release. *(reading)* 'When you heard about the plight of these inner-city children you were moved to tears.'

MIKE Yeah. Reckon I would I have said that.

JAN *(reading)* 'Your heart went out to them and you were filled with a desire to help.'

MIKE Uh-huh. Sounds like me.

JAN Now we've lined up quite a few radio interviews tomorrow. Here's the list.

MIKE Phew. Heavy schedule.

JAN We've got to let people know, darling, the wonderful work you're doing. No point hiding yourself under a bushel.

MIKE *(humble)* Well, it's just great to be able to give of yourself. *(looking at list, whistles)* 'Breakfast radio'?

JAN Too early?

MIKE Quarter to eight – makes it a pretty long day.

JAN We'll arrange a pre-record.

SAM Speaking of which, we're going to pre-record your links for the special.

MIKE When?

SAM Do 'em Thursday, after the show.

MIKE *(excited)* Unreal! I'm going skiing on the weekend. This way I can leave Thursday night. *(leaving)* Hey, we oughta do more of these charity things.

Day ❹

SCENE 20

THE EDIT SUITE

We see vision of the playground special. It is obviously towards the end and features slow-motion shots of swings etc. being built while cute kids look on. Everything has 'Everything I Do' by Bryan Adams or 'Where Do the Children Play' by Cat Stevens over the top. Jon English runs around directing traffic. It looks classy.

We mix out to reveal this is being viewed in the office by all the staff.

SAM Jesus. We putting out a soundtrack album with this special? *(to everyone)* Who's crying?

We reveal Emma, Kate, Shelley and Domenica all with tears in their eyes. Brooke just rolls her eyes.

EMMA God, this is manipulative.

SAM Hey, there was a need.

EMMA Our ratings were sagging.

MARTY Sales department must be rapt.

SAM Hey, these kids wanted a playground.

EMMA They wanted a basketball court.

On the screen, a stream of 'Frontline would like to thank' telemation runs through.

SAM You know the best bit? This whole thing didn't cost us a cent.

SCENE 21

THE MAKE-UP ROOM

Mike is being made up as Rebecca watches.

REBECCA You spend a long time in here.

MIKE It's not just make-up, Rebecca. This is my opportunity to centre myself. For example, I've got a big interview tonight with . . . *(looks at rundown)* um, the head of the Civil Aviation Authority. This gives me time to work out my questions, think about what . . .

Kate enters and drops a sheet of paper on Mike's lap before departing.

KATE Here's your questions, Mike.

MIKE Excellent. Kate must have had a bit of free time on her hands today. If only it was like this every night. *(checks paper)* Yeah, had that. Was gonna ask that. *(to the make-up artist)* Steven, can I borrow that lip gloss? I'm going skiing on the weekend. Don't want to get (burnt).

STEVEN Sure.

MIKE I tell you – I cannot wait to get on top of a run . . .

Geoff enters. He has some papers.

GEOFF Mike, sorry this has come so late.

MIKE What is it, buddy?

GEOFF Information for the charity auction tomorrow. Boy, when I told them Mike Moore was hosting they were rapt. What do you think?

Geoff holds up a pissy poster advertising the auction with Mike's name in big letters.

MIKE Great.

SCENE 22

THE FRONTLINE STUDIO

Mike is at the desk, doing pre-records. On screens behind him are logos for various sponsors: Mitre 10 etc.

EMMA OK, in your own time, Mike.

MIKE Hi, thanks for joining us. Tonight, a very special edition of Frontline. Yesterday we came up with a crazy concept. We heard about some kids in the inner city who had nowhere to play. So I rang an old mate of mine, Jon English. I said: 'Jon, you've got twenty-four hours.' Did he succeed? Let's find out.

FOUR DAYS LATER

SCENE 23

THE PRODUCTION OFFICE

Mike enters, in a ski jacket. He has a sunburnt face, except for where his goggles were.

DOMENICA Hi Mike! How was your weekend?

MIKE *(pretending to ski)* Awesome. *(quietly)* Did you ring . . . ?

DOMENICA The weatherman? *(nods)* I don't think he believed me.

MIKE Really? You told him . . .

DOMENICA . . . your mother was sick up at the snow.

MIKE Who'd they get for the auction?

DOMENICA That host of 'Jackpot' managed to make it.

MIKE Phelpsy? Show pony. Only does it for the publicity. So how'd the show look? The playground thing?

DOMENICA Mike, I cried. My mother – she was crying too. Those kids must have been so happy.

MIKE Suppose Sam's pretty happy too.

SCENE 24

SAM'S OFFICE

Sam, Marty, Emma, Brooke and Stu sit around looking glum. Mike enters and is shocked.

MIKE What?

SAM Mike.

MIKE We've been axed?

SAM Em. (You tell him.)

EMMA Been a few hiccups with the playground.

MIKE What? What?

EMMA A swing broke on the weekend. Kid was hurt.

MIKE Oh no.

MARTY Worse – it wasn't your niece.

MIKE But, well, that's not our fault. That's the builder.

MARTY Which brings us to the second point. Mike, where did you find the builder's name?

MIKE Emma's desk.

Marty puts his head in his hands.

SAM Emma and Marty were organising an exposé on a dodgy builder. That's the name you found.

MIKE Well, the desk was messy . . .

MARTY Thanks to you we ended up hiring an unregistered, incompetent bankrupt currently wanted in three states.

MIKE *(fearful)* Shit. Anything else?

EMMA Only the fact we've just been contacted by the Wilderness Society. A little upset about our use of rainforest timber.

SAM People, I think we're looking at an unmitigated disaster.

Shelley appears at the door.

SHELLEY Sam – ratings.

Sam goes over and takes them.

SAM An unmitigated disaster that rated thirty-two.

Subdued smiles.

EMMA We do another one?

SAM You bet.

Actor Biographies

ROB SITCH: Mike Moore

A founding member as a writer and performer in the D-Generation with Tom Gleisner and Santo Cilauro, Rob's television career began in 1986 with a weekly comedy series on ABC TV (even today he is still recognised as Brains from the 'Thunderbirds' sketch). Since then he has hosted breakfast radio on Melbourne's Triple M and starred in the Logie award-winning 'The Late Show'. In 1994 he breathed life into Frontline's Mike Moore, hailed as one of the most sustained and accurately observed comedic characters ever to appear on Australian TV. He co-created Frontline with Santo Cilauro, Jane Kennedy and Tom Gleisner.

BRUNO LAWRENCE: Brian Thompson

Once described as Jack Nicholson's favourite actor, the late Bruno Lawrence was born in New Zealand and became one of Australia's most respected film and television performers. Acclaimed for his roles in films such as *Smash Palace*, *The Quiet Earth*, *Spotswood* and *The Delinquents*, and in television 'The Feds', 'The Rainbow Warrior' and 'The Great Bookie Robbery', Bruno brought a wealth of experience and golfing prowess to the cast of Frontline.

KEVIN J. WILSON: Sam Murphy

Kevin J. Wilson has been a professional actor since 1964. Apart from working out of Sydney for two years in the late 1960s and two more recent visits to Australia, he has spent his entire career working in New Zealand. Roles include Janet Frame's father in *An Angel at My Table*, and the feature film *Chunuk Bair* where he was co-lead with English actor Robert Powell, playing a Colonel of New Zealand troops at Gallipoli. Recent Australian work includes thirteen episodes of 'The Flying Doctors' as Ted the Pilot, and guest leads in 'G.P.' and 'Chances'. He has also recently appeared as a guest lead in two episodes of the Canadian co-production of 'Mysterious Island', playing the pirate captain.

JANE KENNEDY: Brooke Vandenberg

Producer and on-air announcer on Melbourne radio station 3UZ to Triple M news presenter, Jane was inducted into the D-Generation and removed from the newsroom for laughing during the news stories. (Brooke in fact had a higher cadetship than Jane.) From performing Kylie in the music video 'Five in a Row' to two successful seasons of 'The Late Show'and co-creating Frontline, Jane also played Cassie in the seven-part comedy series 'Funky Squad' which she co-created with Tom Gleisner and Santo Cilauro. In addition to writing, directing and performing for television, Jane also does the same for radio, and with Tom and Santo wrote *The Funky Squad Annual* in 1995.

TIRIEL MORA: Martin di Stasio

With experience on both sides of the camera, Tiriel has had roles in Australian films such as *Strikebound*, *Future Schlock*, *A Kink in the Picasso* and *Official Denial*. His television credits include 'Prisoner', 'Neighbours', 'Embassy', 'Phoenix', 'Secrets' and the narrator in 'Glued to the Telly'. With a booming voice and dry wit, Tiriel looks frighteningly comfortable in his George Negus-style jacket.

ALISON WHYTE: Emma Ward

An accomplished theatre actress, Alison has performed for the Melbourne Theatre Company in plays including *The Dutch Courtesan, The Crucible, Much Ado about Nothing* and *St James Infirmary*. She also played two roles in *A Midsummer Night's Dream* as part of a touring company in the Melbourne Botanic Gardens. Alison recently performed in Steven Berkoff's *Decadence*, the hit of the 1995 Melbourne Comedy Festival, and appeared in *Tape Worm*, a short film screened in the 'eat my shorts' series on SBS TV. Alison trained in classical ballet for eight years and also studied singing – two skills she will probably never have to use on Frontline.

GENEVIEVE MOOY: Jan Whelan

Genevieve brings to life the role of the publicist in such a convincing way she was actually considered to do the publicity for the program. An infectious and bubbly actress, her many roles have included being paid to appear at various business functions and seminars posing as a company executive or a corporate director, as well as theatre, film and television. Genevieve will soon be seen on ABC TV in 'After the Beep'.

SANTO CILAURO: Geoffrey Salter

A co-founding member of the D-Generation with Rob Sitch and Tom Gleisner, Santo's television career started in 1986 on ABC TV. Starting off filming his cousin's wedding on Super 8, Santo is an integral part of the production of Frontline. In addition to writing and producing, he films each episode as well as appearing as Geoff Salter (Mike Moore's friend at the network). Through a career of radio on Triple M and TV on D-Generation specials and 'The Late Show' and co-creating Frontline and 'Funky Squad', Geoff is the first sustained Anglo-Saxon role for Santo.

TOM GLEISNER: Colin Konica

A co-founding member of the D-Generation with Santo Cilauro and Rob Sitch, Tom's TV career started on the ABC in 1986 with 'The D-Generation'. He wrote and performed in a series of specials for the Seven Network in 1988 and had a stint co-hosting the top-rating breakfast radio program on Triple M. As well as being co-creator of Frontline and 'Funky Squad', Tom, along with the rest of the team, co-writes and performs syndicated radio serials for the Triple M network.